More than a dream

Eighty-five years at the College of St. Catherine

Rosalie Ryan, CSJ
and
John Christine Wolkerstorfer, CSJ

Sister Rosalie Ryan
Sister John Christine

The College of St. Catherine • St. Paul, Minnesota • 1992

All photographs and illustrations are from the Archives of the College of St. Catherine except as follows: cover (Craig Perman) and pp. C-1, C-2 top (Perman), C-3 top right (Perman) and bottom, C-4 top left (Perman) and top right (Jim Barbour), C-5 bottom left (Perman) and right (Barbour), C-6 top (Barbour), C-7, and C-8 (Perman) from the College of St. Catherine Office of Public Relations; 1, 4, 10, 13, and 57 courtesy of the Archives of the St. Paul Province of the Sisters of St Joseph of Carondelet; 2 (photo of painting by Robert Beveridge) and 21 courtesy of the Minnesota Historical Society; viii, ix, 20, 37, 124 (APB photo), 127, and 129 courtesy of the St. Catherine Alumnae Association; 81, 88, 98, and 109 from *La Concha* 1964, 1965 and 1966; 131 and 132 courtesy of the Abigail Quigley McCarthy Center for Women's Research, Resources and Scholarship; 112 by Marlin Levison courtesy of the Minneapolis *Star Tribune;* and C-3 top left, C-4 bottom, and C-5 top by John Aitken for this volume.

Illustrations from the Archives of the College of St. Catherine include frontispiece (p. ii) by Menza Van Esvelat; pp. x and 15 by C. J. Hibbard; 7 by Norton & Peel; 12, 35 right, 48, 55, 63, 67, 69, 71, 73, 78, 82, 96, and 105 top by Leo Simmer; 18 left by C. L. Fenney; 22 by Leonard W. Lundgren; by B. C. Golling; 38 left by A. H. Kelm; 39 by John Hines, Jr.; 59 by Kenneth M. Wright Studios; 60 by Raymond B. Scott; 74 by Russell Schweizer; 87, 89, 116, 119, 121, and 135 by Linda Powers; 105 bottom by Act Two; 114 by Robert L. Logman; 128 by Judy Paulson; 130 by Michelle Hines; 134 by T. J. Strasser; and 138 by Janice Ormberg.

Editing, design, production: Ellen Blackman Green '67
Indexing: Suzanna Moody
Printing: Cooperative Printing, Minneapolis
Manufactured in the United States of America

© 1992 by The College of St. Catherine, 2004 Randolph Avenue, St. Paul, MN 55105.

All rights reserved.

Library of Congress Catalog Card Number: 92-072011
ISBN 0-9633553-0-9

10 9 8 7 6 5 4 3 2 1

To Sisters Antonia McHugh and Ste. Helene Guthrie and all the pioneer Sisters of St. Joseph of Carondelet whose labors made their vision of a Catholic liberal arts college for women into much more than a dream

Contents

	Foreword	viii
	Preface and acknowledgments	ix
1.	A vision of excellence	1
2.	An atmosphere of space	31
3.	Part of a larger whole	53
	In color (following page 70)	C-1-8
4.	A variety of ideas	85
5.	In a contemporary way	113
	A note about sources	141
	Index	143

Foreword

Anita Pampusch

I have been struck, in reading the chapters of *More than a Dream,* by the remarkable vision, determination, and high goals set by the early pioneers at the College of St. Catherine and continued by their successors. Though the college has changed considerably in its nearly ninety years, the threefold focus on serving students, providing educational excellence, and encouraging religious faith continues as its outstanding characteristic. The Sisters of St. Joseph have approached and surmounted the obstacles of economic depression, war, enrollment fluctuations, increased competition, and changing demographics with characteristic creativity and energy. Their story demonstrates a constant determination not to let external forces obscure the dream.

This, indeed, is an attitude we continue to hold in 1992. My dreams for the college are no less lofty. I want us to continue to be a thriving institution, offering excellent education programs, with a values-base flowing from our Catholic heritage and ethical beliefs. I expect that, as we conclude our current Capital Campaign, we will see growth on both campuses, the completion of major building projects, cutting-edge academic facilities, and stronger relations with our external community.

We are developing a reputation as *the* place for women to develop leadership skills and improve their self-esteem. The reasons for the existence of the campus have changed from their original ones. St. Catherine's initially provided access to higher education for Catholic women; now, we must look to the specific contribution we can make to women's education at a time when virtually all barriers to that education have been lowered in other institutions. Identifying our uniqueness while maintaining a traditional mission is the key to future success. I believe leadership is the central concept to take us there.

We face many challenges during the 1990s. The high cost of higher education, the erosion of traditional values in society, and competition from other institutions will pressure us to conform or to change. I believe we are surmounting these challenges well and will continue to do so. The spirit of the Sisters of St. Joseph so evident in this history will animate the institution as it looks at its next 90 years.

—Anita M. Pampusch, President
The College of St. Catherine
August 1992

Preface

Wishing to impart to future students and faculty members the achievements and ideals of the early leaders of the college, Sister Rosalie Ryan, formerly of the English and theology departments, began work in the 1980s towards providing a permanent, easily accessible history of the college. Her research and early manuscripts for four chapters, covering each administration through that of Sister Alberta Huber, were greatly enriched and enlivened by a collection of over 500 oral history interviews recorded and/or supervised by Sister John Christine Wolkerstorfer of the history department. The early manuscripts were typed by Ardis Dale and read by Carol Langworthy, Institutional Development, and by Sisters Antonius Kennelly, Immaculata Keenan, and Catherine Litecky.

In 1991 the college reviewed Sister Rosalie's work and, with the intention to publish, recruited Sister John Christine to write a fifth chapter bringing the history to date. Ellen Blackman Green '67 began editing the manuscripts and collecting illustrations. Sisters Mary William Brady and Marie Inez Johnson of the College of St. Catherine Archives provided invaluable research assistance for both writers and editor, as did Sister Mary Kraft, archivist for the St. Paul Province of the Sisters of St. Joseph of Carondelet, and Ruth Brombach, executive director of the St. Catherine Alumnae Association.

Sister Rosalie Ryan

President Anita Pampusch, Assistant to the President Mary Schwiegert Abdul-Rahman, Vice President for Institutional Development Janet Miner, Ruth Brombach, and Sisters Rosalie Ryan, John Christine Wolkerstorfer, Mary William Brady, and Mary Kraft read final manuscript and/or pageproofs before publication. Ellen Blackman Green donated the design and layout and supervised production.

Our heartfelt thanks to these and to the many other former and current faculty members, staff, and students who have responded so graciously to specific questions or helped to verify the fine points. All seem to have been inspired by Sister Antonia McHugh's advice to "Energize yourself."

—Rosalie Ryan, CSJ
—John Christine Wolkerstorfer, CSJ
August 1992

Sister John Christine Wolkerstorfer

Almost a hundred students dressed for a performance of Every Woman's Road *in 1917. Derham Hall is in the background.*

The soul of a pioneer woman is a beautiful thing. It is full of wisdom and hope and self-sacrifice. All pioneer women saw visions and dreamed dreams while facing bare realities.

A vision of excellence

Early in 1905, a bulletin announced that a new Catholic college for women would introduce "the third epoch in the development of the educational work of the Sisters of St. Joseph in the Northwest. In 1851 they opened the first Catholic elementary school . . . some years later they built St. Joseph's Academy, the first preparatory school; and finally they founded St. Catherine's . . . the purpose of those in charge is to make this college the best and highest school of its kind in the Northwest." Twenty-seven sisters had already begun to fulfill this vision in a single building on isolated farmland west of St. Paul.

The College of St. Catherine opened to students in January 1905, but the project had been long in the making. Archbishop John Ireland had begun to plan for the college in the early 1890s, helping his sister Ellen—Mother Seraphine Ireland—acquire 110 acres of land at the corner of Randolph and Cleveland avenues. A financial panic in 1893 postponed the project, and ten years passed before the work continued.

Not everyone greeted plans for the new college with enthusiasm. Institutions for the higher education of women had not found favor in the United States in the late 1800s. Women's education was carried on chiefly by "female seminaries," which gave courses in "domestic training" needlework, manners, and a host of other topics intended to prepare a woman for her place in the home. Toward the end of the century, individual women began asking for more, and the heads of some colleges moved towards providing education in literature and the sciences to prepare women for teaching and other professions. George Schmidt wrote of what this entailed in *The Liberal Arts College: A Chapter in American Cultural History:* "To reach the college level . . . it would be necessary to slough off the many fashionable and vocational scraps of knowledge and concentrate on the solid subjects which sharpened the understanding and disciplined the mind. This meant the higher reaches of Latin, Greek, mathematics, mental and moral philosophy." Efforts to create greater intellectual challenge for women often met with shock, alarm, or derision. "Such an experience," said one critic, "can only be hardening and deforming." Another said, "This borders on the vulgar."

Historian Thomas Woody wrote that the Reverend John Todd, a Protestant minister, absolutely denounced the idea: "As for training young ladies through a long intellectual course, as we do young men, it can never be done. They will die in the process . . . The poor thing has her brain crowded with history,

Mother Seraphine Ireland, superior of the St. Paul Province of the Sisters of St. Joseph of Carondelet, bought land for a new college in the 1890s.

Archbishop John Ireland was convinced that women had something to contribute. In a sermon at the St. Paul Cathedral on August 20, 1902, he said: "I am a firm believer in the higher education of women; I covet for the daughters of the people, for so many of them at least, as circumstances and position permit to aspire so high, the opportunities of receiving under the protecting hand of religion, the fullest intellectual equipment of which woman is capable. In this regard I offer my congratulations to the Sisters of St. Joseph for their promise soon to endow the Northwest with a college for the higher education of young women; and I take pleasure in pointing to this college as the chief contribution of their community to religion during the half-century to come."

grammar, arithmetic, geography, natural history, chemistry . . . metaphysics, French, often German, Latin, perhaps Greek . . . She must be on the strain all the school hours, study in the evening till her eyes ache, her brain whirls, her spine yields and gives way, and she comes through the process of education enervated, feeble, without courage or vigor, elasticity or strength."

The naysayers deterred neither the sisters nor Archbishop Ireland, who had already given material as well as moral support. In 1900 he had signed over to the sisters the rights to his book, *The Church and Modern Society,* which they peddled from door to door, selling 20,000 copies and raising $60,000 for the college building fund. In 1902, Hugh Derham, a wealthy farmer from Rosemount, asked the archbishop to name a special charity. Ireland suggested he support the effort toward a new Catholic liberal arts college for women. Derham donated $20,000 toward the erection of the first building and $5,000 for a scholarship. Later, Mother Seraphine said of the gift: "It may not seem very large . . . but it gave us courage to go on. He well deserved to have Derham Hall named for him."

Because of problems with construction, the school, scheduled to open in September 1904, was not ready for occupancy until the end of that year. On December 26, 1904, twenty-seven sisters walked a mile in a snowstorm from St. Joseph's Academy in downtown St. Paul to board the Grand Avenue streetcar at Seven Corners. They got off the bus at Cleveland Avenue, then walked another mile south to Randolph Avenue. The elements did not discourage their excitement over the new building.

Sister Bridget Bohan later reminisced that on December 27 Archbishop Ireland came out with a team of horses. With him were Mother Seraphine and Sister Celestine Howard. Promptly at 7:00 A.M., the archbishop offered the first Mass. Then he blessed the rooms of Derham Hall: "They had lanterns to light their way around the house . . . a cat followed . . . Sister Jarlath [Noonan] said that Sister Eulalia [Dress] brought the cat from the academy in a bag . . . The cat went into all the rooms as they were being blessed. Whenever the archbishop shook the holy water, the cat went up to receive . . . Finally he said, 'What's *that* doing here?'" Because of the continuing snow, the three guests left after breakfast. A few days later the boarding students from St. Joseph's Academy arrived to become students of Derham Hall.

The sisters had started from scratch in furnishing the new school, and they sometimes came up short. According to Sister Bridget: "We had about ninety boarders, and when their trunks came out with everything, we had sheets enough for about forty-eight or fifty beds . . . And this was the Christmas holidays. Sister Hyacinth [Werden] said, 'I don't know what to do.' 'Well,' I said, 'give us some money, and we'll do the buying.' Sister Edith [Hogan] and I went over to Minneapolis, and you couldn't get sheets ready-made. You had to buy the bolt of unbleached muslin . . . We rented [sewing] machines and Sister Antonia [McHugh] and I sat at those machines from dawn to dark, and Sister Monica [Berghs] made up the sheets. And the boarders took them without being laundered. They made nothing of it . . . Unbleached, oh, it was unspeakable!" Nevertheless, the school shortly offered an "academic" (college preparatory) course, music, art, and domestic arts. In September 1905, college courses formally began, with seven students registered as freshmen.

The challenge of building enrollment engaged the sisters from the start. Brochures extolled the beauty of the campus, and, later, paid advertisements in the *Catholic Bulletin* lured prospective students. The first printed materials read: "On this spot Nature has poured her beauty with a prodigal hand. To the west of the college is the Mississippi, just recovering from its dash over the Falls [of St. Anthony]; further still to the west, the laughing waters of Minnehaha make constant melody, and on all sides alternating stretches of unkempt forest and billowy greensward complete the beauty of the scene."

Later notices stressed the healthfulness of the site. In 1906: "No school in the United States for the education of young ladies is more favorably situated . . . in regard to the healthfulness and sanitation . . . The drainage and plumbing are as nearly perfect as can be found anywhere." Another ad read: "In the construction of the college building the comfort and safety of its inmates were taken into consideration . . . The wide corridors which extend through the whole length of the building afford space for recreation and exercise in inclement weather." And in 1907, signed by Charles Meade, physician for the college: "The site is exceptionally healthful, and the extensive grounds afford ample opportunity for free outdoor life and exercise in the bracing Minnesota air." Would such claims refute accusations of the likes of the Reverend Todd?

The earliest catalog stated plainly the college's objectives:

- to give the students a liberal education to train and develop all their powers simultaneously
- to train Catholic "girls" to be solidly virtuous and religious—to teach all, irrespective of their denominational differences, to respect, appreciate, and encourage religion and Christian morality.

Despite the publicity, enrollment grew slowly, and for the first six years the College of St. Catherine was really a small high school with just a handful of "specials" doing postsecondary work. Most students wishing to continue beyond the sophomore year transferred to the University of Minnesota. Finally in 1911, two students who had completed the sophomore year, Gertrude Malloy and Marguerite McCusker (Testor), returned as juniors. They remained to graduate in 1913, after which student and alumnae news in *Ariston* (the literary quarterly started in 1906) was divided into "College Notes" and "Academic Notes." That year Sisters Frances Clare Bardon, Margaret Kerby, and Antonia McHugh filed a certificate of incorporation for the College of St. Catherine to promote letters, sciences, and the arts through the care, protection, housing, and instruction of students in subjects including the practice of religion.

The next year, at the insistence of Archbishop Ireland, Sister Antonia McHugh was appointed the first dean (chief administrative officer). Building a great college for women was the object of her unceasing labor for the next twenty-four years.

Sisters Bridget Bohan and Antonia McHugh, above on the steps of Derham Hall in 1905, sewed muslin sheets for the first boarders.

Fit for pioneer work

Sister Antonia's background fitted her for pioneering work. She was born Anna McHugh in Omaha in 1873 of an itinerant frontier family. Her father, Patrick McHugh, after several moves in the Dakotas, settled in Langdon, North Dakota, to serve as mayor, postmaster, and bank director. He was elected a commissioner of Cavalier County, then to the territorial legislature for three terms and to the North Dakota legislature for four. Patrick McHugh often took young Anna with him on his business and political travels in the territory.

When she was twelve years old, Anna's father took her to St. Joseph's Academy in St. Paul to study and prepare for her first Holy Communion. Dur-

In 1896, Sister Antonia McHugh visited her family for the first time after final vows. Traveling with her father as a child, she had learned to confront new people and situations with curiosity rather than fear and to associate education with people, travel, and events as much as with books and school. She saw her father work patiently and hard for others. In 1887, after three years of meetings, speeches, and letters to railroad officials, he convinced the Great Northern Railway Company to extend its tracks through Langdon so the farmers would not have to haul grain so far.

ing the next three years, she attended St. Mary's Academy in Winnipeg, which was closer to home. Sister Mary Joseph Calasenz, SNJM, remembered Anna McHugh from her days in high school: "She was remarkable in her practical piety, application to study, and generosity. Her outspokenness was proverbial among her companions; her frankness was of a nature to abash those who were not lovers of the truth." Said Sister Teresa Toomey: "During the whole of her life as an educator, Sister Antonia showed herself to be a true daughter of pioneers, alert, eager, undaunted by difficulties, and bold in her dreams of what Catholic schools in the Northwest could mean for both the Church and the nation she loved."

In 1890 Anna entered the novitiate of the Sisters of St. Joseph in St. Paul, then began teaching third and fourth grades at St. Joseph's Academy. She was among the first group of sisters at the new college. There she threw herself into a routine of cleaning and housekeeping, teaching, supervising resident students, and attending daily prayers. She continued her education with classes at the University of Chicago in summer and correspondence courses during the school year. Professors A. M. Wergeland, wrote on her History of Civilization work: "Very good paper," "very good indeed," and "I shall be very much indebted to your kindness if you would favor me with a copy of this paper." Sister Antonia attended four successive seminars beginning in 1905, with a full year of study arranged for 1908. By December of that year, she had a bachelor's degree in philosophy and education. In 1909 she received a master's degree in history.

Sister Antonia earned the friendship of several outstanding professors at the university. She remembered: "Convocations at which I was privileged to hear President [William Rainey] Harper gave me my first burning desire to have some part, however small, in the work of education in the Northwest." The dean of the faculties became her friend and adviser: "In 1911 Dr. [George Edgar] Vincent came to Minneapolis as president of the University of Minnesota . . . During his administration, from 1911 to 1916, St. Catherine's was in the hazardous days of its beginnings, and it was Dr. Vincent, more than anyone else, who helped to make it secure."

During the first year of Vincent's term, Sister Antonia went on a recruiting trip to Omaha. There she met a non-Catholic student home on vacation from Oberlin College in Ohio. When the student wrote to the university for information about the College of St. Catherine, the registrar replied that "he had never heard of it." Sister Antonia rushed to see George Vincent, saying: "Your Mr. Pierce has made all this trouble for us." Pierce was "called on the carpet" and thereafter remembered the college very well.

Sister Antonia had returned from studies in Chicago to teach at the College of St. Catherine with characteristic enthusiasm. Her classes in history were filled with love of the classical age of Greece and Rome. For study of the Middle Ages she had collected hundreds of pictures of cathedrals and castles. She had spent much time in the study of geology and geography, so the map of Europe became familiar to her students. Her knowledge of music and art was extensive.

Sister Antonia sprinkled her teaching with dozens of maxims and phrases. When she said, "energize yourself," the student moved. She considered some responses "clear as mud" or "windy." Outside of class she might comment that

Students enjoyed classrooms like this one filled with maps, drawings, and charts as well as books, plants, and pictures of the saints.

"things for sale are in windows" or "only horses hang their heads" or "she who would be a woman must avoid mediocrity." From Room 12, she impartially handed out apples and advice. Her classroom was a place where young women found out what was the matter with them even when they didn't want to know. But there was also talk about books and stars and music and pictures. The seriousness of a particular conference with a student could be gauged by whether the door to Room 12 was open or closed.

In these ways Sister Antonia impressed students deeply: "I certainly knew, from the minute I set my foot here, that she was the most important one on the campus. She was the one I loved most, respected most, feared most, and she certainly was running things," said Sister Marie Philip Haley '21.

Spreading the news

When Sister Antonia became dean in 1914, eighteen students were enrolled in the college, but the sisters were determined to attract more. News items, articles, and full-page advertisements in the *Catholic Bulletin* helped make the public aware of the college's facilities: "Come to the College of St. Catherine. Don't put it off. Decide now. If you need financial help, write to us. We will do all we can. Many students earn their way through college. A college education is worth a big sacrifice. Come." On June 3, 1916, pictures first graced an ad. Around the same time, the college began placing ads in the *St. Paul Pioneer Press* and *St. Paul Dispatch* and publishing more and better brochures. The start of a regular run of the no-fare "dinky" from Snelling to Cleveland on Randolph in 1916 supported recruitment for day students, too. Earlier, the nearest streetcar lines were a mile east and north, on Snelling and Grand Avenues. The *Yearbook* became the *College Bulletin,* probably written or edited by Sister Antonia, and in 1918 the college ran a bulletin with thirty illustrations.

Students in area elementary and secondary schools were advised by their teachers of opportunities at the college. Family members, friends, and acquaintances of students spoke highly of it. Sometimes a parish priest recommended a student, and alumnae visitors also spread the news.

In response to laws passed in Minnesota and North Dakota requiring all teachers in elementary and high schools to meet requirements for state certification, Sister Antonia assisted the sisters in her congregation as well as those of others. She received letters from sisters in all parts of the country, asking for help in evaluating credits and meeting the new requirements, usually including a bachelor's degree. She gave advice and education, tuition-free at the college, in the hope that the recipients would send future students to their alma mater. In 1921-22, for example, five Sisters of the Holy Names from Vancouver, two Missionary Sisters of the Most Holy Trinity from Alabama, and two Sisters of St. Joseph from Crookston, Minnesota, registered at the college.

These strategies all helped toward increasing enrollment from 30 students in 1914 to 218 in 1920. But the most direct recruiting method—the personal visit—met with the most success. Genevieve Lamb (Oberly) recalled that every year the sisters stayed at her grandmother's home while visiting her hometown of Michigan, North Dakota. A teenager of fourteen or fifteen, she was called upon to drive a surrey carrying the sisters and their lunches to neighboring towns such as Clary. Obtaining the names of Catholic girls from the parish priest, the sisters then visited them in their homes. With no Catholic college in the state, North Dakota was a rich field for recruitment, and enrollment from the area increased from one in 1911 to thirty-one in 1919.

The sisters traveled to Minnesota towns, branching out to Wisconsin and Montana. They went to and from the coast on the Northern Pacific and Great Northern railways on passes granted by the railroads on the assumption that students would come back as paying fares. Each pair of sisters carried fifty dollars in cash to cover six weeks' travel expenses. They stopped in every fair-sized town along the way, staying without cost in convents or hospitals and in the homes of students or alumnae. They visited the homes of those who had inquired about the college or who were known as prospective recruits by students or alumnae from the town. Difficulties were compensated for by their success at bringing in registrants and the chance to see the West—including Yellowstone and Glacier parks, as arranged by alumnae or parents of students.

Sports were part of the good news of the college. For more than sixty-five years every Katie learned to play field hockey, as above in 1927.

According to a note on the back of the photo above, these Katies won eight of nine games: (left from bottom) Regina Hurley (Sister Jeanne d'Arc), Marion Connole (Brandt) '23, Florence Williams; (center) Modesta Reichert (Gamble) '20, Margaret Smith, Irene Bourgois; (right) Hilary Mikschl, Loretto Galvin '21, and Leona Knapp.

The college took a step forward in recruiting techniques in 1924-25 with the production of a movie on campus life called *A Day at St. Catherine's*. Its plot centered on the adventures of a new student. Athletic events (including a field day and a tennis tournament), music classes, the dedication of the chapel, and a commencement procession were shown. Two years later, the college announced the availability of honor tuition scholarships in Catholic high schools throughout Minnesota and surrounding states. This strategy, coupled with a student service program initiated in 1922, helped to increase enrollment even during the economic depression of the 1930s.

Sister Antonia clearly was not interested in enrollment for enrollment's sake, however, and she carefully planned for every facet of college development. Sister Teresa remembered that she labored, usually in several areas at once, to carry through this fourfold program:

1. to obtain national and international recognition for the scholastic work at the college

2. to offer to the sisters of the college the opportunity for a wide cultural background and for professional education at outstanding American and European centers of learning

3. to work out a schedule of study and activity ensuring education at once religious, humanistic, and professional

4. to secure funding for the erection of new buildings, the maintenance of an adequate library, and the establishment of an endowment fund.

Official recognition

Between 1916 and 1920, the college was accredited by the North Central Association of Colleges, the National Educational Association, the National Catholic Educational Association, and the Association of American Colleges. During the same period, graduates were made eligible for membership in the American Association of University Women. Sister Antonia's old friends served her well in the process. "With his characteristic generosity and splendid spirit of service, [George Vincent, who in 1917 had left the University of Minnesota to become president of the Rockefeller Foundation in New York] made it clear to me what to do, how to organize, and how to bring about the improvements that made the accrediting of the college possible," she said later.

Accreditation by the North Central Association of Colleges had been particularly complicated, since the financial organization of public universities and colleges differed from that of private colleges, especially Catholic ones. During the winter of 1915-16, the college prepared a self-study and was visited by an accrediting team from the association. The sticking point was the matter of endowment. The college had very little, most of its resources being invested in buildings and faculty development. Sister Antonia worked to convince team members that the contributed services of the sisters constituted a considerable endowment. Team member Charles Judd, a friend from the University of Chicago, seemed to understand the concept, for he wrote in his North Central report: "These teachers do not receive any pay and have no private contracts with the institution but are under the general control of the orders to which they belong. Many of the institutions undoubtedly receive in this way services that represent a large endowment."

The students shown above in 1925 may or may not have been dressed for the recruiting film produced by the college that year. Left to right are Mary McNally (Cashman), Katherine Moroney (Kenney) and Eleanor McCahill (Denny), all Class of '26.

But the larger commission did not at first accept the concept. Judd wrote to Sister Antonia: "The committee . . . is not including the name of your institution on the tentative list . . . on the grounds set forth in this report." She replied immediately, on March 18, 1916: "I note with complete satisfaction your just appreciation of the endowment question for Catholic schools . . . With this matter settled in our favor, I am at a loss to know why our name is not included on your approved list, as I know we more than meet every other standard recommended by the Association."

The committee evidently reversed itself; the Spring 1916 *Ariston* crowed: "On Saturday, March 25, the announcement was made to us that our college had been placed upon its list of schools accredited by the North Central Association of Colleges." That year college recruitment ads replaced the line "accredited by the Minnesota State Board of Public Instruction and by several prominent universities" with "the only college for women in the Northwest belonging to the North Central Association, which places it educationally on a par with Vassar, Wellesley, and Smith."

Professional educators

Indeed, the teaching services of the sisters constituted an extraordinary endowment. Sister Antonia had given high priority to the professional and cultural education of the faculty. The teaching sisters were to be as well educated as their equals at other colleges and universities. To Sister Antonia, that meant attending and receiving degrees at great universities in the United States as well as travel and study abroad, and the process had begun before the college opened. Sisters Hyacinth, who taught German, and Bridget, who taught music, had studied in France and Germany in 1903. Sister Antonia had begun her correspondence course at the University of Chicago, unheard-of for Catholic sisters at the time.

At first, the faculty was small, and some teachers formed entire departments alone. From 1905 to 1910, Sister Clara Graham, for instance, was the only English instructor, and she taught eighteen of the twenty-one English courses offered during the next five years. Essays printed in *Ariston* were frequently taken from those done in her classes, and she led a weekly Dante Reading Circle. But with the cooperation of the superiors of the Sisters of St. Joseph, Sister Antonia sent many young sisters for further study as soon as they left the novitiate, conveniently constructed just east of the college in 1912. (The provincial house moved there in 1927 and Bethany Convent, for the senior sisters, in 1954.) As they finished their graduate work, these sisters became the core of the St. Catherine faculty. Sometimes they started teaching before finishing their studies, working on dissertations in their free hours or while sitting up to check in residents returning from concerts and other events.

Sister Agnes Rita Lingl reflected: "To the horror of some people, sometimes bishops, Sister Antonia sent the sisters out to many non-Catholic or rather secular universities . . . We studied at the University of Chicago, and [when the university] wanted to start a three-year master's program, they picked out a number of colleges—I think only thirty-seven across the country—St. Catherine's was *the* Catholic representative . . . the sisters from other communities were all being sent to the Catholic University or to Notre Dame."

In 1920-21, five degreed and experienced members of the faculty—Sisters Clara Graham, Mary John Ryan, Charitas Farr, Eva McDermott, and Frances

Edna St. Vincent Millay sent this autographed portrait to Sister Antonia after reading her poems at the college in November 1927. On her several visits, Millay became special friends with Sister Ste. Helene and sometimes sent her poems for critique before publication.

Rita Ryan—were given other assignments by the St. Joseph provincial superior. Sister Maris Stella (Alice) Smith reflected many years later: "I was here for a year with Sister Clara as principal of Derham Hall. She wasn't here when I was a senior . . . perhaps there was an element of Sister Clara and Sister Antonia not seeing eye to eye . . . Sister Clara was more conventional. Sister Mary John and Sister Eva were also of that more conventional school . . . I think you might call them casualties."

Sister Antonia quickly chose for advanced study Sisters Maris Stella, Teresa Joseph Griswold, Helen Margaret Peck, Antonius Kennelly, and Agnes Rita Lingl in 1922, and Sisters Angele Gleason, Jeanne d'Arc Hurley, and Cecilia Manion in 1923. She freed some instructors for a quarter, for summer school, or for the an academic year to pursue graduate studies at prestigious universities. Sisters Anna Goulet and Alphonsine Welp attended Columbia and Sisters Eleanore Michel, Mona Riley, and Anna Margaret Normile went to Chicago. She arranged study abroad for Sisters Ste. Helene Guthrie and Jeanne Marie Bonnett in 1924, for Sisters Maris Stella and Antonine O'Brien in 1927, and for Sisters Antonius and Agnes Rita in 1929. Sisters Anna and Cecilia studied music under Marcel Dupré and Alfred-Denis Cortot in Paris.

A schedule of study . . .

Some faculty members taught in more than one subject area, but as the faculty developed, so did each department and its curriculum. Sister Ste. Helene Guthrie, who had earned a bachelor's degree from the University of Minnesota in 1907 and taught two years before entering the novitiate, joined the English department in 1911, though for some years she taught mostly in the high school. She was the first sister to study at Oxford University in England, in 1924-25.

While Sister Ste. Helene studied at Oxford, Sister Jeanne Marie Bonnett worked in Louvain, Belgium. She had entered the novitiate in 1915, received a bachelor's degree from the College of St. Catherine in 1917, and earned a master's in psychology and education from the University of Minnesota in 1919. She became head of the St. Catherine "psychology and education" department the next year. After one year of study at Louvain she received a *Doctorat en Pedagogie,* in 1925.

Sister Anna Margaret came to the college to teach in 1914. She was one of the first sisters to complete graduate degrees at the University of Chicago—a master's degree in classics in 1919 and a doctorate in 1927. She became a distinguished teacher of Latin and Greek and head of the department of classics, where she was joined by Sister Mona. Agnes Keenan '31, one of the first lay teachers at the college wrote later: "We who knew Sister Anna Margaret well were affected most by her love of truth . . . but it was never a cold truth, or truth divorced from human love." Because of ill health, Sister Anna Margaret left teaching in 1934.

Geraldine Haley '21 (Sister Marie Philip) also entered the community with a bachelor's degree. After graduation from the college, she received a French government scholarship for two years of study in France and earned a baccalaureate degree from the Acadamie de Paris in 1923. After her return, she taught for several years before entering the Sisters of St. Joseph and joining the St. Catherine faculty. She continued graduate study at the University of Minnesota, earning a master's degree in French and a doctorate in 1936 and

Sister Ste. Helene Guthrie, the first sister to study at Oxford, became dean of the college in 1929, when Sister Antonia became president. One alumna wrote upon her death in 1949: "The success of the college program depended in no small part on Sister Ste. Helene . . . maintaining a spirit of optimism and of extraordinary courage . . . facility in handling a large professional correspondence, realization of the problems connected with school finance, the power of making decisions in the absence of the head of the college, and in the midst of all her work, a sense of humor and willingness to meet others socially, which won friends for herself and above all for the college."

becoming head of the French department that year. Sister Marie Philip wrote many articles for *PMLA (Publication of the Modern Language Association)* and was a cofounder of *Renascence,* a journal of criticism of modern literature. In 1938 her doctoral dissertation, *Racine and the Art Poétique of Boileau,* was published by Johns Hopkins University Press.

Sister Teresa Toomey was among the most scholarly of the early sisters. She began teaching history at the college in 1918 while working on a degree at the University of Minnesota. She received a bachelor's degree in 1917 and a master's degree in 1922, then continued working on her dissertation, "Florentine Renaissance Painting as a Source for Social History," finally earning her doctorate in 1943. She received her degree "in absentia" because sisters did not then go out at night.

Sister Eleanore Michel had joined the faculty in 1915. Always scholarly, always friendly and helpful, she never imposed her knowledge upon others. She received a bachelor's degree from the college in 1916, a master's degree in German from the University of Minnesota, and a doctorate in Romance languages from the University of Chicago in 1930. She studied for a year at the University of Madrid and continued her study of the history of art in Madrid, Florence, and Paris. For over forty years she was a professor of Spanish literature and history of art; she was the adviser to international students for much of that time. She carried on a large correspondence with alumnae from other countries, receiving so many Christmas greetings each year that she could not finish her individual replies until the following July.

Sisters Mona Riley and Eleanore Michel, above in 1936, studied at the University of Chicago. Sister Eleanore then went on to the University of Madrid. Encouraged by Sister Ste. Helene, she designed the college coat of arms based on models found in European museums, especially the Bargello in Florence, Italy. She made the needlepoint coat of arms displayed on occasion in O'Shaughnessy Auditorium.

With the well-educated sisters donating their teaching services, the college had little need for full-time lay teachers. The earliest years saw a succession of part-time teachers for subjects such as piano and violin, voice and elocution. Sister Antonia brought in competent part-time instructors for areas in which the sisters were not yet prepared to teach. From the University of Minnesota she recruited Richard Burton, Mary Ellen Chase, Robert Cushman, William DeHorn, Melvin Haggerty, Frank Rarig, Martin Ruud, and Anna Von Helmholz Phelan. The Reverends P. F. O'Brien, John Seliskar, and others from St. Thomas and the St. Paul Seminary also taught part time, as did George Klasse from the Minneapolis Symphony Orchestra.

Spencer Stoltz, who had earned a doctorate at the University of Chicago, worked full time as the college's first and sole chemistry teacher in 1921. Sister Antonius Kennelly and Lucille Bristol (Smith) '24 joined the department three years later as assistants and by 1927 were teaching chemistry full time. Stoltz was a quiet, honest man. Once when he found a student had cheated on a test, he merely remarked, "All I can say is . . . it's nice to be able to go to bed at night and to be able to face your own conscience."

Among the most loved teachers from the University of Minnesota was author and scholar Mary Ellen Chase. She taught English at the college for three school years beginning in 1929 and for three additional summers. She devoted a chapter in her book *A Goodly Fellowship* to the college and the friends she made there, saying: "I have never seen happier people, or funnier for that matter, than the nuns at St. Catherine's. Many of them were Irish by inheritance, some by birth, and their sense of humor was inimitable. I have never known so much laughter elsewhere or such good, rich cause for it. I like the thought, which I learned first at St. Catherine's, that those virtues resulting in sainthood are, first of all, simplicity and joy in the Lord rather than meekness, humility, patience, and other less attractive forms of holiness. Knowledge of the saints was not encouraged in my Maine upbringing; but in the years since then I have had a great good time in reading of some of them, and they have added immeasurably to my enjoyment of life.

"St. Catherine's, so far as I know, never looked upon me as either a heretic or a heathen. I shared, in so far as my 'heresy' allowed me, in its life, from which I gained blessings immeasurable. I liked the peace of its chapel, the quiet of its garden, the friendliness and fun of its nuns, the good manners of its students. I liked the shuffling off of a hundred trivialities, the release of which seemed not only possible but inevitable within its gates . . . I liked the single-mindedness . . . the sense that religion was not something to be seized upon in uneasy moments, but natural, like one's hands and feet, and waiting only to be discovered."

The Reverend P. F. O'Brien, from St. Thomas, brought classics to life through his references to people the students knew. Sister Helen Margaret Peck he called a "daughter of the gods, divinely tall," quoting from Tennyson's "A Dream of Fair Women." He demanded that translations be appropriate to the exalted tone of the original. At one commencement he read in Latin the citation for an honorary degree being presented to Mary Rahilly McCahill, then for the sake of the "barbarians" repeated it in English.

Religious, humanistic, and professional

As the faculty developed and enrollment increased, the curriculum expanded to keep pace with new demands. Sister Lioba O'Brien joined the English faculty in 1921, continuing her teaching there for more than fifty years. She taught classes on Shakespeare, Tennyson, Browning, the novel, and the short story, and had a facility for remembering the names of students and any of their mothers who had attended the college earlier. Once she remarked to a class: "It's all right for you to tell me that your mother went to school to me, but don't any of you tell me that your *grandmother* went to school to me." She had a strong and somewhat Victorian sense of humor. Every now and then she interrupted a lecture to say, "Will the young ladies in the back row please uncross your legs?" She locked the door of the classroom to latecomers and said, "Knock, knock, knock. Let them knock." After they had waited awhile, she let them in.

In 1927 Sister Helen Margaret returned from the University of Chicago with a doctorate, enriching the English faculty. Two years later, Sisters Antonine and Maris Stella, who had followed Sister Ste. Helene to study in England, returned with an Oxford sense of language and a regard for history, the tutorial method of teaching, and the intricacy of the Oxford system.

The two sisters' letters had drawn vivid images from their first landing in England: "It was a perfect moonlight night, and we had about three miles to go to our harbor. As we came to land a thick fog settled around us, and we could see nothing but eerie, winking lights and heard only the weird bells on the buoys and the harsh whistle of the tender, feeling her way through the fog. The first impressions I have of England are all colored by this night of arrival in Plymouth."

A weekly meeting with a tutor, to present an essay, was an integral part of the Oxford experience. Sister Antonine wrote to Sister Antonia on April 8, 1928: "We are both doing nineteenth-century literature and Middle English by way of language. I am somewhat tremulous about Miss Wardale, but perhaps I

The wheel (sometimes shown as broken), symbol of St. Catherine of Alexandria, represents the one on which she was to be martyred. The wavy line stands for the Mississippi River flowing near the college. The lily of France denotes the French origin of the Sisters of St. Joseph and the virginity of St. Catherine. The torch of learning relates to the mission of the college. On a scroll above the shield is the college motto: Progressum tutatur pietas *(Devotion to duty safeguards progress). An inverted sword represents St. Paul, patron of the archdiocese, and the sword of St. Catherine's decapitation.*

can do passing fair. Miss Dimsey, with whom I am to tutor in literature, is very young, as Miss Wardale is old." The, on October 31, 1928: "The seminar we have just come from is one of the most interesting ones we have had . . . Miss Brockhurst is young and Scotch and charming, and a convert besides . . . We go to her own room, which is an ideal tutor's room—literally packed with books, fine pictures, and intriguing curios—and incidentally a few chairs for those who do not care to sit on the floor."

The two sisters enrolled for tutorials or lectures on medieval romances, on Chaucer, Shakespeare, and English comedy. They heard lectures on Middle English texts by Charles Talbot Onions of *Oxford English Dictionary* fame. Sister Antonine wrote: "Unfortunately he stutters very badly, but that does not prevent him from bursting out in the middle of his lecture with 'Young lady, have you your gown? (A meek 'yes') Well, put it on . . . I have known young ladies to be sent home for just such offenses.'"

And on June 10, 1928: "We were fortunate enough to be at Convocation last Tuesday when [Henry] Craigie received his D. Litt. *Honoris causa,* in celebration of the completion of the Oxford Dictionary. Mr. Craigie's name was also on the King's birthday list the preceding week. He will therefore go back to Chicago [as] Sir Henry Craigie . . . Mr. Onions, assistant editor of the Oxford Dictionary, and the three printers to the University press . . . were also given honorary D. Litts. There was some excitement about these latter four; for Dr. Farnell, a member of Convocation and ex-vice-Chancellor, got up and entered a protest against the conferring of higher degrees for services not sufficiently scholastic."

Shortly before Sisters Antonine and Maris Stella returned from England, Sister Antonia read in the newspapers that Geheimrat Wieland of the University of Munich had won the Nobel Prize for chemistry. She decided two sisters should study in Germany: Sister Antonius in chemistry and Sister Agnes Rita in German literature. At the end of July 1929, they left for Munich. On the way they were to meet Sisters Antonine and Maris Stella in Paris.

In August 1929, Sister Antonius wrote of their landing to Sister Angele Gleason, who had joined the history faculty after earning a master's degree at the University of Chicago: "You must know that we were not met at all when we landed here. A message from the sisters informed us after we had boarded the special boat train at Le Havre that they would meet us at the Hotel de Chevreuse in Paris on Saturday. Imagine it being some fifteen months since I had attempted to pronounce a French word, but after four hours in the 'funny compartment' we were in Paris, and an obliging French porter, at my halting 'Expres Americain,' led us up to an American Express man who spoke perfect English and sent us on our way rejoicing to the *wrong* Hotel de Chevreuse (there being two of the same name, unknown to him), but in no time we were welcomed by an old French couple (again not a word of English) who said no sisters *ever* stayed there before, much to my interior misgiving, and they gave us a good clean double room for much less than a dollar a day."

The four sisters traveled through France and Germany in August. Upon their arrival in Munich, the sisters found political unrest a result of the growing influence of national socialism. Four years later Sister Agnes Rita wrote to Sister Antonia about the Nazi developments: "Everything is quiet here in Germany but consistently and forcefully heading toward Fascism. A few Catholic meetings were already forbidden here, and shortly before Pentecost the Catholic young men who are learning a trade and who were to have a con-

Sister Maris Stella Smith, some time after her study in England. She wrote: "We took a lovely bus trip across Dartmoor to Tintagel on the Cornish coast. The black cliffs are a great contrast to the reds and greens of South Devon. There is little left of the castle . . . in which Uther besieged the fair Igraine. A steep path ascends to a sheltered cave with towering rocks on either side, and the waves washing on the smooth sand beach. Under the cliffs is . . . Merlin's cave. The entrance is very dark, but as you go, light comes suddenly from the opposite side where the waves come in and there is a great clamour of water and whistling wind. Merlin himself almost rises from the shadows."

vention were forbidden to meet . . . Last week the government changed its mind and allowed the convention to take place but *only* within the stadium . . . The bishops of Germany met about a week ago . . . Among other things they demand freedom for every citizen, freedom for the Catholic youth societies, freedom of the Catholic press. The latter is an important point because all newspapers have been nationalized to the extent that an unimportant little Catholic weekly published near Munich was forced to dismiss its editor, a priest, and put in his place a secular . . . Hitler was in charge and was forcing National Socialism on the hospitals and schools, many of which were staffed by sisters. All the sisters in this vicinity (Bavaria, you probably have learned, is under a National Socialist dictator, a Catholic) seem to have only the one fear that pressure will be exercised on their schools. There are hundreds of lay teachers without positions, and the danger exists that the government may force some of them upon the convent schools, which are also under state control. That would not only put out some of the sister-teachers, but it would also place a financial burden on the schools which would make it impossible for them to exist."

Sister Antonius wrote in November 1933 of the difficulty of graduate study in a new language: "I miss all the jokes, or most all of them, which is very tragic in my young life, and I'd never dare ask a fellow German student to repeat them. My lab teacher, Herr Professor Doktor Fischer, has infinite patience with my murderous use of his mother tongue. I spend four hours a week taking the foreigners' course at the U, and while it is the 'berries,' compared with the Berlin one, I [still] hope to learn a great deal—knowing so little to start with."

Earlier, she had written of problems in adjusting to the chemistry labs: "The laboratories, as everybody predicted, are beautifully inconvenient. Perhaps I shall develop a better technique as a result. The stock room system is widely scattered, one place for glassware, another on the opposite side of the building for chemicals, special apparatus has to be ordered from a firm in the city, matches, towels, and the like . . . My fellow Americans and the Englishman are very indignant about our having to *buy* practically all our glassware. The Englishman plans to have an auction when he leaves."

Sister Antonius was accepted by Wieland for work on her doctoral dissertation. He was eager to learn more about America, she wrote Sister Angele in March 1931: "I cannot imagine that Geheimrat Wieland would be terribly impressed on Sister Jeanne d'Arc's announcing a connection with me when they met in Chicago, though I flatter myself that he would know of whom she spoke, being as I am the only sister in organic chemistry and for these two semesters the only one in the building . . . I have conferred with him three times all told so far, and he has been amiable enough, even eager to practice his English on me, and manifesting great interest in Minnesota and CSC [College of St. Catherine] chemistry. I finally satisfied his curiosity on the subject of CSC head of chemistry when he, at the third conference, asked if Mr. [Spencer] Stoltz were a monk. His astonishment knew no bounds when I said that Mr. Stoltz was not only a layman but a non-Catholic: 'Ach, Sie sind viel mehr tolerant in America als wir in Deutschland.'"

When Sister Antonius went to make arrangement for her preliminary oral examination, Wieland told her about his recent travels in America. Then, she wrote on May 23, he said: "'Now you want to take your examination.' 'Yes,' quakingly. 'How about tomorrow at 10:30?' Nothing to do but say I'd be there. How's that for German speed?"

In 1931, Sisters Antonius Kennelly, Anna Goulet, and Agnes Rita Lingl visited Cambridge, England, on their way to study in France and Germany.

On the next day she took the oral: "Well, if I ever murdered the German language I did it to perfection in the next hour. When I was dismissed with a funereal air by the three present, I was absolutely certain I had failed. There was little to be hoped for from Professor Fajans, who had been absent that day in the hardest of branches (physical chemistry), but I dragged myself back on the following Monday. Fajans had just been granted a neat sum from the Rockefeller Foundation to build an addition to the lab exclusively for physical chemistry—a million marks, gossip says. Well, you never saw anybody so amiable. After I had struggled along for ten minutes or so in German, he said I might speak English if I wished. Did I! Henceforth I shall regard Rockefeller as a personal benefactor. I could feel that I was going to get through, and sure enough, at the end of half an hour he sent me down to Wieland with a note, which must have been the deciding factor. On reading it he said, 'Then you have passed the whole exam. Ich gratuliere Ihnen.'"

Sisters Antonius and Agnes Rita also managed some travel in Europe. During one Christmas holiday they went to Vienna, visiting the home monastery of Gregor Mendel. They went to Brunn, where Mendel had lived in an Augustinian monastery, hoping to find some Mendel artifacts for placement in Mendel Hall, then under construction on the St. Catherine campus: "One of the monks took a flashlight and rushed us to the museum . . . and thus we saw in the little 10 x 10 museum, all they have of Mendelia originals—apparatus, manuscripts, etc. The plaque already sent to you was there too, made by a Brunn artist for the centenary of 1922 . . . Then we were shown Mendel's garden . . . very small, if my judgment was not impaired by the twilight—I should say about 30 x 12 feet, and as the Procurator said, 'In that very plot, he established the law that made him known to the ends of the earth.'"

Through the influence of the National Minister of Education in Paris, Sister Antonius had an opportunity in May 1933 to visit, while in Paris, the Pasteur Institute, the Institute of Industrial Physics, and the Institute of Radium. She was conducted through the Institute of Radium by Marie Curie's daughter, Irene Curie. After the tour, she and another visitor were ushered into a small office where Marie Curie, looking very old and weak, thanked them for coming to the Pasteur Institute. Madame Curie died a year later.

Meanwhile the art department on campus was growing, especially the painting classes. The first art instructor was Sister Berissima Boog, among those who had opened the college in 1905. She had attended and studied at St. Agatha's Conservatory, a St. Paul facility of the Sisters of St. Joseph, devoted to the arts—music, painting, sculpture, drama, and elocution. Sister Berissima had just returned from study in Europe, where she copied many masterpieces. These and many of her later works were displayed at St. Agatha's and at St. John's Academy in Jamestown, North Dakota. She painted the portraits of St. Catherine and of Hugh Derham now hanging in Derham Hall. Sister Berissima was succeeded by Sister Anysia Keating, recently returned from a two-year sojourn in Europe, especially in Florence and Munich. Gifted in painting and ceramics, she was probably in charge of the art department through 1913-14. After many encounters with administrators, she developed a shrewd strategy, saying: "If you act a little queer, they will leave you alone."

In 1914 Sisters Marie Teresa Mackey and Cosmas Shea joined the college art department, which under the guidance of Sister Marie Teresa progressed rapidly. For years she planned study with some renowned artist each summer. According to Agatha Hynes Miller '18: "She couldn't wait to bring all of that

Sister Agnes Rita Lingl, above, especially admired Bavarian religious customs—the Advent calendar, Advent wreath, Jesse tree, and observance of St. Nicholas Day—and introduced these to students upon her return from Europe in 1933.

Copying masterpieces and painting from plaster casts were acceptable methods of study for art classes. These students painted from live models (sometimes each other) as well.

knowledge back to us." Sister Philomene McAuley joined the art department when Sister Cosmas left the college in 1914, and she became head of the art department in 1933. She had received a master's degree from the University of Chicago in 1931. Sister Philomene was a member of the Minneapolis Art Association and of the Catholic Art Association, and she became national secretary of the latter in 1924. She helped to frame its objectives: to foster a truly Christian social art after discovering what human art is and what Catholic art is, to work for eliminating "the blasphemy of ugliness" from Catholic churches, and to encourage and facilitate art activity in Catholic schools. The association had little success in defining "human" or "Catholic" art.

Sociology and social work curricula also developed remarkably in the 1920s and 1930s. The *College Bulletin* announced: "The new part that women must take in solving social problems makes it imperative that the department of social and political science furnish a standard of judgment, and include courses like Racial Backgrounds and Americanization." To help meet the need for specially trained workers in the field of social service and to encourage students to become interested in social work, the department listed four senior courses in applied sociology, later called "social case work." The dean's report for June 1932 announced the addition of an organized course in social service work, leading to a social service major. The course consisted of one quarter of social psychology, one of social psychiatry, and one of supervised field work.

Interest in the social sciences on campus reflected the growing involvement of women in fields of social service in the United States. The Reverend Frederick Seidenburg, SJ, dean of Loyola University School of Sociology, addressed an enthusiastic St. Catherine audience in April 1924: "I take it that the new citizenship [his topic] primarily refers to the citizenship of women endowed with the ballot [the 19th Amendment was ratified in 1920], but I think it could be applied to the citizenship of the male, because we are entering not only on the new age of woman, but let us hope, in the new age of social justice . . . Woman's instinct and her sympathy naturally gives her vision for better things, and hence it was natural that women . . . were the instigators and promoters of most of our social reforms. We can thank them for the fight on child mortality, on tuberculosis, and child labor, on underfed children. We can thank them for their advocacy of a living wage, for housing reforms, for vocational guidance, for supervised public recreation . . . To repeat, their standard is the normal life for all citizens and hence logically their goal is social justice to all!"

Sister Marie Philip, later reflecting on social work experiences of students in the 1920s, said that a social worker named Ruby Boughman was teaching at the college during that period. She took students to visit a street along the Mississippi River called "The Levee": "There was something like a frame schoolhouse—just one room, as I can remember. And you would go in there and there would be . . . just the nicest Italian chefs and bakers—all men. The women didn't go out at night . . . We were trying to teach them. Of course, we knew nothing about teaching English to foreigners—absolutely nothing . . . But I remember those nights, the warmth of them and the gratitude of those men . . . We kind of prepared them for Americanization. For citizenship papers you need to know a little civics. And we felt perfectly safe. Nobody worried about us walking from Seventh Street to the Levee and back."

New emphasis was also placed on educating teachers for preschool children. Particularly gifted in teaching young children, Sister Ann Harvey, who had earned a master's degree in childhood education at Columbia in 1930, took over the nursery school opened by Ruby Blackhurst in 1929, continuing until her retirement in 1974. Over the years she taught several thousand children, some of whom became prominent St. Paul professionals.

Continuing emphasis on the importance of science brought several new members to the science departments in the late 1920s. Sister St. Mark Wirtz received a bachelor's degree from the college and a master's degree from the University of Minnesota in 1932 and taught general biology, ecology, botany, histological techniques, heredity, history of biology, embryology, nature study, local flora, ornithology, plant morphology, and zoology. She later taught geography in Russia Area Studies for the five-college consortium. Sister St. Mark pursued many hobbies. She made slides of the campus, of killdeer nesting, of flowers in bloom. She made jelly, did weaving, crocheting, knitting, and photography, winning several prizes at the Minnesota State Fair. She made and sold rosaries, investing the proceeds in a camera for the biology department.

Science faculty member Sister Teresita Judd entered the novitiate in 1922. Sister Antonia, who was at time working to obtain a chapter of Phi Beta Kappa, soon sent her to the University of Minnesota to study for a degree in biology and "get elected to Phi Beta Kappa." Sister Teresita graduated *summa cum laude* and was elected to Phi Beta Kappa and to Sigma Xi, an honor society in biology. She continued with graduate study, receiving a master's degree in 1940 and a doctorate in 1948 with research on the effects of chemical and physical elements in experimental animals. Later she continued postdoctoral research at Roswell Park Institute in Buffalo, New York, for eight summers. In the summers of 1944 and 1945 she worked at Institutum Divi Thomae, in Cincinnati, looking for a medication for dysentery.

Sister Teresita had many interests besides teaching and research. She ran the printing press for faculty and staff and made original greeting cards for them. For the biology department she made over a hundred charts used in

Sister Ann Harvey composed songs and dances, correlating rhythms with activities like running or skipping and describing the sounds as tripping fairies or lumbering giants. Then she gave the flowers and butterflies (above) a chance to try for themselves. Her work was published as Rhythms and Dances for Pre-School and Kindergarten *in 1944.*

teaching biology. She helped various faculty members, especially the priests in the theology department, by running off their tests and having them corrected by machine.

Sister Marie James Gibbons returned from Columbia University in 1936 with a doctorate in chemistry. She was especially interested in preparing students for research in chemistry. She received several grants from the National Science Foundation to do so, and in 1964 St. Catherine student affiliates of the American Chemical Society and of Iota Sigma Pi (honor society in chemistry) were cited as "outstanding." Sister Marie James, like many of the broadly educated sisters, would show great flexibility, playing many roles at the college.

Spencer Stoltz left the chemistry department for industrial work in 1936, later taking a position at the College of St. Scholastica in Duluth. He returned to the College of St. Catherine faculty when Sister Antonius, who had rejoined the chemistry department after her studies in Germany, became president in 1943. He remained until his death in 1951.

Sister St. Mark Wirtz took her ornithology class birdwatching. She was for a time in charge of the college grounds, where she planted many trees and worked in the greenhouse with gardener Salvatore Cerri in experiments to produce the "papple," a cross between a pear and an apple.

Of buildings, bucks, and books

Increased enrollment and expanding programs necessitated buildings in addition to Derham Hall, and Sister Antonia had embarked on a large-scale construction program. With friends from the University of Chicago and elsewhere, Sister Antonia set out for New York more than once to submit proposals for new buildings to various funding institutions.

When Sister Antonia was appointed dean in 1914, work on a second major building for the college had already begun. With the Derham Hall dormitories filled to overflowing, some provision had to be made for housing. The November 12, 1912, *Catholic Bulletin* commented: "The excavation of the new building to be added to St. Catherine's College is about completed and work on the basement walls has begun. It will have a frontage of 198 feet on Randolph Street, near Prior, and will have a depth of 173 feet. It will be a brick building of reenforced concrete, and will have four stories and a basement." In the fall of 1914, College Hall (at first called simply "the other building"), for housing

Two boarders, above, studied in their room in College Hall, opened in the fall of 1914. Sisters Maris Stella and Antonine returned in 1929 from studies in England with the idea of renaming the building for Hilda of Whitby Abbey, a center of learning remarkable for its intellectual progress and for being led by a woman. Jeanne d'Arc Auditorium, attached to Whitby Hall, was for years the scene of a weekly convocation, above right, attended by every Katie dressed in an academic gown purchased upon registration. After graduation she could hand in the gown for recycling—or put a piece of it in her scrapbook!

college students and college facilities, was opened. The central section of the first story was designated Music Hall, East Hall housed the art department, and the west wing—Science Hall—housed home economics and science. The residence corridors could accommodate 250 students. Jeanne d'Arc Auditorium, an extension, soon welcomed students, teachers, and speakers, as well as music department concerts and dramatic productions.

Ecstatic about its lovely new building, members of the St. Catherine community watched the beginnings of war on the other side of the world. Sentiment was strong against U.S. involvement both across the country and on campus until, after some provocation, Congress voted to help France fight Germany, on April 2, 1917. Then, much of the discussion on campus turned towards how best to serve. The Summer 1917 *Ariston* included an editorial called "College Women and War" as well as poems such as "War Hymn to Mary" and "Flag of Peace." A later editorial countered a suggestion that the college close so students could work for the war effort. After all, well-trained minds would be needed to put the world back together: To continue school, pray for peace, and join the Red Cross effort seemed the better course.

The college stayed open. Sister Eleanore Michel worked to retain the teaching of German and build the department despite the growing regulation of German texts by the Minnesota Commission of Public Safety. Students variously put on war benefits or continued antiwar efforts, expressing their positions in poems and editorials. And though not all students and faculty members agreed on American involvement in the war, almost everyone on campus became involved in knitting or making dressings for the St. Paul Red Cross, setting up the Derham Hall dining room every Friday afternoon for the purpose. All were happy to hear "The Great War is over" ringing through the hall at midday on Friday, November 8, 1918. A bit prematurely, Sister Antonia gave the rest of the day off, but on the following Monday, the armistice was signed.

Despite suggestions that college students go to work, the war had in fact brought enrollment up. On December 14, 1918, the *Catholic Bulletin* noted that "twenty music rooms have been converted into dormitories and thirty single rooms have been transformed into double rooms. The intention of young women to prepare themselves to fill positions of men who have gone to the front is thought to be one of the reasons for breaking all records."

Sister Antonia was ready. To make her vision concrete, she had drawn up a complete building and landscape plan. The next step would be a building for the music department, to be named for the patron of music, St. Cecilia. She set out on one of several visits to George Vincent at the Rockefeller Foundation, returning from New York with the promise of financial help and advice to establish a board of trustees.

On January 27, 1919, the Board of Trustees of the College of St. Catherine met for the first time, in the "Alumnae Parlour" of College Hall. Listed in attendance in the minutes were Sister Seraphine Ireland (ex officio, provincial superior), Sister Antonia McHugh (ex officio, president of the college), the Very Reverend Monsignor Humphrey Moynihan (president of the College of St. Thomas), Marion Leroy Burton (president of the University of Minnesota), John J. Toomey (vice president and treasurer of Northwestern Trust Company and father of Sisters Teresa and Joan Toomey), Michael. J. Dillon (general manager of Pacific Mutual Life Insurance Company), E. (Edward) M. McMahon (general secretary of the St. Paul Association of Public and Business Affairs), Thomas D. O'Brien (former chief justice of the Minnesota Supreme Court and an attorney with O'Brien, Young, Stone, and Horn), Michael W. Waldorf (president of Waldorf Paper Products), and William C. Carroll, M.D. (St. Joseph Hospital). Mrs. James (Mary Rahilly) McCahill of Lake City and Mrs. George T. (Charlotte Hill) Slade of St. Paul, also new trustees named in the bylaws of the amended certificate of incorporation, had telegraphed their regrets. The twelve-member board was to hold and invest endowment funds and to approve mortgages, indebtedness, purchase and sale of property, and the erection of buildings. The trustees elected Burton as chair, Waldorf as vice-chair, and Sister Antonia as secretary and discussed the foundation already laid for a first-class college. They appointed a committee to plan an endowment campaign to raise $200,000 as a match for a $100,000 grant from the Rockefeller Foundation and planned to entertain Wallace Buttrick, president of the foundation's General Education Board. At the next two meetings, they agreed with Buttrick on the terms of the grant, including that it not be used for theological instruction, and approved plans for the new music hall.

On April 14, 1921, Burton resigned from the board and Archbishop Austin Dowling, who had succeeded Ireland in 1919, was elected a trustee. He immediately was named chair, and the archbishop for many years thereafter served as the titular head of the board. The board usually met only once each year, mostly to approve new construction. Dowling was just beginning an archdiocesan capital campaign of his own. He immediately offered to grant the college $200,000 from the Archbishop Ireland Educational Fund—provided that Sister Antonia refrain from mounting a separate campaign. She did, earning the college's one and only archdiocesan subsidy, and used it to match the Rockefeller grant. In the fall of 1921, Caecilian Hall opened with studios for the faculty, practice rooms for students, and a recital hall for performances.

The first college homecoming, sponsored by the St. Catherine Alumnae Association in June 1923, marked the twentieth anniversary of the laying of

After Caecilian Hall opened in 1921, students enjoyed the tradition of decorating a Christmas tree reaching up through the staircase wells. The new building was named for St. Cecilia, patroness of music.

During the 1923 homecoming, a statue of the Sacred Heart, gift of the alumnae, was blessed and installed in front of Derham Hall.

the college cornerstone. Since the first graduates had completed high school only (forty Derham Hall graduates started an alumnae group in 1908), the college alumnae association did not meet officially until June 7, 1917, when it elected Margaret (later Sister Mary Cecilia) Carnel '14 its first president. In 1919 the college was approved for listing by the Association of Collegiate Alumnae, and by 1920 the association had twenty baccalaureate members. In 1921 graduates teaching in the state began the custom of meeting on campus during the annual fall convention of the Minnesota Educational Association in the Twin Cities.

A year after the 1923 homecoming, *Ariston* noted that at the annual alumnae business meeting Lillian Busian (Lord) '24 was elected editor-in-chief of the *Alumnae News,* to be issued three times each year. In June 1929, the alumnae constitution was revised to include resident corresponding and financial secretaries—Sisters Mona and Eleanore, respectively. The *Alumnae News* became the *Alumnae News Letter,* a mimeographed bulletin of three or four pages. So it remained until March 1941, when it resumed its earlier name and printed format. In 1932 Sister Eleanore became secretary of the association, serving until 1943. The association undertook to contribute to an endowment for the college, and by 1936, its members had signed pledges of $120 each, to be paid in twenty-four annual installments. The funds were used to buy life insurance on six sister faculty members at $10,000 each, for an eventual endowment fund of $60,000. In 1967 the alumnae honored Sister Eleanore with a citation "because of your concern for the college and your complete devotion from the earliest days of the college to Mother Antonia's vision of a great St. Catherine's."

In 1923, the same year the statue was erected, the entire campus was enclosed by a wrought-iron fence with elaborate gates, and planning was initiated for a separate chapel. It would be large, Romanesque, and beautiful—from the high bell tower to the tiled roof and tile facing on interior walls and pillars. H. A. Sullwold was chosen as architect and Paul Steenberg as contractor. Sullwold was sent to Europe to visit Spanish and French medieval cathedrals so he would understand what the chapel should look like. He visited the Church of St. Trophime at Arles, France, which Sister Antonia had admired in 1922. She told him that with a few adaptations, the chapel at the college must follow suit.

Work on the chapel progressed rapidly, with many conferences among Sister Antonia, the architect, and the contractor. When the workers laying concrete for the floor were unable to finish before Thanksgiving of 1923, Sister Antonia promised to provide Thanksgiving dinner if they would work through the holiday to finish. And so they did. On another occasion, when the tile company did not want to work on Saturday, contractor Paul Steenberg persuaded the carpentry foreman and bricklayer foremen to lay tiles themselves. Sister Antonia was so pleased she gave each of them a box of cigars. Years later, Steenberg wrote: "I was much pleased with doing this chapel for many reasons. First, it was a place to worship God. It was a beautiful chapel, and I believe I had satisfied Sister Antonia's wish, which I was told could not be done. [She] was a woman who knew what she wanted and was pleased when she got a real job."

On October 7, 1924, the chapel was complete, and it was dedicated on the feast of Our Lady of Victory, for whom it was named. Three days earlier, the *Catholic Bulletin* had given fourteen pages almost exclusively to the college and its new chapel. Archbishop Dowling reportedly said: "Sister Antonia asked to build a chapel, but she built a cathedral." Sister Lioba, an enthusiastic obser-

The neighborhood was still full of empty lots when the chapel was built in the 1920s. Clockwise from left: College Hall (Whitby), Caecilian Hall, Derham Hall, the Chapel of Our Lady of Victory, and the beginnings of the Dew Drop. These images at the main entrance of the chapel honored college founders and patrons:
- St. Catherine of Alexandria, patroness of the college
- St. Joseph for the Sisters of St. Joseph
- St. Teresa of Avila, on whose feast day in 1650 the sisters had become a congregation
- St. Michael the Archangel for Mother Seraphine Ireland, provincial superior and founder
- St. Anthony of Padua for Sister Antonia McHugh, first president
- St. Rose of Lima for Mother St. Rose Mackey, provincial superior during construction
- St. Agnes for the Reverend Mother Agnes Gonzaga, general superior (St. Louis)
- St. John for Archbishop John Ireland, instrumental in founding the college
- St. Augustine for Archbishop Austin Dowling, in office during construction
- Thérèse of Lisieux, the Little Flower, because Sister Antonia hoped she would be canonized.

ver, wrote to Sister Ste. Helene at Oxford University in England: "That great day dawned . . . summer sun, summer warmth, summer green on all sides—and through this loveliness of combined beauty there passed from College Hall to the Chapel of Our Lady of Victory, the procession of dedication—the Archbishop in Cappa Magna, monsignori in such a blaze of glory that it communicated itself to the entire line, priests to the number of at least seventy, the college student body, and people world without end . . . Father [Francis] Missia and the seminarians sang the litany all the way down the aisle, and the reverence of students and congregation can never be forgotten.

"Father [Aloysius] Ziskowsky presided in the sanctuary and his prowess in the church service kept things moving with both grace and precision, but with no sign of obtrusiveness . . . Some of the college girls were ushers in the true sense of the word, for they seated a throng which must have numbered 1,000. All the pews were full with six in a pew besides hundreds of chairs. Mr. [Leopold] Bruenner's Mass was divine—parts of it like the Agnus Dei really inspired—and never did Anna [Goulet] play nor the sisters sing as on last Tuesday. The seminarians sang the gradual and the proper of the Mass in Gregorian chant and the change from their voices to the choir was most affecting . . . there is no telling when [Anna] will again come down to foot locomotion."

Sister Anna had first use of what the *Catholic Bulletin* described as: "a fine, three-manual organ . . . That this organ might thoroughly harmonize with the beautiful new building, the Reuter Organ Company sent their experts to St. Paul to go over the plans and details of the building with the architects . . . It . . . has character, one that is admirably well fitted for concert purposes as well as for chapel services."

With the dedication complete, faculty and staff helped move the library from Derham Hall to the ground floor of the new chapel. A new closed stack system meant that student assistants in large numbers paged books to waiting patrons. The library science department, at first called the "School of Library Science," moved there, too. Beginning in 1918 with a nine-credit course in school librarianship, the program had quickly grown under Sister Marie Cecilia Marzolf, who had graduated from the college in 1920 and received a bachelor's degree in library science in 1926 from the New York State Library School in Albany. In 1926 a principal sequence, distributed over the junior and senior years and leading to a bachelor's degree in library science, was offered.

Sister Marie Cecilia, named head librarian in 1926, also presided over a growing book collection, partly the result of a gift of $5,000 from the Carnegie Corporation that year. In 1929 Sister Marie Jose Matchinsky, who was to receive her bachelor's degree in library science from Columbia University in 1930, became head librarian, and Sister Marie Cecilia devoted her full effort to the library science department, revising the program to meet a new requirement of the American Library Association that the entire senior year be devoted to the principal sequence. Then, according to the president's report for 1930-31: "The library school was examined and provisionally accredited by the Board of Education for librarianship . . . In the spring of this year it was re-examined and received final accrediting."

According to Ariston, *April 1924: "No one could have imagined that [the library beneath the chapel] would be so spacious, so bright, and so attractive. The bookstacks are all behind the charging desk as the closed shelf system is now employed. The students feel this to be a great improvement. Reserve books never disappear mysteriously as they did of yore . . . The reading room . . . tempts even the least studious to work there."*

In the meantime, Sister Antonia had attended to the construction of a new building for the sciences. A second grant of $100,000 from the Rockefeller Foundation in 1926 made possible the erection of Mendel Hall, named for the great Austrian biologist and discoverer of the laws of heredity. Sister Antonia again gave credit to George Vincent, saying he encouraged "our plans for the upbuilding of our science department. . . it was largely through his support that we received the necessary financial aid." The *Catholic Bulletin* noted upon its opening in September 1927: "Mendel Hall is to be used exclusively by the science departments. It is a five-story building of variegated red and terra cotta brick . . . The building is divided by a tower, the center of which is ninety-four feet from the east end . . . The new hall was designed to hold approximately fifteen laboratories, as well as lecture rooms, study hall, and faculty office." But Mendel Hall soon accommodated the art department, the education department, and a Montessori child care facility as well. And the sisters who had returned from Oxford set up Mendel Hall 200 as a seminar room, filled with books and pictures of England, including a complete set of carved wooden figures of the Canterbury pilgrims from Chaucer's tales.

In 1929, the Rockefeller Foundation granted $300,000 to help develop the health program at the college. The new building, at first known as the Health Center and later as Fontbonne Hall, particularly was to provide space for training in basic sciences for nurses and in physical education for teachers. Sister Antonia, in the president's report for 1931-32, stated that the new Health Center, open that year, "embodies the complete realization . . . of the health unit in our expansion program." The burgeoning library school also moved to the Health Center. The new office for the department chair, a laboratory room for technical processes, and a large classroom there meant more room for the crowded library beneath the chapel.

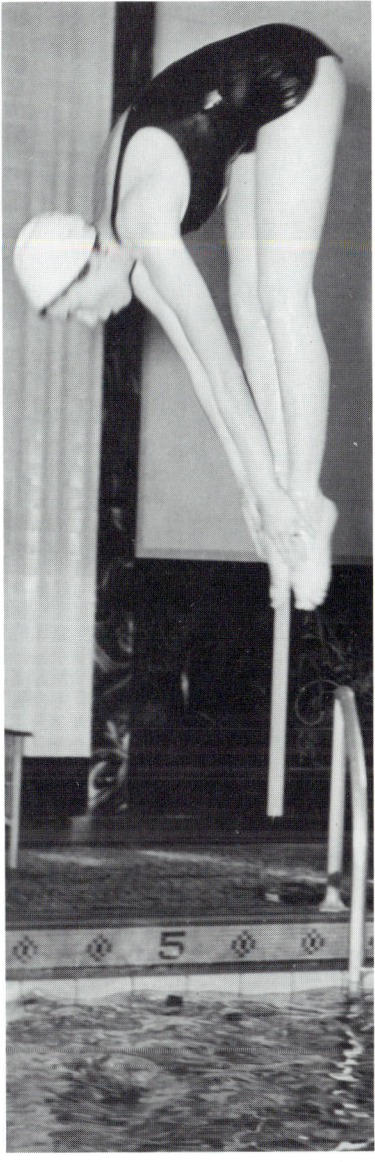

Praise with pots and pans . . .

The care and maintenance of six buildings and the hundreds of students filling them demanded much of the nonteaching staff of the college. Among those working behind the scenes was Sister Georgia Morrisson, beloved friend and counselor of students living in Whitby Hall. She had greeted the first students arriving from St. Joseph's Academy in 1905. Among other responsibilities, she had charge of the laundry, which at that time meant washing all the students' clothes. Sister Georgia assigned each sister, including faculty members, a part of the laundry work according to her own estimate of the other's intelligence. When a task was not well done, she might say: "And you with your Ph.D!"

Sister Georgia often shared her memories of the "old days" with the younger sisters: "We had a horse named Dolly. She was kept in a stable below the library [at that time in Derham Hall]. We cut hay for her in the field by Cleveland Avenue . . . We used to grow ever-bearing strawberries and all kinds of vegetables and potatoes. The sisters planted the potatoes by following the plow . . . It was hard work, hard on your back. We had to pick off potato bugs too."

Well known among students, too, were several Sisters of St. Joseph who had come to America from Ireland as lay missionaries. (The United States was considered mission territory until 1921.) The Irish sisters—Odelia Murphy, Jarlath Noonan, Candida Gallahue, Elerius Hennessy, and others—provided

The college's definition of liberal arts education for women included the physical and scientific. Students (above left) participated in a chemistry lab in Mendel Hall, opened in 1927. Legend has it that Sister Antonia ordered the new hall built slightly to the east of the original plan, to prevent the extension of Prior Avenue through the campus. Four years later, every Katie was required to take swimming in the Health Center, later named Fontbonne Hall, for Mother St. John Fontbonne, who refounded the Sisters of St. Joseph after the French Revolution and first sent the sisters to America.

Sister Georgia Morrison for many years presided over Whitby Hall. She liked to tell the younger sisters of the earlier days when the sisters owned a horse.

Riding was for years a student activity, too. Phyllis Hale, Catherine Thornton, and Mary Helen Thornton (Haaker) '39, rode at Fort Snelling in 1937 as members of the college's Western Saddles Club.

a warm, loving atmosphere, consoling many a homesick freshman with an extra cookie or piece of cake. Magdalen (later Sister Marie David) Schimanski, a student in the late 1930s, remembered: "Sister Odelia . . . used to provide our work-a-day spreads on a summer evening because we always stayed during summers and vacations . . . the painters, the electricians would have to work in the buildings, so we would move every month to a different building . . . I was very fond of all those kitchen sisters from Ireland: Sister Candida, Elerius, Jarlath. I remember them standing in the chapel—it would be the grand entrance to the chapel overlooking the Dew Drop. They'd be looking at the sunset there. I could almost draw them from memory—those silhouettes of those great big women. There was something beautiful about their peacefulness and their joy and the way they were friendly to us students."

Another admirer, Mary Ellen Chase, wrote in *A Goodly Fellowship:* "They praised the Lord with pots and pans as cymbals and harps and with good food. I used to go into their huge kitchen below the chapel cloister and talk with them as they beat, stirred, and kneaded. The four of them were ample women of great good humor. They wore large gray aprons over their black habits and usually had a touch of flour somewhere on their black veils. As they bustled about in their convent garb intent upon the means of existence, they somehow connected the religious life with the ageless, and surely religious, necessity of daily bread."

For many years Frank Trojan was the ever-faithful chef, never so happy as when he was baking bread or rolls for the evening meal. For special occasions he produced beautifully decorated cakes.

The building and grounds crew included Salvatore Cerri and his wife, Evelyn. For more than twenty years, Salvatore worked on the grounds crew and Evelyn as custodian in Fontbonne Hall. Salvatore, known on campus as Cerri, cared for the trees, flowers, and lawns under the supervision of Sister St. Mark. At times Cerri pruned the trees almost to extinction, much to her distress. Years, later, when Sister Mary William Brady was president of the college, Cerri one day burst into her office, exclaiming in Italian-English: "Mud, Mud, come quick. Chap fall in lake," meaning "Mother, mother, come quickly. The chapel is falling into the [Dew Drop]." Sister Mary William assured him that the chapel would not fall into the lake and that the crack in the foundation would be repaired soon.

Gardener Dave Bacigalupo, for many years wintered over and transplanted plants in the greenhouse attached to Mendel Hall. His specialty was growing poinsettias for Christmas decorations in the chapel. He made date palms and grapefruit trees flourish in the greenhouse and started many plants for transplantation on the grounds.

Tim Feeney was a railroad man for twenty-four years before he came to the college. Hired for painting, he soon took over carpentry and general repairs, and for twenty-three years he was in charge of all door and furniture repairs. Asked why he stayed so long, he said, "I liked the work and I liked the people."

And beyond

Sister Antonia oversaw the construction of five college buildings from 1914 to 1932, but her vision for the students reached beyond buildings, beyond campus, beyond city and nation. To her mind, one could not be fully educated without travel in Europe. She emphasized that basic to preparation for travel was intensive study of the appropriate language: "I am quite sure of this, that encouragement should be given to our young people in schools to acquire a language sense. They should be encouraged to learn at least one or two modern languages which they could use with facility—other than our mother tongue. Many times I have had parents ask me, 'What is the good of learning French or German? Our daughter will not speak these languages here in America.' True, there is rare occasion for their use, but let us hope that most of our boys and girls will have a chance to visit the countries where these languages are spoken. Certainly it makes for cultural background in every way."

If students could not get to other countries, she found a way to bring other countries to them. One way to accomplish that was to offer scholarships to international students. Several students from Canada and one from Mexico had attended the college earlier, but the first European students were Lucienne and Angele Petit, at the college from 1918 to 1920. Emerging from the postwar devastation of France, they had had little preparation for the United States. Sister Mona Riley recalled: "I can remember them sitting with babushkas over their heads, not knowing any English, but they turned out beautifully. Lucienne finished at one of the universities—I think it was Columbia—and then she taught at Adelphi College on Long Island."

After these first two students from France, a steady stream of international students—from Puerto Rico, Panama, Peru, and Brazil, from Germany, Hungary, Italy, Spain, Greece, the Philippines, Iraq, Israel, and Japan—registered at the college. In the 1970s and 1980s many students came from Africa—Kenya, Tanzania, Nigeria—and from the Orient—Japan, China, Malaysia, and Pakistan. Many years after her own student experience abroad, Sister Marie Philip said: "International outreach has been one of the marks of the college . . . In my own life, certainly nothing was as important, academically, as my having gone to France, ill-prepared as I was. It opened so much to me, and it was a very formative period in my life. I was young, I was *very* receptive, and I think if I was able later to do rather outstanding work with the [French] Institute, it was really that I am kind of half French, in the sense that French values were imprinted upon me so ineradicably during the two years that I was a student in France."

Sister Antonia also encouraged international-mindedness by inviting teachers from other countries as native speakers to help students improve their language skills. Among the early exchange teachers was Marthe Devaux, from the northern part of France. She studied at Hamline University in St. Paul, then in 1927 came to teach French at the College of St. Catherine. After several years she returned to France to enter the Sisters of St. Joseph of Bourg, where she received the name Sister Madelaine Alice.

Isabella Schmitz-Dumont '32 from Cologne, Germany, was first an exchange student and then a teacher at the college. Arriving in 1929, she earned a bachelor's degree while teaching intermediate German, anatomy, and physiology. She then took a premedical course at the University of Minnesota. Looking back, she said: "I accepted a one-year scholarship from Mother Antonia. That one year extended to six years, and those years became very important and decisive for my future life." In 1934 she entered the Women's Medical College in Philadelphia, where she earned an M.D. degree. She served a residency in surgery at St. Mary's Hospital and in obstetrics at St. John's Hospital in Philadelphia. During this time she met Joan Mulder, a medical technologist and artist. They shared a dream of being missionaries in Africa. In St. Vincent's Hospital in Birmingham, Alabama, the two young women met

Sisters Elerius Hennessy, Candida Gallahue, and Jarlath Noonan, above with a friend in 1939, were among the Irish "kitchen sisters" working at the college from its earliest days.

Students could learn about quantity cooking from chef Frank Trojan, above in 1950.

Archbishop Thomas Toolan, who urged them to help the work of the Edmundite missions in Selma, Alabama, rather than go to Africa. In September 1944, they opened a Selma clinic connected with Good Samaritan Hospital. For thirty-six years, Schmitz-Dumont was the only physician on call at "Good Sam." She delivered thousands of babies and performed hundreds of emergency procedures.

Schmitz-Dumont served as president of the Dallas County Medical Association, as charger fellow of the American Academy of Physicians, and as a member of the board of directors of Good Samaritan Hospital. In 1961, Pope John XXIII conferred the Medal *Pro Pontifice et Ecclesia* on Schmitz-Dumont and Mulder for their heroic service for the poor of Selma. They also received the Good Samaritan Award from the National Catholic Welfare Conference in 1975 and the *Lumen Christi* from the Catholic Extension Society in 1979.

Students unable to travel abroad learned much from international students and teachers on campus, as well as from other visitors and events of the day. In the vanguard of American women preparing for new participation in the world, they were independent in spirit and sometimes broke college rules designed to limit "radical behavior." Lucy Sanschagrin '25 (later Sister Marie Ursule), for instance, was almost expelled for bobbing her hair, and Mary O'Brien '27 (Sister Antonine's sister) was accused of "suffragetteism" for carrying a swagger stick. There seems to have been little activity related to women's suffrage (most students were not old enough to vote), but after women's right to vote was ratified in 1919, mock presidential elections were held. The first, apparently in response to the election of Calvin Coolidge, was described in the 1924 *La Concha* (student yearbook begun in 1919-20): "Not to be outstripped by any other independent women in America, we of the College of St. Catherine decided to use our privilege of franchise and held our own election. It was with much agitation and anxiety that the girls gathered at eleven o'clock on a certain Wednesday morning in the auditorium. After several days electioneering the students met ready to assert their opinions and support their candidates. In fact, the meeting resembled a Republican caucus."

Then interest in social and political events grew, and with faculty members returning from study in other lands, the discussion of world issues flourished. Activities of the campus League of Women Voters included participation in state and national conventions, presentation of a radio broadcast written and performed by students, participation in the Model Disarmament Conference, and hosting the state convention in 1932 and the fourth annual meeting of the Model League of Nations in 1934. The dean's report for that year noted that "the League has been one of our most enterprising organizations. Since its inception in 1929, it has attracted some of the most promising of our students."

The students retained their ability to challenge what they heard. A *Wheel* editorial on April 12, 1935, discussed a speaker at the Woman's Club of Minneapolis: "Dame Rachel Crowdy, head of the humanitarian committee of the League of Nations, was scheduled to speak on 'Women in International Affairs.' She was astonished when told of her topic and said, 'I could not speak for five minutes on *women* in international affairs. There are none.' We, who are vitally interested in international peace, will some day answer Dame Crowdy's challenge and give her ample opportunity."

Some students combined artistic, entertainment and economic activities to good effect. Proceeds from a grass-roots attempt to produce plays on campus were donated to a fund for a new elevator in Derham Hall in the early 1920s,

Isabella Schmitz Dumont '32 from Cologne, Germany, above received an honorary degree from the college for her work as a physician among the Selma, Alabama, poor. On June 28, 1980, the St. Catherine Alumnae Association presented her the St. Catherine Alumnae Award.

for example. Sister Marie Philip recalled: "It was kind of up to the students to organize any play or anything that we had in my day, because I don't think that we had a dramatics teacher. So we would hire Miss [Mary G.] Kellett . . . from Visitation. We would choose the play with her, and I think she chose the people acting in it and did that part, but we saw that the girls got to rehearsals and so on. The play that stands out in my mind because I think I had charge of it was *Quality Street,* by [James] Barrie, my senior year. We borrowed the setting from St. Cloud Normal School . . . We sat all night outside of Whitby watching for the truck to come."

Among the more formal musical and dramatic productions was *The Messiah,* presented by the Choral Club and assisted by the men of the St. Paul Municipal Chorus. On March 2, 1926, the *Lantern* (a weekly published by the sophomores for one year only) mentioned Austrian composer and pianist Percy Grainger's visit and the two programs he gave in Jeanne d'Arc Auditorium. Inspired by Edvard Grieg, he had collected English and Irish folksongs and arranged them for concert use. Sister Antonia's voice rang forth: "This event is one of the greatest privileges which are given to the students, probably a privilege which to some may not again be granted . . . It is your duty, girls, to let the public know of his coming and invite them."

The combined choral clubs of St. Catherine and St. Thomas presented operettas directed by Cecil Birder of the St. Thomas music department. During the 1930s, he directed works such as The Mikado, Patience, The Gondoliers, *and* Ruddigore. *At left is the cast of* H.M.S. Pinafore, *in 1932.*

An unusual program was presented by a Mr. Wilfred, who played the "clavilux," a machine that threw shadowy, graceful figures on a screen, while playing soft music similar to that of an organ. Among his numbers was "The Chicago Nocturne."

The French Club presented *Cyrano de Bergerac* by Edmond Rostand, and the *Lantern* commented: "The play calls for selected talent and a good deal of ability, but the French club is a fertile field to draw from, and we are assured it will be a success." The play, directed by Marthe Devaux, was received with enthusiasm by students and faculty.

Student productions sometimes took the form of a pageant, like that in 1936 celebrating the centennial of service by the Sisters of St. Joseph of Carondelet in America. The April 17, 1936, *Catherine Wheel,* a student newspaper started in March 1935, noted: "The centenary celebration, centered in St. Louis, was designed especially to commemorate the six French sisters who in 1836 arrived in St. Louis and subsequently established in Carondelet (now a part of St. Louis) the first motherhouse of the congregation in America." For the

St. Paul celebration, a spectacular pageant, *The Fire Bringers,* was given on the terraces west of the chapel. More than six hundred people took part in the outdoor spectacle. The pageant, said its author, Sister Maris Stella, "was completely symbolic, not about historical events. Because the purpose of the Sisters of St. Joseph has always been the worship of God through active service, this commemorative pageant was based on the ancient story of the bringer of fire to earth, symbolizing those who from the beginning of time have been devoted to the service of mankind."

Despite her many responsibilities, Sister Antonia kept in touch with the students, making sure the world of each was expanded through cultural activities outside the classroom. Sister Ann Harvey recalled: "Someone sent Mother Antonia four tickets to the symphony, and the seats were very good. She asked me if I wanted one and I said 'Yes,' because I was a poor little girl and did not have any money . . . a telephone call came from Mother Antonia about twenty minutes after she gave me the ticket, to please come to her office because she wanted to tell me what to wear, and how to look. She told me to wear a hat and bring my purse and wear gloves . . . In true Sister-Antonia-fashion, she waited up for us after the symphony and got our enthusiastic ideas on the music. It was my first symphony, and I thought I was in heaven."

According to Sister Antonia, the accumulation of knowledge was not the sole purpose of a college education. Character training or "the building of a life" was most often the subject of her assembly talks. Sister Marie Philip noted: "Wednesday after Wednesday she lashed us into a fairly homogeneous student group. She drove at practice, at homely virtues—honesty, cleanliness, industry, dependableness, a nice consideration for others. Who could ever forget her urging us to 'chisel our characters,' to accomplish hard things, to be women of good sense? She taught us that the ideal of sound and strong Catholic womanhood is big, simple, noble, and practicable."

Mary Ellen Chase wrote in *A Goodly Fellowship:* "Sister Antonia went at the realization of St. Catherine's College with everything she had in her . . . *Laborare est orare* was sound doctrine to her . . . She saw architects and remade their plans; she sat on stone heaps and inspired workmen. She laid out grounds and planted trees . . . She had read widely and seemingly she had forgotten nothing that she had ever read. She was the best of teachers . . . Her feverish activity made her not only apparently omnipresent, but completely master of every scene and situation as well . . . In the chapel she could be intent upon her own devotions and aware of any lack of devotion in her girls . . . She was a handsome woman with an alert, eager face and a fine carriage. When she swept down the corridors of her college in her black habit on her way to the chapel, or the garden or the kitchen or the powerhouse, everyone upon her swift approach straightened head and shoulders."

In 1936, Sister Antonia became ill, suffering several strokes. In 1937 she resigned because of increasing disability, to live quietly in Whitby 106. Friends and alumnae still visited, and the honors poured in as before: President Herbert Hoover invited her to the White House Conference on Child Health and Protection. Pope Pius XI awarded her the *Pro Ecclesia et Pontifice* medal. She was elected president of the Association of Minnesota Colleges and awarded an honorary degree of Doctor of Laws by the University of Minnesota.

Sister Antonia McHugh died quietly on October 11, 1944. The Spring 1927 *Ariston* had written of her: "Sister Antonia succeeded in building up not only the physical plant but the curriculum and the faculty as well . . . Our develop-

Sister Antonia McHugh, wrote Mary Ellen Chase, "prayed while she hustled and she hustled while she prayed . . . everyone upon her swift approach straightened head and shoulders."

ment in every line is due to her farsightedness, her zeal in furthering the course of Catholic education in America. Under her wise guidance, courses of study have been organized and the college standardized until it is now recognized by the highest authorities. All the best in American universities, all the advantages, all the benefits of foreign travel, have been utilized . . . in the preparation of superior teachers."

Five years after her death, *Ariston* was still paying her tribute: "Always to her St. Catherine's has been a great college. Even when it was only a dream. Never just a building on a hill, it was a growing family of buildings: Caecilian, Mendel, the Health Center, the Chapel. All these she planned, built, and peopled in her mind long before the architects were ever summoned. The pews of Our Lady of Victory Chapel were filled with girls in cap and gown when the old chapel on fourth Derham was still adequate to the college needs. It is that vision for the future, that aspiration for excellence, and the creative power to convert vision into reality that has distinguished Mother Antonia's work." That vision of excellence was her legacy.

On March 12, 1942, six hundred students and faculty members practiced artificial respiration in Fontbonne Hall. With the assistance of the American Red Cross, the college offered the first-aid course as part of its defense program during World War II.

The atmosphere of a Catholic college should be conducive to the student's arriving at the highest percentage of truth.

An atmosphere of space

After the retirement of Sister Antonia, the college struggled to keep its momentum as a growing institution in a country struggling to overcome the effects of economic depression. Franklin Roosevelt was president. The New Deal was in full swing. Japan was uneasy. Naziism was on the rise in Germany. But for a few years the college did not greatly feel the effects of international tension.

In 1937 the college was enjoying a strong intellectual life, recognition for high standards of scholarship, accreditation by the North Central Association of Universities and Colleges, and a good physical plant. Another fine fruit of Sister Antonia's labor came shortly after her retirement. She had worked with zeal and persistence to obtain a chapter of Phi Beta Kappa, applying several times without result. Her successor, Sister Eucharista, had been aware of these efforts and later recalled: "The inspectors told her . . . the library wasn't sufficiently built up, and that especially the French department was very weak. So she put on her shawl and went down to Carleton (I think) and *that* was accredited and asked to see the French department. She said, 'You know, the whole library of the French department was on the professor's desk.' She reported that to the people who [said the French library at St. Catherine] was insufficient. I think they were properly amused and probably somewhat amazed."

Finally in October 1937, the United Chapters of Phi Beta Kappa awarded a chapter of the society to the College of St. Catherine, the first Catholic institution to receive one. Mathematics professor Alphonsus O'Toole, chair of the Phi Beta Kappa committee, on his return from the meeting of the United Chapters in Atlanta, reported: "I wish every [student and alumna] could have been there with me to hear the unanimous acclaim given Sister Antonia from famous scholars all over the country. She is universally considered a great educator . . . standards of our chapter of Phi Beta Kappa will be kept very high."

The formal installation of the Gamma Chapter of Minnesota of Phi Beta Kappa took place in Jeanne d'Arc Auditorium on May 17, 1938, also Sister Antonia's birthday. Sister Eucharista gave the address of welcome, and Guy Stanton Ford, acting president of the University of Minnesota, presided. The initiation of honorary and alumnae members—Sisters Antonia, Eleanore, and Jeanne Marie—preceded the induction of Sisters Antonia as president and Jeanne Marie as secretary-treasurer. Then came the initiation of new members—senior Maridee La Pointe (Johnson) '38 and alumnae members Clara Glenn '20, Ellen Lord '24, Genevieve Ahern (McVay) '27, and Anne Condon

Collopy (McKeown) '28. The principal speakers were Archbishop John Gregory Murray, who had succeeded Austin Dowling in 1931, and Marbury B. Ogle of the University of Minnesota. For a long time thereafter, the College of St. Catherine was the only Catholic college holding the distinction of a Phi Beta Kappa chapter. Other honor societies on campus included Pi Gamma Mu for the social sciences, Delta Phi Lambda for creative writing, and Kappa Gamma Pi for high academic standing and leadership among Catholics.

An independent thinker

In 1937 Sister Eucharista Galvin, a quiet, thoughtful, and determined leader, was named president of the college. Born in Waverly, Minnesota, in 1893, she entered the Sisters of St. Joseph in 1915 and took her final vows in 1920. Friend Elizabeth Cochran wrote after Sister Eucharista's doctoral exam at the University of Chicago: "You are a credit to them with your brain, good judgment, and the very admirable quality of standing on your two feet and thinking for yourself. You are the first sister to take a doctorate in the department, and he [one of the professors] is proud of you. He's had many sisters in his class, and he remembers you as being the most independent thinker and one of the most charming personalities of the crowd." Sister Eucharista began teaching history at the College of St. Catherine in 1929, also assuming the duties of registrar until she became president.

Sister Eucharista was a strong advocate of independent thinking and judgment. She had written in an address on the teaching of history in Catholic colleges: "The duty of the Catholic college is to encourage the student to search into and learn the facts about controversial questions, not in order to prove his group right, but in order to come to a true understanding . . . The atmosphere of a Catholic college should be conducive to the student's arriving at the highest percentage of truth . . . By the time a student reaches the college level he [sic] must be willing and ready to learn the unpleasant and sometimes embarrassing facts in the human element in the history of the church."

Sister Eucharista gave a wide berth to new ideas such as those espoused in the developing liturgical movement. In 1937, the Liturgy Club was organized under the direction of Sisters Helen Angela Hurley and Angele Gleason. Leaders of the movement including the Reverends William Busch of the St. Paul Seminary, Virgil Michel of St. John's University and editor of the *Orate Fratres* liturgical magazine later called *Worship,* and Gerald Ellard, author of *Christian Life and Worship*, addressed the club.

Sister Antonia, whose basic interest had been the intellectual life of the college, had not slighted the religious life of students. Indeed she had required evening prayers and started an annual three-day student retreat, directed by churchmen later including Gerald Ellard, John LaFarge, SJ, and F. P. LeBuffe. Nevertheless, according to Sister Helen Angela: "The liturgical movement centered at St. John's, which aimed to diffuse social charity and understanding through increased lay participation in the official worship of the church, was something with which Sister Antonia would have nothing to do. 'Why, I have been in all the churches in Rome,' she would say, 'and I never heard a Missa Recitata. What is good enough for the pope is good enough for me.'"

Students of the late 1930s and 1940s also participated in a greater way in teaching religion. Each week Sister Jeanne Marie instructed a class of sophomores and juniors in the catechetical methods of the Confraternity of Christian

Sister Eucharista Galvin, named president in 1937, received a bachelor's degree in history from the college in 1924, a master's degree from the University of Chicago in 1925, and was one of the first sisters to receive a doctorate from Chicago, in 1929.

Doctrine (CCD), using a series of books called *The Spiritual Way*, by Mother Margaret Bolton. About twenty-eight students taught CCD classes to children released from St. Paul public schools one hour a week for religious instruction.

For better understanding . . .

Another result of a penchant for openness was the involvement of faculty in two cooperative studies—one dealing with general education, the other with teacher education. In 1938 the college was invited as the only Catholic institution of twenty-two colleges participating in a cooperative study that aimed, according to the introductory letter, "to evaluate programs of general education in a variety of institutions." Each institution was "to develop its own program in the light of its philosophy of education, its objectives, and its financial and human resources." The director of the study was Ralph Tyler from the University of Chicago. Sister Annette Walters was the local coordinator. She was at the time working on a doctorate in experimental psychology at the University of Minnesota. She completed the degree in 1941, when she also became chair of the psychology department at the College of St. Catherine.

In the course of the general eduation study, the college was visited by the director, the associate director, and nine research associates in humanities, social studies, natural science, personnel, and curriculum construction. Most of the staff visits included several days of intensive work, including addressing the faculty, meeting with committees, and consulting with individuals who had previously submitted problems. Sixteen faculty members were able to take advantage of workshop experiences during the study at the University of Chicago and Northwestern University in humanities, social sciences, natural sciences, and curriculum improvement.

In 1943 Sister Annette reported these outcomes for the study:

- better understanding of the needs of youth
- greater interest in problems of general education
- increased understanding of social factors indicating new emphases and revisions in the curriculum
- awareness of the limitations of various techniques
- solution of immediate problems, such as determining the next steps to be taken in the teaching of new courses, selecting appropriate evaluation instruments, and relating instructional materials to course and institutional objectives
- increased awareness of the contribution of other members of the faculty.

In addition, the faculty received expert assistance in the fields of administration, evaluation, personnel, social understanding, and human development. And courses developed in the early 1940s as a result of the study included An Experiment in Humanities by Sister Mona Riley, Contemporary Readings by Abigail Quigley (McCarthy) '36, Catholic Literary Revival by Agnes Keenan, Creative Writing by Sister Maris Stella, Introduction to Psychology by Sister Annette, and survey courses in biological, physical, and social sciences.

Sister Mona Riley had done extensive work on the humanities course, beginning with two summer workshops in 1939 and 1940 at the University of Chicago. Under the direction of Harold Dunkel, director of the workshop, she designed and began to offer an Introduction to the Humanities course. She said later: "The 1939 report showed that I was attempting a 'functional' course, that

Participating in the Palm Sunday liturgy were, left to right, students Mary Ruhr (Kranz) '44, Betty Luther, Betty Ann Meyers, and Mary Louise Nolan (Skaife) '44.

34   More than a dream

As a result of educational studies done at the college in the 1930s and 1940s, Sister Mona Riley, above, offered a course called An Experiment in the Humanities. Meant to influence the daily lives of students, the course inspired some to enjoy cultural activities outside their majors. Ritamary Reynolds (McGovern) '48 and Dolores Bowman (Lammers) '50, above right, participated in a joint orchestra rehearsal with Tommies Vernon Humbert and James Jude.

is, a course which would be useful in the present and future experiences of my students. Was it such a course? Throughout the year the objective which was emphasized and consciously kept uppermost in the minds of both teacher and students was that of influencing the daily lives of the students."

One humanities student told the April 1952 *Wheel*: "During the three quarters, a tremendous amount of material is covered, including a survey of architecture, classical and modern music, modern poetry, and an exhaustive study of the world's best paintings. According to Sister Mona, more important than merely memorizing buildings or paintings are the underlying aims of the course. In humanities you listen carefully, you look carefully. Gradually you develop a greater awareness of the world . . . You begin to see and hear more clearly, deeply, and broadly, and to derive greater intellectual and emotional enjoyment from the arts. Through critically analyzing your own taste, you become more confident of it, and more able to express yourself concerning it."

Several instruments of evaluation, including a "Religious Attitudes Questionnaire" by Sister Marie Philip, who had become interested in teaching religion, and a "Life-Situations Questionnaire" by Sister Annette, were designed to assess student attitudes toward justice, social responsibilities, and religious ideals. With several other sisters, Sister Marie Philip published "An Attitude Scale in Religion for Catholic Colleges" in the *Journal of Religious Instruction,* in June 1941. She also became involved in the liturgical movement.

In 1939 the Standing Commission on Teacher Education of the American Council on Education invited the college to participate in a cooperative study of teacher education. The administration decided to participate in this study as well, hoping it would supplement and reinforce the education study already under way. Again St. Catherine was the only Catholic college of the thirty-four participating. The director of the study was Earl Armstrong, who had broad experience as a public school teacher, school administrator, college professor, education dean, government official, and chief of an accrediting agency. He was a field coordinator for the Committee on Teacher Education of the American Council on Education. The campus coordinator was Sister Helen Margaret.

When the teacher education study began, most members of the faculty were satisfied with the program at the college and were willing to leave improvement to the education department. They agreed that provisions for student teaching were inadequate. The study was one way to develop a four-year sequence for teacher education, and it commanded the interest of the whole faculty. New survey courses in general education would prepare students to fill a demand from the smaller school systems for teachers "who could handle not one social science . . . and not one natural science, but all of them." As a result, a plan was adopted for divisional majors in social or general science.

A planning committee was chosen for general education—Sisters Mona for the humanities, Antonius for the natural sciences, and Teresa for the social sciences. In professional education were Sisters Annette for psychology, Mary Edward Healy for social understanding, Jeanne Marie for curriculum and methods, and Helen Margaret for personnel management and guidance. Agnes Keenan was active in the discussion of student teaching. Each group submitted a statement of goals, methods, and courses and a statement of competencies needed by teachers in their fields. The coordinator, Sister Helen Margaret, compiled a unified statement, which was adopted with minor changes. The final stage, listing resources at the college that would enable students to develop the required competencies, was completed in time for Armstrong's visit in October 1941. He was highly pleased with the progress made.

Before Armstrong's visit, three discussion meetings on Syracuse University's publication, *A Functional Program of Teacher Education,* were held. On April 7, 1940, Sister Annette discussed the study of adolescent psychology, insisting there be a more integrated course in human growth and development and that guided observation of children be part of the course. These elements eventually became the Introduction to Psychology course.

On April 21, 1940, math professor Kenneth Wegner led a discussion of the sociological bases of education. At that time students could choose any course

Sister Helen Margaret Peck, campus coordinator for the teacher education study, had master's and doctoral degrees from the University of Chicago and had been a member of the English department from 1927 to 1937. That year she became registrar, a position held until 1963. Through the years she assumed other jobs at the college, nearly always maintaining duties taken earlier. She wrote many scholarly articles, including several related to the teacher education study. The study resulted in new science survey courses for prospective teachers: at left, Margaret Murray (Wylie) '38, Genevieve Ozark (Leverone) '39, and Dorothy Bartelme (Hensien) '39 studied biology.

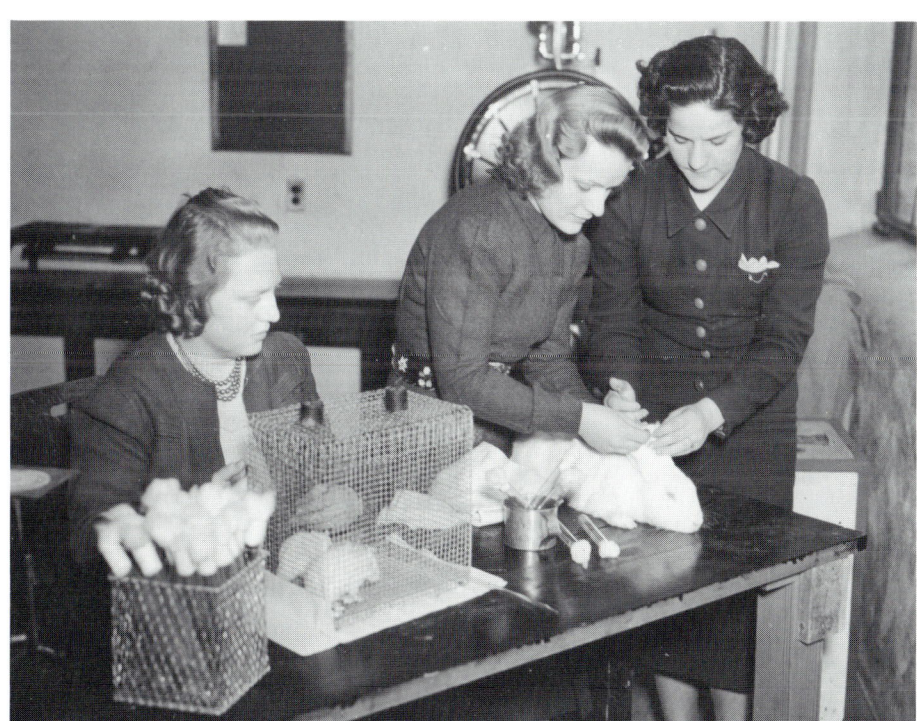

in the social sciences to fulfill the graduation requirement. The social understandings acquired were largely a hit-or-miss affair. Eventually two courses required for the junior year—Social Psychology and Community Backgrounds of Education—were developed. In the latter class, students were called upon for more active participation than listening to lectures, reading, and taking occasional field trips. Each student (most were from small, middle-sized, and urban environments) was to choose a community, preferably her own, for a survey. They found that communities of the same size might differ greatly in cultural and economic qualities. Those writing family histories for Sister Eucharista's American history course had additional background. Both courses enriched the Special Methods and Student Teaching classes for seniors.

Work on student teaching began early in the study. Most students of the past had done student teaching in Derham Hall, an arrangement unsatisfactory to both the high school students' parents and the college education department. In October 1939, Sisters Jeanne Marie and Helen Margaret visited the superintendent of St. Paul Public Schools to ask for more extensive opportunities for student teaching. He granted the same privileges accorded other teacher training institutions in the city. He asked that uniformity of procedure mark the activities of all such institutions and, after consultation with school supervisors, drew up regulations for practice teaching in city schools. The regulations dealt with such matters as distributing student teachers among schools, number of student teachers per critic teacher, number of student teachers in the system, and communication between critic teachers and teacher training institutions.

The student teaching committee—Sisters Jeanne Marie, for the education department, Antonius for the subject fields, and Marie Ursule Sanschagrin, French teacher and principal of Derham Hall—drew up a plan indicating the type of teaching, responsibilities of the critic teacher, hours of observation, and the period to be covered by student teaching, as the superintendent requested.

A second conference including Sisters Jeanne Marie and Antonius, the superintendent and director of the city high schools, and representatives of the other teacher training institutions resulted in a guide for student teaching applying to all such institutions in St. Paul. On campus, student teaching was scheduled for mornings during the fall quarter with special methods courses in the afternoons. Methods courses paralleled student teaching so that students could present teaching problems as they arose. The addition of a history and philosophy of education course helped to integrate and summarize the program while encouraging students to form their own philosophies of education.

The end of the teacher education study in 1942 saw these outcomes:

- greater understanding of and interest in teacher education by the faculty
- ability to see the program as a whole, a four-year sequence
- more integrated and experience-based curriculum
- a list of teacher competencies on which each student could rate herself.

Agnes Keenan, above, wrote "The Differences between Catholic and Non-Catholic Education" for the November 1939 Journal of Religious Instruction, and the article became part of the report on the teacher education study. To get a broader view of student teaching programs, she visited Syracuse University as well as the Commission on Teacher Education in Washington, D.C.

And development

Departments not directly involved in the studies developed during Sister Eucharista's presidency, too. The social sciences had received impetus from new faculty members including Sister Edouarda La Qua, whose Labor Problems students attended meetings of the St. Paul City Trades Federation, composed mostly of craftsmen. Earlier, according to the *Wheel* of December 18, 1936, the Reverend Francis J. Gilligan of the St. Paul Seminary, who taught part time in the social sciences, had challenged his Immigration and Racial Relations class with this statement: "There is more economic discrimination against the Negro in St. Paul than in the average American city . . . The first step toward solving the race problem would be taken when people were brought to talk about the question coolly, calmly, and rationally." Distinguished lecturer and sociologist C. J. Nuesse left the college to teach at Marquette University midway through 1943-44. Sister Mary Edward Healy took over his classes.

Agnes Keenan '31 had been teaching in the English department since 1938. She had a master's degree in English and philosophy from Catholic University and had spent a summer studying at the British Library in England. There she became interested in the writings of Alice Meynell and wrote her thesis on the topic. Keenan was an indefatigable lecturer who became known in the Twin Cities for talks such as "The Outlook for Catholic Literature," "American and English Libraries," and "The Writings of Alice Meynell." She is best remembered for her Catholic Literary Revival course, which traced Catholic literature from Newman's *Apologia Pro Vita Sua* to contemporary writers like Jacques Maritain, Frank Sheed, Sister Maris Stella (Alice) Smith, and Thomas Merton. Her sense of humor, inexhaustible fund of anecdotes about writers and philosophers, and keen interest in students made her a valued teacher and friend.

Abigail Quigley graduated from the college in 1936 and joined the English department in 1940 while working on a master's degree from the University of Minnesota, completed in 1942. She entered into campus activities with enthusiasm, becoming known for her speaking and writing abilities. She debated the topic "World literature should supersede traditional English and American literature courses" with Jean Gardiner Smith, librarian at University High School, at a meeting of the Minneapolis English Club, defending world literature on the ground that it gives students a better sense of the continuity of western culture as well as a world point of view. She taught popular classes until her departure in 1945 to marry Eugene McCarthy, who became a U.S. Senator and later ran for president. Abigail Quigley McCarthy became a well-known writer of columns for *Commonweal* magazine and books including *Private Faces/Public Places*, *Circles: A Washington Story,* and *One Woman Lost* with Jane Muskie.

Abigail Quigley McCarthy '36 joined the English faculty in 1940, quickly became involved in the general education study, and developed the Contemporary Readings in Literature course. She was a St. Catherine Alumnae Award winner in 1987, above.

Agnes Keenan's younger sibling, Sister Immaculata Keenan, had been the first to enter the Sisters of Saint Joseph with a doctoral degree. She received a bachelor's degree from the college in 1931 and master's (1932) and doctoral (1936) degrees from the University of Minnesota, where she specialized in the works of Francis Thompson. Following graduate studies, she taught English literature at Good Counsel College in White Plains, New York. A year later she entered the novitiate. From 1941 to 1981, except for five years as novice mistress for the Sisters of St. Joseph, Sister Immaculata taught English at the college, beloved as a Dante scholar, trusted adviser, and inspiring teacher of gentle ways. After her retirement from teaching, she continued to assist students in the Writing-Reading Center.

Sister Immaculata played a part in the development of continuing education as well. In May 1941, she became faculty adviser (later "faculty representative") of the *Alumnae News,* with Nadine Winterer (Molter) '40 as editor. The St. Catherine Alumnae Association had in 1936 taken tentative steps into adult education, sponsoring six lectures by speakers including the Reverends William O. Brady and Edward Keenan, and Sister Antonius. Their success led to more ventures in adult education, including the publication of a bimonthly book review called *Books Abounding* in 1946-47 by the St. Catherine chapter of Kappa Gamma Pi, a national honor society for Catholic women's colleges. Florence Baskfield (Myslajek) '46 and Abigail Quigley McCarthy coordinated the publication, with issues centered on themes such as the place of women, the French literary revival, poetry, social problems, and philosophy. The July 15, 1947, issue explained: "There have been as great changes in Catholic education and in the context of the life of lay Catholics in America in the last ten or fifteen years as there have been in the history of the world. This change has been reflected in Catholic literature. We want this review to help Catholics out of school to keep in touch with the Catholic center."

Two years later in 1948, Anne Dolan Kelly '43, association president, had remarked in her letter to members: "Weren't you pleased with the [recent] announcement of the Alumnae Lending Library service? It was Sister Immaculata's suggestion that the Gleason Memorial Fund [from the estate of the Reverend Leo Gleason] be designated for this purpose . . . Most of us have a limited time to devote to reading and this service should be to our advantage. The books will be selected by a committee who will strive to choose only books of interest and benefit to you." Twin Cities alumnae could borrow books in person, while others could have books mailed to them. The lending library continued even when, in July 1950, *Books Abounding* ceased publication because of prohibitive printing and postage costs.

Mabel Meta Frey of the drama department, said of her job interview: "Sister Ste. Helene took me to this big area under the auditorium. She said, 'I want you to build a little theater here some day. There is no money, but I want you to build a little theater.'" The Players' Club she started, shown at right in 1937, managed to complete the little theater in a year. She secured membership for the college in National Collegiate Players in 1941.

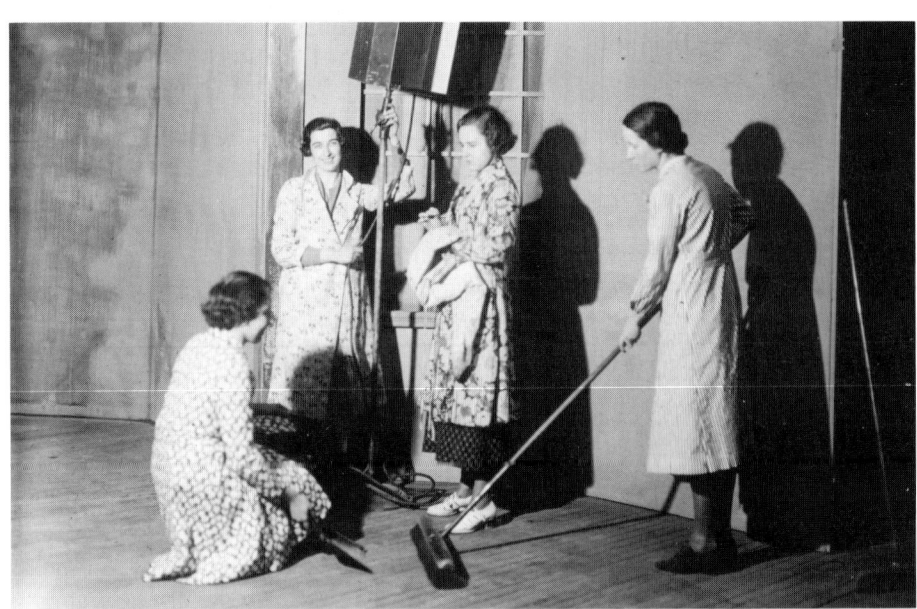

The drama department had taken a great leap forward when Sister Eucharista hired Mabel Meta Frey in the fall of 1937. At first, she said: "We put on plays in Jeanne d'Arc, but we couldn't practice there because the music department was there all the time . . . They couldn't find me an office . . . Then they found this little room upstairs, and there was half a radiator in it . . . The linoleum was holey on the floor, and an old couch was there, and that was it. So I started renovating it right away, and I know I was scrubbing the floor when Sister Antonine [then dean] walked by, and in an hour workers came, and it moved very fast from then on. They put in a radiator and I had an office."

Despite the hardships, Frey found time to develop the department professionally. When she arrived at the college, all the parts in plays, including men's roles, were customarily taken by women. She refused to follow suit, saying, "I won't play girls in men's roles . . . it ruins their voices." She established the Players' Club with members from the College of St. Catherine and St. Thomas in 1937, and the next year it became a charter member of the Catholic Theater Conference. The members of the Players' Club worked very hard, and in about one year the little theater requested in her job interview was finished. The wiring of the stage and theater was done by a professional for about $600, but the rest of the work was done by students. The $600 was paid off in four years with money raised through charging admission to the plays.

Mabel Frey was the chief and only play director and producer for many years. Contemporary plays, the classics, and musicals were all part of her repertoire. She put on *The Joyous Season, Riders to the Sea, Brief Music, As You Like It, The Merchant of Venice, Our Town, My Fair Lady, The Sound of Music*, and scores of others. During her production of *Romeo and Juliet*, the two principals fell in love, and later they married. Mabel Frey remained as head of the department until her retirement in 1971.

The music department was enriched by the presence from time to time of visiting teachers and musicians. Sister Anna Goulet had many friends in the music world from her studies in France and elsewhere. In 1936-37 she had published two volumes of *A Pageant of Our Musical Heritage,* long in use in her classes. In 1938 she spoke on "Purposes and Needs of Music in Catholic Schools" at the National Association of Music Teachers in Washington, D.C. She acted as chair of a round table talk on parochial school music at the National Music Clinic at the University of Minnesota.

With the building of a new power plant in 1940, the old red brick building behind Derham Hall was turned into a reserve library, relieving the crowded main library beneath the chapel. Sister Marie Jose, head librarian, died in 1942, and Sister Marie Inez Johnson '29, who had earned a master's degree in library science at Columbia in 1939-40, succeeded her, maintaining the position until her retirement in 1974.

Sister Anna Goulet brought to the college great musicians including pianist Frank Mannheimer of London and Marcel Dupré, with whom she had studied in Paris. He visited first in 1923, then again in 1929 and 1949. Above, he worked with music students Marcella Flaten (Wartman) '49, Elizabeth Maguire (Moeller) '50, Helen Boening (Bambenek) '49, and Kathleen Daly (Malone) '49.

In 1940 the old power plant (later the bookstore) became a reserve library, left. It had a stack capacity of 10,000 volumes with some shelves open to patrons. Its reading room, decorated in knotty pine, could accommodate 150 students.

Towards a peace bred of justice

Less scholarly student activities reflected a strong college commitment to social and political issues. The International Relations Club and League of Women Voters held serious discussions. A network—the Mississippi Valley International Relations Clubs—had met at the college in April 1935. The Carnegie Endowment for International Peace supplied books and pamphlets; its purpose was explained in the *Wheel* by Nicholas Murray Butler as "not to support any single point of view so as to know how to treat the conditions which now prevail throughout the world, but to fix the attention of students on those underlying principles of international conduct, law, and organization which must be agreed upon and applied if peaceful civilization is to continue."

In 1937, the League of Women Voters hosted the annual convention of the All-College League. Among the topics discussed were tariffs, equal rights, protective legislation, collective bargaining, and professionalizing public service. The St. Catherine League remained active until 1953, then disbanded at the request of the state league because it was the only remaining campus league.

In 1937, too, the campus had been the scene of a strong peace movement. According to the October 22, 1937, *Wheel,* the president of a national Catholic peace group that had requested affiliation with the Catholic Association for International Peace wrote to the college: "A Catholic program for world peace has come into existence to help the American public, and especially Catholics, to foster a better understanding of international relations, that they may be just, charitable, and peaceful." Earlier that year, *Wheel* fashion notes suggested that students might be expected to contribute to a military effort: "Knee-high skirts with their accompanying knee-high socks are in vogue for hiking, skating, and biking. New box pleats and swing skirts give plenty of room for action . . . There has been a stampede for corduroy, but the demand cannot be met, as Uncle Sam's aviators get first choice. It is used to line their uniforms."

By 1939 war had begun in Europe, but there was still a current of antiwar sentiment in the United States. The *Wheel* declared in an editorial on November 10 that year: "[The average college student] is not unpatriotic. He is willing to take up arms in defense of American soil, but he will refuse to fight on the battlefields of Europe. They are determined to take no part in the organized destruction of life and goods." A *Wheel* poll found only 4 of 350 students favoring entry of the United States as an armed force in the European war. On April 16, 1941, the *Wheel* was still pleading: "We must steel ourselves against the emotionalism of war hysteria. We must consider slowly and deliberately the far-reaching effects of each new course of action which we adopt."

By that time the country's relationship with Japan had become strained, and on December 7, 1941, Japan attacked the U.S. naval fleet in Pearl Harbor, Hawaii. President Franklin Delano Roosevelt asked Congress to declare war, which it did on December 8. Germany and Italy declared war on the United States three days later. The college quickly swung into a defense position, generally following the country, which was solidly behind President Roosevelt. Sister Eucharista, in her annual address to the freshman class, warned students about the complexity of life in a warring country: "We must get behind the government 100 percent and accept our responsibilities. This is no time to criticize the administration . . . While we are fighting a just war against rightful enemies, we should not hate people of these nations, who are really our brethren, but what their government stands for." Echoing Sister Eucharista's speech, the

Students were active in the peace movement before the United States entered World War II. In 1939, students marched in the May Fete parade as world leaders—Cecelia Bonemeyer '42 as Uncle Sam and Grace Mary Ederer '41 as Hitler, Loraine (later Sister Catherine Ann) Tauer '41 as Mussolini, and Magdalen Schimanski '41 as Chamberlain.

December 17 *Wheel* said: "There can be peace for a nation at war . . . greater than the ignoble ease we have been enjoying. It is a peace synonymous with virtue . . . the conviction of the justice of our cause, and our consequent responsibility . . . It is a peace bred of courage . . . to accept and double the sacrifice required of us."

A collegewide campaign to help in the war effort began, and a War Activities Board including students and faculty initiated these activities:

- Red Cross first-aid courses for students and faculty, with Marvel Mee of the physical education department in charge
- nutrition classes by Sister James Agnes Fogarty of the home economics department
- campus sale of defense bonds and stamps along with contributions to the Red Cross led by Kenneth Wegner with assistance from members of the social science honor society, Pi Gamma Mu
- a prayer campaign organized by the student government and Sodality
- a monthly Mass for deceased soldiers
- sewing and knitting for the Red Cross by students (The *Wheel* reported on January 16, 1942: "Anyone who does not know how to sew or knit will be instructed on Friday or Saturday evenings by Sister Angela Therese [Eisenmenger].")

Many local citizens entered into campus activities, some attending first-aid classes, others the nutrition courses: "One hundred St. Paul women attended the first Red Cross nutrition course . . . consisting of ten weekly two-hour periods, at the end of which the Red Cross nutrition certificate will be granted," reported the *Wheel*. Some faculty members and students felt the cause of defense (or the lure of higher wages) so strongly that they left the college to work in a defense-related industry. The pay was excellent, and the war effort made more jobs available to women than before; others quickly filled their places.

Some other American citizens had fewer opportunities than they had enjoyed before the war. Early in 1942, influenced by a fear of Japanese invasion of the West Coast, the government interned 117,000 persons of Japanese background in relocation camps, mostly in arid mountain states. Many were forced to sell their homes, farms, or businesses at a great loss.

Sister Eucharista, always concerned for justice, offered Japanese women an opportunity to attend the college as an option to internment. Ruth Matsuo and Mary Jane Kinoshita (Hashisaki) '47 were the first to attend; six more students arrived the following year. Ruth Matsuo said: "I haven't been to school for almost a year, and it feels good to go to classes again." She and her mother had been ordered to Pomona Fair Grounds in Los Angeles for four months before being sent to a relocation center at Heart Mountain in Wyoming, where life was "certainly different." There were thirty blocks of barracks, six families to a building, and mess halls in each block. Heart Mountain, which housed about 1,800 people of Japanese descent, was operated like a town by Caucasian administrators and mostly Caucasian teachers. Said Ruth Matsuo in a March 1943 *Wheel:* "No trees, no sodas, no elevators, and we shopped by mail . . . We did have a camp newspaper and movies of Mickey Rooney when he still had blond hair." The experience prepared the Japanese students for easy adaptation to life at the college, and several became graduates.

Because of her zeal in supporting the war effort and particularly her work with air-raid wardens, Sister Eucharista received a certificate of merit: "For the

Sister Eucharista provided an opportunity for American-born Japanese women confined to internment camps to attend the college. Above, students Dorothy Kanegaye (Sawada) '46, Mamie Lee (Joe) '45, and Florence Nora examined a Chinese vase to be sold for a China relief fund in 1944.

many courtesies extended so graciously and granting of such splendid accommodations, we bring our humble thanks to Mother Eucharista and bestow on her honorary membership of the Air Raid Wardens of the 24th precinct of the 11th ward, St. Paul, Minnesota, Jan. 11, 1943."

But the presidency of the college had been coupled with the position of religious superior there when Sister Antonia took office, and according to church laws of the time, a superior's tenure was six years. In the middle of the war, Sister Eucharista returned to her teaching position.

The Civil Air Patrol was active on the St. Catherine campus during World War II. At right, Warrant Officer Helen Masterman taught student rookies Alice Zrust and Doris Olson how to salute. Below, Ruth Weber (Aberwald) '42 and Mary Hilbert (Tyrrell) '43 set up to sell bonds in 1942.

She left the college a new self-awareness, a renewed curriculum, and a cleaner financial slate. In addition to conducting the two educational self-studies and encouraging intellectual and religious growth, she had, after a long series of negotiations, consolidated and refinanced the college's $700,000 debt through the Ziegler Company of Milwaukee in 1938. The college agreed to pay the company $45,000 each year until the debt was paid, and by June 1945 the balance was only $375,000. The negotiations revealed the need for a more sophisticated legal structure, and in March 1943, the college filed "A Certificate of Amendment of Certificate of Incorporation" approved by the Sisters of St. Joseph of the St. Paul Province. Its bylaws designated the archbishop a trustee of continuing tenure and made him chairman. The provincial superior of the sisters, the president of the college and the president of the St. Catherine Alumnae Association were also to be trustees during their tenures, and all other trustees were to serve six years. In addition to its former duties, the Board of Trustees could recommend actions to the college. The bylaws name these trustees: Archbishop John Murray, the Right Reverend Monsignor Humphrey Moynihan, Lieutenant Commander Eugene P. McCahill, U.S.N. (also president of McCahill & Company), William C. Carroll, M.D. (by this time a surgeon at the St. Paul Clinic), Mrs. Henry (Minnie L.) Turrish, Robert Butler (financier-builder who had been contractor for Fontbonne Hall), Herbert H. Keefe (attorney and business manager for the St. Paul Clinic), William A. O'Brien, M.D., Sister Antonia McHugh (president emeritus), Mother Agnes Gonzaga Kelly (provincial superior), Mother Eucharista Galvin (president of the college), and Dorothy Mahood '29 (teacher at Monroe High School and president of the St. Catherine Alumnae Association).

After teaching history two years Sister Eucharista served as the superior of the St. Paul province of sisters from 1945 to 1951, then taught history at the college again before being named general superior of the Congregation of the Sisters of St. Joseph of Carondelet in St. Louis from 1954 to 1966. She established missions in Japan in 1956 and in Peru in 1962 and worked as a missionary and language teacher in Japan from 1969 to 1973. She died at Bethany Convent in 1985.

An advocate for the sciences

Sister Antonius Kennelly, who followed Sister Eucharista as president, had a strong background in both education and experience. She had taught rural school near her home town of St. Thomas, North Dakota, for two years before attending the college for one year in 1918. In 1922 she entered the Sisters of St. Joseph, receiving her bachelor's degree in 1926. She attended the University of Minnesota for four quarters of graduate work in chemistry before receiving an International Exchange Fellowship for study in Munich. On returning from Germany, Sister Antonius taught in the chemistry department. She was its chair from 1936 until she became president of the college in 1943.

Sister Antonius was always interested in progress and new developments. Thomas Whelan of St. Thomas, North Dakota, once wrote her: "We own and operate the Pembina Airport and with it a flying school. Now you remember what happened to the cardinal who flew around the world. When he landed he became the new Pope [Pius XII]. Now I understand that you drive your own car, and the progressive thing to do would be to learn to fly . . . If you want to become a pilot, we will give you 'the works,' including ground school, and it will be 'on the house' . . . you could get a private pilot's license in eight days." She replied: "As for driving our car, I hasten to protest that no sister of St. Joseph is allowed to drive a car to date. In any case, this particular one has driven little since she all but pushed the back out of the garage on the Kennelly farm with the old Studebaker in 1917. Aside from this, I would be all for flying."

As both teacher and administrator, Sister Antonius Kennelly was vigorous in her advocacy of the sciences. In an address to the University of Minnesota Faculty Women's Club in 1937, she had said: "No one can be said to possess true culture who has not acquainted himself with the rudiments of scientific knowledge. Only with a knowledge of science can we come to a realization of the harmony and beauty of the universe."

The increase in enrollment through the war years had spurred additions to both faculty and programs of study. In 1942, the college had reorganized the department of nursing, placing it in the upper division and granting a baccalaureate degree with a major in nursing. Katherine Sehl was named the first director of the nursing department that year. The St. Joseph's and St. Mary's Hospital schools of nursing requested that they became part of the College of St. Catherine nursing department, with control given to the college. The college then operated both baccalaureate and three-year nursing programs.

In 1943, the cadet nursing program at the college became an official part of the U.S. Cadet Nursing Corps. Some resources of the college—space and personnel—were severely strained by the influx of cadet nurses—100 in the fall and 80 in the spring. Katherine Sehl resigned at midyear, 1943-44, and was succeeded as director of the department by Gladys Sellew, a graduate of Catholic University. She had worked with the Reverend Paul Hanly Furfey, author of *Fire on the Earth,* and was deeply influenced by his ideal of poverty. The U.S. Cadet Nursing Corps program remained at the college through the end of World War II with about 130 cadet nurses graduating each year until 1948, the year after Sister Agnes Leon Mahowald took over the department.

An influx to the United States of German professors fleeing the Nazis before World War II had included Franz Mueller in 1935. He taught at St. Louis

University, then moved to St. Paul and taught at the College of St. Thomas. With master's and doctoral degrees from the University of Cologne, he began teaching economics and social thought part time at the College of St. Catherine in 1943.

Continuing the traditions

With a bit of adjustment, the drama department continued its performances during the war. Said Mabel Frey: "We tried to find plays, musicals, and so forth that didn't have many men in them. One was [Engelbert] Humperdinck's *Hänsel and Gretel*. There was one man, the father in it. It wasn't very hard to get [just one] . . . The boys from St. Thomas were almost nil, you know, not old enough to take the part."

Adjustment or not, students at the college continued many other traditional student activities as well. For many years the college had celebrated Winter Carnival in late January or early February. At first called "Sports Day," it consisted of intramural tournaments in basketball, volley ball, ping-pong, and bowling in Fontbonne Hall. It also included speed skating, figure skating, and snow sculpture. As Sports Day developed, it became more like the St. Paul Winter Carnival, with a campus queen and attendants, chosen by the students. The identity of the queen was kept a secret until she was crowned by St. Paul's Carnival King Boreas at a convocation on Winter Carnival Day.

In 1944, Winter Carnival was called "Victory Day." That year the student association president, Mary Ruhr (Kranz) '44, crowned Alberta Ashton '44 (later Sister Mary Madonna and Minnesota Public Health Commissioner) as "Bond Queen"—the person who best enticed students to buy war bonds and stamps. The celebration included outdoor winter sports as well indoor events like bowling, right, in Fontbonne Hall.

After a National Eucharistic Day held at the state fairgrounds in St. Paul in 1941, the college had decided to hold an annual day honoring the Holy Eucharist. Sister Teresa was usually chair of arrangements. Archbishop Murray opened the day with Mass at 9:00 A.M. There were lectures, discussions, a holy hour, and an outdoor procession to four altars representing the four corners of the earth, and closing benediction in the chapel.

The largest religious organization on campus was the Sodality of the Blessed Virgin Mary, a Catholic action and spiritual life group admitting about a hundred students each year. One Sodality objective was to help students to grow in holiness through daily Mass, rosary, mental prayer, and spiritual reading. The Sodality functioned through committees advised by the sisters, concentrating its activities on definite aspects of religion. The Apostolic, Liturgy, Eucharistic, Catholic Literature, Catholic Truth, and Our Lady's committees were as active as their members were willing to be. A general meeting was held once a month, a Missa Recitata once a week during Advent, and a Christmas party for wards of Catholic Charities. The Sodality sponsored an annual Vocations Day and after the war helped collect clothing for Europe in cooperation with the War Relief Service of the National Catholic Welfare Conference.

During the war, the Sodality worked to erect a shrine to Our Lady of Peace in the woods south of the chapel. In 1942 the *Wheel* urged students to spend a lot at May Fete since proceeds would go towards the shrine. An annual celebration held at the beginning of May, the fete was an all-day fair with booths for food, raffles, and games. Some years students paid a penny to wrap themselves in a sheet and slide down the spiral fire escape installed in Derham Hall in 1944-45. In others, faculty members might be "arrested" and held in a mock jail until they could persuade onlookers to post their bail or pay a fine. An outdoor supper usually followed a parade through the campus of clowns and floats, presented by the clubs of the college at 5:00 P.M. The Sophomore Skit performed in the morning for the Winter Carnival was rivaled only by the Senior Varsity Show presented on the evening of May Fete. Members of the faculty and staff were often the targets of student satire.

Students after the war . . .

Despite the traditional activities, everyone at the college looked forward to the end of the war. In 1943, Sister Eleanore wistfully told the *Wheel* of being awakened in the early hours of November 11, 1918, at the end of World I, by a student: "Sister, Sister, what'll we do? The armistice has been signed." Sister Eleanore replied: "Dear, you can go back to your room. Now!"

When World War II ended in 1945, students looked forward to more than peaceful studies. A September 27 *Wheel* editorial read: "For the first time in our college careers, Katies, we entered the gates in a peaceful world . . . The war is over, the tension is gone, and we can enjoy the frills of college life. There'll be parties, dances, and a 'real date,' football games, shopping tours, and, of course, assignments, cramming, and tests."

But campus life was irrevocably changed. Unexpectedly, many women war veterans decided to return to college, and twenty-four veterans enrolled with benefits of the G.I. Bill of Rights in 1946. Most had been WAVES, WACS, Marines, or members of the Army Nurse Corps, and their determination and purpose marked them as a special group on campus. Soon they organized a veterans' club to provide service and entertainment for campus veterans. They also raised money to help ship food and clothing overseas. The return of students who had held war-related jobs combined with the arrival of the veterans caused an acute shortage of rooms. The *Wheel* observed on October 10, 1946: "New temporary quarters had to be found . . . The west end of Mendel Commons was partitioned to make room for five girls, and five more in the recreation room on third Derham. They are waiting for presently occupied rooms to become vacant." Enrollment leveled off but never decreased to prewar levels.

With an influx of veterans and other students, residents began to assemble for night prayers at 10:15 on the dormitory floors instead of in the chapel as in

Chaplain Donald Gormley led a dedication service for the shrine to Our Lady of Peace, above, on October 8, 1943. Students walked in procession, singing hymns and reciting the rosary. The Wheel *noted: "Under the pedestal of the statue of Our Lady of Peace is a ridge containing rocks brought by the students from their home states."*

years past. At first they recited the rosary; later they said Compline, using a booklet published by Liturgical Press in Collegeville.

Dormitory regulations were still strict. Freshmen were to be in their rooms for study at 5:00 P.M. until dinner at 6:00. Study (or at least quiet) time was maintained from 7:15 to 10:00. From 10:00 to 10:30 students could visit, take baths, or receive telephone calls. To leave campus for shopping or other business, the student needed a permit from the floor supervisor. For overnight visits, the name of the person visited was to be on file with written permission from the parents. Security was strict, and quiet for study closely supervised.

Though the world had surely changed, faculty and students carried on the old traditions, as summarized in the *Wheel* in 1946: "Fall Quarter—Opening Mass, Big-Little Sister Luncheon, Junior Tea, Freshman Assembly, Christmas Party complete with Santa Claus and 'whopping' Christmas tree, and quarter exams. Winter Quarter—Winter Carnival with its queen, basketball games, snow sculpture, general culture and world affairs tests, annual retreat . . . and quarter exams. Spring Quarter—Vocations Day, Honors Day Assembly, Eucharistic Day, May Fete, quarter exams, Baccalaureate Mass, and Graduation." Students didn't worry too much when an activity of the Sodality was not financially successful: According to the minutes of a meeting on November 4, 1946: "The treasurer reported that fifty cents was realized at the All Hallows party."

Students continued the traditions started before the war. Above, Lois Dinessen, Jane Irish, and Virginia Bohmer (Walsh) '40 enjoyed Winter Carnival in 1938. At right, other students danced in 1943, touched by the sadness of a world at war. Afterwards, they looked forward to reading again of matters considered in the Wheel in 1937: "A whiff of net or marquisette afloat in the spring breeze . . . is the way to romance and loveliness."

They became members of new organizations, too. In 1946, the National Federation of Catholic College Students (NFCCS) organized with the college a charter member. According to its constitution, the NFCCS was "to assist student groups to give energetic and practical application to the teachings of the Holy Father and the church's leaders regarding the formation of a Christian-minded apostolate among the Catholic laity, and to contribute to the spreading and deepening of a highly trained Catholic opinion."

And in aftermath of World War II, students provided continuing assistance to people in Europe. In 1946 the *Wheel* reported: "Pleas from alumnae and former students in France, Germany, Hungary, and Rumania have begun to arrive at St. Catherine's. They were in dire need of clothing, food of all kinds, especially canned meat, dry milk, macaroni, and rice. The collection and mailing of the bundles is being supervised by Sister Antonius, Sister Stella Marie [Berthiaume '32], and Sister Eleanore." The gratitude of people in Germany for the relief was expressed in a letter in 1948 to Sister Mary William: "Since we have been without potatoes for some time, I had to make the difficult decision to exchange potatoes for lard . . . you can imagine the joy when we saw the large can of lard as we took out the contents of the package. Then the *cheese,* the milk, the sugar, the cocoa, the chocolate, and the other *precious* things . . . Since 1945 we have not eaten any because none has been allotted to us."

And teachers . . .

In 1945 the college opened an occupational therapy department, with Sister Jeanne Marie Bonnett as director. She had earlier been head of the psychology department and an excellent recruiter. A Milwaukee public school superintendent testified: "Sister Jeanne Marie, who visited Shorewood High School today in the interest of securing the right type of student for your college . . . radiates charm and grace." In preparation for new work, Sister Jeanne Marie finished her studies at the Boston School of Occupational Therapy in just one year, receiving her certificate of national registration in 1945.

The new department had its problems. Some faculty members in the liberal arts were unhappy about introducing another professional department. Sister Jeanne Marie herself championed the liberal arts as a basis for professional majors. Sister Antonius reflected years later: "We did start the occupational therapy department . . . I had some doubts about it because they were both [nursing and occupational therapy] non-liberal . . . and I was supposed to be standing up for a liberal arts college. But I felt that it was patriotic to do it to help out the war effort and also to take care of the increased enrollment."

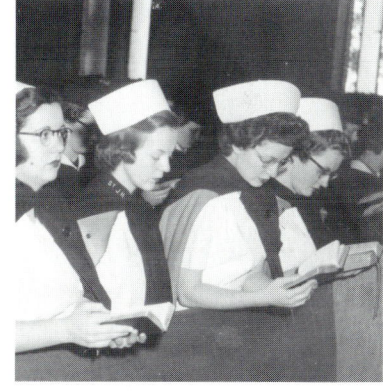

Class of '51 nurses Agnes Belair (Bohnet), Kathleen Pull (Henry), Estella Whittaker (Lukoskie), and Mary Frances O'Grady (Chaix).

Sister Antonius noted the developing profession of occupational therapy during the war, and chose Sister Jeanne Marie Bonnett to train for and head the program. At left, Mary Domler (Ochs) '47, Althea Ashton (Harman) '47, and Celine Abbott (Beaubien) '48 were some of the first students in the field.

The accreditation process was difficult, but friends of the college, including Joseph Ryan, who had been college physician from 1939 to 1941, did all they could to help. A member of the Manhattan Project at Oak Ridge, Tennessee, during the war, he had afterwards joined the staff of St. Joseph Hospital to work towards a nuclear medicine laboratory, the first in a private hospital in Minnesota. He said that to obtain accreditation for the new department: "Sister Jeanne Marie set up a committee of physicians, psychiatrists, orthopedists, and internists. We were to meet with an examining team from the American Medical Association [AMA] . . . Fortunately one of the examiners had been one of my patients in the army. That may have been a big help. Anyway, we had no trouble after that." The AMA granted accreditation on June 8, 1947.

In 1946 Therese Mueller, wife of Franz Mueller, began to teach social thought at the college in place of her husband, who had too heavy a teaching load at St. Thomas. She also had master's and doctoral degrees from Cologne. Therese Mueller was a pioneer in the liturgical movement, especially in family liturgical practice, having published *Family Life in Christ* and *Our Children's Year of Grace.* The two professors occasionally spoke to student groups on Advent and Christmas customs in Germany. Their three daughters—Mechthild Mueller (Ellis) '54, Hildegard Mueller (Kerney) '55, and Gertrud Mueller (Nelson) '58—all graduated from the college.

When Peter Lupori joined the art faculty in 1947, he was already a prominent sculptor. He received a bachelor of fine arts degree from the Carnegie Institute of Technology and a master's degree from the University of Minnesota. Over the years he received many awards, including second and third prizes in the Prix de Rome competition and first prize in the Beaux Arts competition in New York. Among his many commissioned works are the mahogany statue of St. Joseph in the lobby of St. Joseph Hall, stations of the cross for Holy Childhood Church in St. Paul, and a thirty-six foot ceramic bas-relief depicting the highlights of medical history for Fairview-Southdale Hospital in Edina, Minnesota. He has been a member and officer of many Twin Cities arts groups, including president of the Society of Minnesota Sculptors. With the help of Sister Leon Lefebvre, longtime member of the art department, Lupori taught classes in ceramics, wood, and metal sculpture.

In 1950 Sister Marie Ursule Sanschagrin, above examining the alumnae publication SCAN with two students, was awarded a Fulbright scholarship to study folklore in Paris. There she collected (as a hobby) crib figures of clay representing the common people from all parts of France. Known as santons—the "little saints" were painted in traditional clothing by the families in each town.

Sister Marie Ursule Sanschagrin, from Benson, Minnesota, also joined the college faculty after the war. She had entered the novitiate in 1922, begun teaching in 1925, and served as the principal of Derham Hall from 1925 to 1933. She received a master's degree from the University of Minnesota in 1930, and from 1945 to 1947 she studied French at the University of Laval in Quebec. While in Canada, Sister Marie Ursule began to collect sayings and songs about the people of Sainte Brigette de Laval, a village twenty miles from Quebec, for doctoral study. Because her father was originally from that village, she was received by the people as one of their own, and they readily shared their lives and their music. Her thesis became a compilation of more than 45 fairy tales and 278 songs of French-Canadian origin. Most of the music she collected dated to songs of seventeenth-century France. Luc Lacourciere, professor at Laval University, wrote: "All those who have had occasion to know the work accomplished by Sister Marie Ursule . . . qualify it as extraordinary. This is the opinion of M. Marius Barbeau, the foremost Canadian au-thority in folklore and also that of M. l'Abbe Savard . . . our best Canadian writer . . . this thesis will be epoch-making in folkloristic and historical studies in Canada."

Sister Marie Ursule had earned the accolades, sometimes traveling by dogsled through the mountains in temperatures forty-five degrees (F.) below zero, wearing heavy boots with felt soles and three or four pairs of stockings and a knit cap, to do her research. Her work was published by Laval University Press in March 1951, when she was awarded "Le Prix Raymond Cosgrain." The head of Laval University congratulated her for her "abundant" original documentation about the geography, history, customs, and oral traditions of the people of Sainte Brigette de Laval. Meanwhile Sister Marie Ursule had returned to teaching at the College of St. Catherine.

Loretta (Sister Helen Joseph) Sanschagrin joined the novitiate four years after her sister. She had taken a year's course at a normal school, and she taught in a country school two years while struggling with her vocation. Her aunt, whenever she saw Loretta, would say, "Well, that one is going to be a nun." Sister Helen Joseph said later: "I used to get so angry about it . . . my mother always taught us we should pray so that we would know what God wanted us to do . . . I used to make these novenas, but I always added to the end, 'Don't let it be a sister.' But God wanted it."

Sister Helen Joseph entered the Sisters of St. Joseph, received a bachelor's degree from the college in 1940, and a master's degree from the University of Minnesota in 1947. She disapproved of students who did not wear stockings, who walked on the grass, and who sat on tables, and she told them immediately of their failings. She was a great fan of the Minnesota Twins and once arranged to listen to a baseball game while undergoing surgery on her knee. She had happy memories of her childhood in Benson: "We always sat around the big dining room table, and my mother supervised our homework . . . Then we had the family rosary. . . We'd go out camping, we gardened . . . We always had lots of fun at home." She was as much at home in Mendel Hall, where, at the sight of a "delinquent" she flew out of her office with a reproach.

Sister Helen Joseph Sanschagrin began teaching biology at the college in 1941. Above, she worked at a microscope with Sister Teresita Judd.

Courses in theology and philosophy, a priority for college administration and faculty from the earliest days, at first were taught by priests from the St. Paul Seminary, among them the Reverends Lawrence O. Wolf, William O. Brady, Louis J. McCarthy, Rudolph Bandas, and Richard Doherty. Topics included Old and New Testament, logic, ethics, and the history of philosophy. With the arrival of the Reverend William Murphy, OP, in 1945, a new era began. At first he taught logic and ethics, but with the arrival of the Reverend Edward Emmans, OP, he began to conceive a new program. The enthusiasm of the Dominicans for St. Thomas Aquinas, a neo-Thomistic revival flourishing at the time, and some dissatisfaction with the program as it stood led to the proposal for a four-year sequence of philosophy and theology based on the work of Thomas Aquinas. The philosophy and theology sequences would require two two-credit courses in each subject every quarter of a student's four years. A faculty committee studied the alternatives.

The faculty divided on the program. One group feared the elimination of Scriptures and little or no work on the church and the sacraments. The other group pointed out the superior organization of the proposed program, its intellectual discipline, and solid foundation of thought. After much discussion, the proponents won, and the program was approved in 1946 for institution with first-year students in the fall of 1947. The text for the course was Walter Farrell's *Companion to the Summa: Volume 1*.

Murphy and Emmans did most of the teaching, with occasional help from priests at the seminary, and their work did much to sell students on the course.

Mary Ellen Chase, an earlier member of the faculty, was one of many nationally known writers to speak at the college in the 1940s.

On four different visits, Mortimer Adler spoke on topics related to the Great Books program he founded with Robert Hutchins.

Emmans was an inimitable wit and satirist. He enlivened philosophy classes with the presence of "Cucufat," an invisible being who helped to take philosophy from abstract to concrete terms. Emmans was famous for epigrams such as (on St. Patrick's Day): "I am not Irish and proud of it." To a student who asked an irrelevant question, he said: "May your hair turn green and grow out of the end of your nose." Some students found the going difficult, but respect for the intellectual content of the philosophy-theology program increased. As the years passed, succeeding volumes of the *Companion to the Summa* were used.

Student comments on the program were generally favorable. One said, "Theology is the substance of our religion; once we have some understanding of it the liturgy becomes much more meaningful and beautiful." Another was sure that "If I had learned nothing else, the program would have made the four years [at the college] worthwhile." Still another said, "I think the theology and philosophy program is one of the most important programs on campus . . . one of the reasons I stayed four years at St. Catherine's." Murphy and Emmans were soon joined by the Reverends Joseph Angers and John Reardon, both Dominicans, and the program remained much the same until about 1960.

The intellectual life of the college, through the administrations of both Sister Eucharista and Sister Antonius, was stimulated by an amazing procession of visiting speakers. Dorothy Day, editor of the *Catholic Worker*, spoke at the college three times, in 1937, 1946, and 1947. She had founded the House of Hospitality in New York to help feed homeless, jobless men during the depression. She told students during her first visit: "Catholicism doesn't mean sitting piously in church on Sunday and dropping a dollar on the plate; it means giving of your abundance to those who have nothing." She encouraged students to prepare for the apostolate with a thorough education. After her visits, several students volunteered for work at the House of Hospitality.

Maisie Ward Sheed and her husband, Frank Sheed, spoke on campus twice. They were cofounders of Sheed and Ward, publishers of Catholic books in New York and London, and of the Catholic Evidence Guild in London, a group of street preachers who spoke about Catholicism in Hyde Park. Charles De Koninck, philosopher and chairman of the philosophy department at Laval University, visited the college three times, and Mortimer Adler, of the University of Chicago, four. Mary Ellen Chase, Ade Bethune, Baroness Catherine de Hueck, Rudolph Allers, Alfred Noyes, Baroness Maria von Trapp, Helen C. White, Dietrich von Hildebrand, the Very Reverend Monsignor Fulton J. Sheen, and the Reverends Gerald Vann, OP, and John Tracy Ellis, SJ, were among the illustrious writers and thinkers who addressed student convocations. Students often knew nothing about the speaker in advance, and they sometimes fretted about compulsory attendance. Later they realized the intellectual feast that had been set before them.

Making difficulties a challenge

Sister Antonius Kennelly's six-year term as president ended in 1949. She immediately entered a program in medical technology at St. Joseph Hospital in Kansas City, becoming a registered medical technologist by the fall of 1950. From 1950 to 1956 she served as chief administrator (and religious superior) at St. Joseph Hospital in St. Paul, after which she resumed teaching chemistry. Chair of the department from 1964 to 1969, she retired from teaching in 1977 though she remained active in her field until her retirement to Bethany in 1984.

Some resources were tight during the war, but La Concha, *which had skipped publication in 1930, stayed on press through the war. At left, Mary Jane Lewis, Marcia Black (Carmody) '37, Gertrude Nelson (Breidenback) '39, Mary Frances Hay (Dolan) '37, Carol Hankee (Nelson) '38, Mary Palcich (Sinclair) '40, and Alice Promer '38 took their turns in a long line of class editors for the yearbook.*

The spirit of openness maintained at the college meant open doors to nontraditional students like these ex-servicewomen gathered on the Dew Drop bridge in 1946: left to right, Florence Dezurik '48, Florence Sletner (Miller) '47, Barbara Cardinal, Margaret Power (Patrone) '48, Margaret Pavlik, Catherine (later Sister Anne Joachim) Moore '47, Mae Reed, Elizabeth Dusek (Langevin) '50, and Elizabeth Freeman.

The end of the depression and the war and postwar years had been a time of stress. Expanding enrollment, pressure on resources, an overworked faculty and staff, and a shortage of materials meant heavy demands on everyone at the college. But a sense of camaraderie and dedication to Catholic education had made the difficulties a challenge. Agnes Keenan reflected on those years: "There seems to have been an atmosphere of space about the years we worked together: openness and clarity that come from a willingness to look, to listen, to examine, to enjoy, no matter what the idea. And there was much controversy, the clash of thought springing from firmly held principles, and the clang of opinions just as firmly held—with points made lightly and in good humor."

Carmen Legarda, the Philippines, and Louise Gradstein (Dillery), France, rode at the front of a 1951 May Fete float.

We pray that we too may be open as our founders were open, and inherit from them the prudence and the wisdom that move us to try all things.

Part of a larger whole

The College of St. Catherine was in many ways a mature institution by mid-century. Enrollment had increased from 234 in 1921 to a total of 1,434 (including special classes) in 1950. The faculty in 1949 included 55 sisters and 53 lay teachers. There were six major buildings on campus. But there was room for growth—in programs, collections, plant, professions, methods, and perspectives. The college would enfold a larger world within its gates as it expanded without, learning to cooperate with other institutions to enlarge opportunities for students, graduates, and faculty, encouraging involvement in the social apostolate, and extending its international outreach.

Many services and abilities

Sister Antonine O'Brien was named president of the college in 1949. After earning a bachelor's degree in 1926, she attended the University of Minnesota for a short time, then traveled with Sister Maris Stella to England. The two sisters returned from Oxford University in 1929, qualifying for master's degrees in English in 1933. Sister Antonine became an assistant professor of English in 1929, retaining that position until she became dean in 1937. As dean she saw a rapid expansion of enrollment and faculty. In 1945 she was named assistant provincial of the Sisters of St. Joseph, remaining in that position until she became president.

Shortly after Sister Antonine became president, the Sisters of St. Joseph celebrated the tercentenary of the founding of the community at Le Puy in France in 1650. Sister Teresa wrote a pageant for performance by the students. The program for *The Little Design of the Rev. Jean Pierre Medaille, S.J.*, explained: "The Institute of the Sisters of St. Joseph, whose members seek first to grow in the love of God through prayer and to express this love through external works of charity and zeal, was the first uncloistered congregation of women to receive general episcopal approbation." The pageant, written for many performers, had four acts: Father Medaille Plans His Little Design, The First Sisters of St. Joseph Receive the Holy Habit, The Sisters Rejoice in Suffering for the Name of Christ during the French Revolution, and The Scene of the Harvest Becomes World Wide: The Sisters Go out to Asia, India, Africa, America.

Sister Antonine, known as a charming hostess, good writer, and stickler for propriety, had written a short history of the sisters, entitled *Heritage*, in 1936.

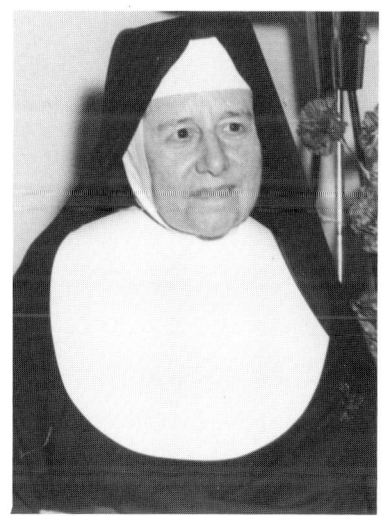

Sister Antonine O'Brien was born in Minneapolis and attended St. Anthony High School. She entered the St. Joseph novitiate in 1921 and earned a bachelor's degree in English and Latin from the college in 1926.

There she noted the founding of the college and summarized its objectives: "Modern life demands of young women students many services and abilities . . . not required of the women of fifteen centuries, or three centuries, or one century ago. Theirs is a time of specialization—for which St. Catherine's prepares them. Out of its doors have gone teachers, librarians, social service workers, writers, artists, musicians, business women, and homemakers . . . nurses, dietitians, laboratory technicians, research workers, and health and physical education directors. But . . . the college remains first of all a college of the liberal arts . . . in which the end of education is the same as it was in the days of St. Catherine of Alexandria, or the struggling sisterhood of Le Puy."

During Sister Antonine's tenure as president, the college became the scene of a struggle between proponents of the liberal arts and those of the professional fields. To assure the right proportion of each, the faculty began in 1952 a study of the liberal arts curriculum that continued for several years. The college catalog for 1954-55 noted: "A liberal arts education implies the ability to think clearly and critically, to express one's thoughts effectively . . . The ability to read literature with perception, an understanding of the role of science and its method, some knowledge of historical method . . . An understanding of the nature of man and of reality. A Catholic liberal arts education views this knowledge as part of a larger whole, and through the study of philosophy and theology relates all these studies to each other and to divinely revealed 'truth.'"

A concept of integration

The college had already shown an interest in becoming "part of a larger whole" when in 1950 its elementary education program became affiliated with the Diocesan Teachers' College. At the suggestion of the Reverend Roger Connole, archdiocesan superintendent of schools, students majoring in elementary education began to take their first two years of liberal arts courses at the College of St. Catherine and the last two years at the Diocesan Teachers' College, housed in the former home of James J. Hill. The four-story mansion (complete with art gallery), given to the archdiocese by Hill's daughters, also housed the diocesan Bureau of Education and the superintendent's office.

Connole had already made an impact on elementary education in the archdiocese. After receiving master's and doctoral degrees in education from Catholic University, he taught at the Diocesan Teachers' College from 1934 to 1950. There the sisters who had not yet earned bachelor's degrees enrolled for Saturday and summer school sessions. Because earning a degree that way took so long, it was facetiously called "the twenty-year plan."

Connole's dissertation, "A Study of the Concept of Integration in Present-Day Curriculum Making," conceived a unique approach to curriculum and classroom presentation/management. As superintendent of Catholic schools and head of the teachers' college, he gathered the finest teachers of the area and with them developed an archdiocesan curriculum based on his ideas. The schools were his laboratory. He visited them often, teaching various classes, supervising student teachers, and constantly reevaluating his work. He kept the curriculum guides in mimeographed form to allow for constant revision.

Much of the success of Connole's program was due to the work of Sisters Mary Ellen Cameron and DeLourdes McAulay, archdiocesan supervisors of parochial schools staffed by the Sisters of St. Joseph. For twenty-five years the two sisters traveled through the archdiocese, advising and encouraging teach-

Students majoring in elementary education began to take their first two years of liberal arts courses at the College of St. Catherine and the last two years at the Diocesan Teachers' College. At left, student teachers practiced in a Catholic elementary school in the diocese.

ers, especially young ones, to improve their techniques. When the Diocesan Teachers' College became the education department of the College of St. Catherine in 1950, Sister Mary Ellen became coordinator of student teaching for elementary education students. She taught classes such as Curriculum and Methods of Teaching Social Studies. She was the adviser of many prospective teachers until failing health forced her retirement in 1965.

In 1961, after more than twenty years of revision and rewriting, Connole collaborated with Sisters Jean Ann Eckes, Aline Baumgartner '53, Judith Stodola, and Angela Schreiber '58 in putting the religion portion of his integrated curriculum into a textbook, *The Christian Inheritance*. Sisters Ansgar Holmberg '62 and Joanne Emmer '54 illustrated the text. Teachers of the archdiocese carried these plans and methods back to more than sixty communities, and Connole became known as a force for educational change. As Connole and the sisters worked on the curriculum, he taught Philosophy and Curriculum of Elementary Education to St. Catherine juniors and seniors majoring in elementary education. These students also became familiar with the concept of curriculum integration and *The Christian Inheritance* series.

And cooperation

Meanwhile an exciting experiment in intercollegiate cooperation was in progress. Georgiana Slade Reny, granddaughter of James J. Hill and a trustee of the Hill Reference Library, first suggested cooperation between the librarians and libraries of the colleges of St. Paul and the Hill Reference Library downtown. Though the Hill Family Foundation had funded a project for cooperative use of faculty and visiting lecturers by area private colleges and Macalester College was experimenting with an area study program, no Catholic colleges had been invited to participate to date.

Upon Reny's suggestion, Macalester dean Wilhelmus Bryan helped by recruitiing Macalester College and Hamline University presidents Charles Turck and Hurst Anderson. Along with Sister Antonine and the Very Reverend Monsignor Vincent Flynn, president of St. Thomas and a trustee of the Hill

Reference Library, they joined in conversation with A. J. Heckman, executive director of the Hill Family Foundation, and with Roger B. Shepard and George A. Morgan, president and vice-president of the Hill Library.

After several discussions, they turned Reny's idea into a request on April 8, 1952, to the Hill Family Foundation for funds to survey the five libraries. The request was granted, and A. F. Kuhlman was selected to perform the survey. Kuhlman was favorably impressed by the colleges, finding "some great and exciting possibilities in the libraries." In the preface to his *Cooperation in Library Development and in Higher Education in St. Paul,* he mentioned "leaders with imagination, energy, and good will to discover some new patterns for the improvement of higher education and for the enrichment of human life." And in his report: "The four colleges mentioned are all fully accredited, sound liberal arts colleges that hold great promise for St. Paul and the larger community they serve. Their administrations are characterized by good will and an eagerness to find out how they can increase the usefulness of their institutions through cooperation with their sister institutions and through a utilization of the resources of the Hill Reference Library."

By October 1952, a four-college joint planning committee (consisting of the four presidents, the deans and librarians, and the president and librarian of the Hill Reference Library) had formed. Cooperation on curriculum matters was discussed, as were plans for further cooperation among libraries. The first project of library cooperation produced two editions (1954 and 1959) of *Periodical Holdings and Subscriptions in Eight Minnesota Libraries.* The work listed almost five thousand periodicals available in the state, providing access for students and faculty at the cooperating colleges to much of the research material in the Twin Cities. Also under discussion by the committee was a suggestion by Yahya Armajani of Macalester "that we establish a Hill Center of Area Studies in St. Paul. This center will use the [Hill] library as its library and will closely cooperate with the four colleges of the city. Every year this center in cooperation with the four colleges will offer studies in two or three areas open to all of the students of these colleges."

By February 1953, the joint committee had prepared another petition for funding from the Hill Family Foundation. It stated the underlying philosophy of the program: "The cooperative aspect of these programs is their most important feature . . . that four colleges, two of them affiliated with the Roman Catholic church, one with the Methodist church, and one with the Presbyterian church, have been able to plan resolutely and sympathetically for this joint intellectual endeavor is in itself a matter of supreme importance for all those who value the underlying unity of America."

Sisters Marie James Gibbons and Angele Gleason enjoyed a carriage ride in Ireland. Sister Marie James was on her way to visit the Middle East in connection with her teaching for Area Study. Later she went to Russia. Others went to Japan, Taiwan, and Hong Kong.

And culture

The first Area Study, of Russia, was taught at the Hill Reference Library in newly renovated rooms in 1953-54. Two professors from each college taught the twenty-eight students enrolled. Sisters Eucharista and Marie James Gibbons first taught for the College of St. Catherine. Sister Mary Edward began teaching Area Study the next year, when Sister Eucharista was called to St. Louis to be general superior. For seventeen years, each Area Study class began with this prayer by St. Thomas Aquinas: "Grant, O merciful God, that I may ardently desire, prudently examine, truthfully acknowledge, and perfectly accomplish what is pleasing to Thee for the praise and glory of Thy name. Amen."

Russian Area Study was followed by Middle East and Far East Area Studies, one each year; then the three-year cycle repeated. Enrollment was small—usually about twenty-eight to thirty students—but participants were enthusiastic despite a few problems. How to get students from their colleges to the Hill Reference Library was one, where faculty members could park was another, and the reference library's policy of not lending books still another. The no-lending policy eventually was waived for Area Studies students.

The preparation of Area Studies faculty was key to the strength of the program. Some members attended great universities like Harvard, Yale, and Stanford; others visited the countries they taught about. The Hill grant also made possible the establishment in each college of a core of the best books and periodicals for each area, so faculty and students could share in the enrichment.

Broad cultural experiences relating to each area were offered to the larger student bodies of each college and to the general public in a three-day cultural institute each year. For Russian Area Study, these offerings included an institute on Soviet-American relations, a series of Soviet films, and student dramatic productions. Later, more concentrated institutes offered outside speakers, films and/or slides, demonstrations, and other cultural experiences.

The College of St. Catherine had instituted its own Fine Arts Festival, which sometimes fit in well with the Area Studies program. The two-week annual festival, beginning in late April 1952, included student and faculty performers in art, music, dance, literature, and drama. Twin Cities artists and music groups often participated in forums, concerts and workshops, providing a community dimension. A Greek drama produced during the first festival, *Iphigenia in Taurus,* integrated literature, dance, and drama in one performance, with original music composed by Sister Lucina (Catherine) Kessler. *Alcestis, As You Like It, Medea,* and *The Grass Harp* were produced for the festival in succeeding years. The Russian Area Study class discussed the festival production of *The Cherry Orchard* in 1953-54.

Sister Mary Virginia Micka chatted with Catherine Pribyl, another who joined the English faculty in the 1950s. Both were advisers to student publications.

Contributing to these events were some new faculty members. The English department had gained the talents of Sisters Mary Edmund (Eleanor) Lincoln and Mary Virginia Micka, both graduates of the college. Sister Mary Edmund had begun teaching library science in 1948, while working on a master's degree in American studies at the University of Minnesota. She continued toward a doctorate after receiving her master's degree in 1955. More interested in literature than in the professional studies, she transferred to the English department in 1958, though she taught in the library science department at Rosary College in River Forest, Illinois, during the summers of 1968 and 1973. Eager to enrich her teaching by continued study and travel, Sister Eleanor studied at Oxford during her sabbaticals in 1969-70 and 1980-81. On her second sabbatical she joined a tour of Israel with St. Mary's University, San Antonia, Texas. She led student tours of England during summers and January terms.

Sister Mary Virginia Micka began to teach at the college in 1950. She had graduated from the college with a degree in English in 1943, and she received a master's degree in English from the University of Notre Dame in 1956. Involved in creative writing, especially poetry, since her undergraduate days, she became interested in writers of fiction, especially Flannery O'Connor and May Sarton, whom she met when they visited the college.

In 1980 Sister Mary Virginia began to devote more time to writing poetry, and many of her poems were published in journals like the *Southern Review,* the *New Yorker,* and the *Kentucky Poetry Review.* In 1979-80 she took a sab-

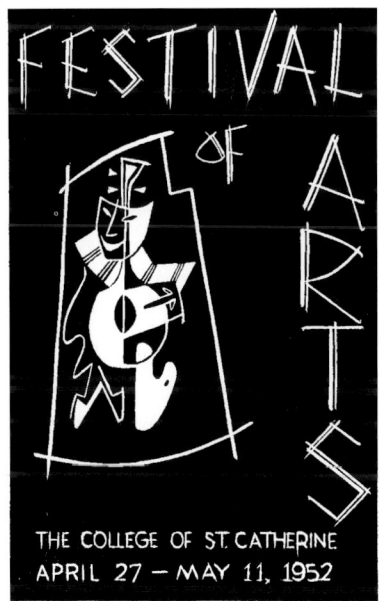

batical from teaching to devote more time to writing. She spent some time in Cazenovia, New York, which she described as "a Rip Van Winkle kind of a town." "Leaping out into the unknown," she rented a guest room above a mortuary on Sullivan Street, there writing nearly forty poems and short stories. She visited with the townspeople, listened to their stories, then wrote poems about her landlady, about neighborhood children, and about an antique fair. After reading for a group of women, she said: "I read to them about themselves." Her writings were chosen with those of 3 others from 170 manuscripts for a new theater project, "Writers on Stage," at the Southern Theater in Minneapolis, sponsored by the Loft, a local literary organization. She has since won many prizes and read her poems to many other groups.

Sister Marie David (Magdalen) Schimanski began teaching at the college in 1946. As a St. Catherine student she had received the *Atlantic Monthly* poetry prize and the Breadloaf Scholarship for summer study. She studied art at Catholic University of America and received a master's degree in 1952, afterwards returning to the St. Catherine art department. Eventually she taught painting, jewelry, philosophy of art, and African art history.

Sister Paul (Catherine) Litecky received a bachelor's degree in chemistry from the college in 1946, then entered the novitiate. After a year teaching high school in Graceville, Minnesota, she arrived at the college to teach chemistry. After receiving a master's degree in biochemistry at the University of Minnesota in 1954, she did postgraduate study at St. Louis University.

Further enriching the cultural mix and perspective of both students and teachers at the college was the first exchange student from Africa in 1954. Emily Maliwa lived in the town of Melanji in Nyasaland, which with the two Rhodesias constituted the Federation of Central Africa, and spoke the language of the area—Nyanju. Before arriving in the United States, she believed all Americans were fabulously wealthy. She changed her mind rather quickly. Before arriving on campus, she spent some time in Washington, D.C., where unrest among black students was strong. From them, she got the idea that all Americans are racists and that she was being discriminated against at every turn. She liked the snow on campus but said, "I will die if it gets any colder."

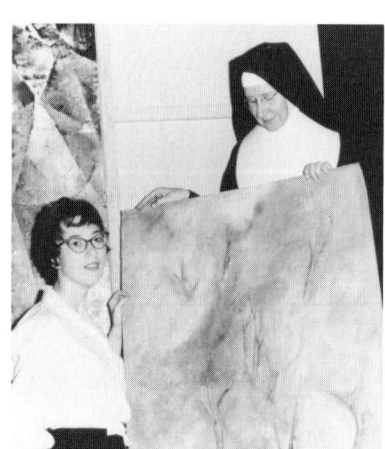

Sister Marie David (Magdalen) Schimanski worked with art student Sonia Daleki (Helton) '59, above. Sister Marie David, who has exhibited paintings in several local art galleries, received a Fulbright grant for study at the Pius XII Institute in Florence.

And graduate study?

With libraries and colleges cooperating in new ways, the training of professional librarians was more important than ever. That the college had the first accredited library school west of the Mississippi and the first accredited Catholic library school in the country was a matter of great pride to Sister Marie Cecilia, its director from 1918. She was a woman of action, devoted to her vocation and the people she worked with, and she had toiled ceaselessly to build the finest library school in the country. Deeply interested in every student enrolled in the program's classes, she worked continually to place graduates in their first library positions, following with help to get them even better jobs. Then, on July 13, 1951, the American Library Association Council adopted *New Standards for Accreditation,* requiring that undergraduate instruction be discontinued and graduate-level study be directed towards a master's degree. Library schools offering undergraduate instruction would not be accredited after 1955.

The college had long been proud of the quality of its instruction, but the idea of offering a master's degree in a professional field was not attractive to faculty members who feared graduate programs might upstage undergraduate instruction. Others did not want to abandon a flourishing field in which the college had a distinguished record. After much discussion, the library science department received faculty approval in September 1953 to plan a master's program and arrange for a visit from the Board of Education for Librarianship.

The first step to accreditation was to make a self-study of resources available for graduate work. Committees under the general coordination of Sister Annette and Agnes Keenan began preparing reports for the various departments. A "statement dealing with the plans and resources for the proposed graduate program in library science" was submitted to the North Central Association of Colleges and Universities in January 1954, and on April 16 the college was advised to continue with its plan. In September 1954, the department offered the first full program of studies leading to a master of arts degree, its stated purpose "to prepare its graduates to take their place in society and to assume responsibility in college, public, special and school libraries. It stresses principles no less than techniques, in all phases of the service. At the same time it emphasizes the broader educational and social aims of the profession. It encourages its students to continue studies in those disciplines which make for understanding of the problems of modern society."

The library science master's program held many of its classes in Fontbonne Hall. Sister Christina Varner, a high school teacher and librarian in Princeton, Minnesota, before entering the novitiate, was its only full-time instructor. In 1966, she received a certificate of merit from the Minnesota Library Association in recognition of her contributions to library science, devotion to the growth of undergraduate and graduate education, and inspiration to colleagues in academic librarianship.

The program allowed completion of the degree in one calendar year for students starting with all the prerequisites but permitted up to six years for completion on a part-time basis. Sister Marie Cecilia was full-time director, and Sister Christina Varner, called back from doctoral research at the University of Chicago, was the sole full-time instructor. She had earned a bachelor's degree in English and education from the University of Minnesota in 1938, a bachelor's degree in library science from the college in 1945, and a master's degree in library science from the University of Chicago in 1950. Five other faculty members taught part time in the library science program. By the summer of 1955, twenty-four students were enrolled.

And space

Though programs had grown and enrollment increased, the college had seen no plant expansion since the early 1930s. In 1947 Sister Antonius had urged the establishment of a fund for a building to house food service and social activities, appealing to alumnae for help. The St. Catherine Alumnae Association already had some experience at fundraising—it sold more than 9,000 tickets to a concert by Father Flanagan's Boys Town Chorus in 1946 and sponsored a lecture on "Communism in Action" by the Very Reverend Monsignor Fulton J. Sheen in 1947. When Ellerbe and Company drafted plans in 1951 for a four-story building to include dining rooms, cafeteria, snack bar, student and faculty lounges, office space, a centralized kitchen, alumnae suite, and space for home economics, the estimated cost of $1,800,000 clearly indicated more fundraising. Sister Marie Ursule, named adviser of the association in 1951, would visit chapters in many cities. She would direct an annual fund drive, Children's Carnival, Memorial Mass, and class reunions as well as the Continuing Education Program, starting in 1954-55 with evening classes such as Ceramic Sculpture with Peter Lupori, Tailoring with Alice Clark, Psychology of Mental Health with Sister Annette, and Christian Appraisal of Modern Literature with Sister Mary William. Before that, however, on March 6, 1952, she directed the association in sponsoring a performance of Beethoven's *Missa Solemnis, Opus 123*, at the St. Paul Auditorium in support of the building fund.

Ann Gideon '52, Catherine Heinz (Quigley) '51, and Constance Keefe (Smith) '51, above, enjoyed ice cream at the soda fountain of the Whitby Tea Room, which opened in 1944. One source says that at 11:00 A.M. everything stopped for a twenty-minute break during which students could order Eskimo Pies and olive butter sandwiches (but not brownies).

The association may have been inspired to help provide less crowded facilities by the visit a few weeks earlier of the famous Dionne quintuplets—Annette, Cecile, Emelie, Yvonne, and Marie—who as rare examples of multiple birth, had caught the imagination of the city and the college. Their parents, Oliva and Elzire Dionne, had accepted an invitation for the family to participate in the St. Paul Winter Carnival, January 25-30, 1952, as the guests of Charles A. Ward, president of Brown and Bigelow. They stayed in the college guest house, attended Mass in the chapel, and took meals in Derham Hall.

On January 25, the quints held their first press conference. Reporters, radio announcers, and cameramen crowded into the founders' parlor on first-floor Derham. They questioned the girls about sports, school activities, boyfriends, and college and career plans. St. Paul Police Chief Charles J. Tierney stood guard at the front door. That evening the college entertained the Dionne family in Mendel Commons. The French department presented a program of French and American folksongs and dances. The Dionnes joined in, singing a few songs of their own. They seemed to enjoy the party, apparently at home in a Catholic setting. The next day they rode in the Winter Carnival Parade. Five days later, the Dionnes boarded the train for Canada.

The following spring, with funds still insufficient for building, a loan of $1,000,000 was negotiated with B. C. Ziegler Company of Milwaukee. There were major gifts from I. A. O'Shaughnessy, the Elizabeth Quinlan Foundation, Mrs. Fred (Marie Brule) Berthiaume (mother of Sister Stella Marie), and other parents, friends, and alumnae. Mr. and Mrs. T. Merritt (Katherine Callaghan) Coughlan, whose daughters, Sister Jeremy (Helen) Coughlan '46 and Maura Coughlan Robertson '49 were alumnae, donated the rough-cut Mankato stone for the exterior. Digging for the new facility began in June, with the Steenberg Construction Company as contractor and Ellerbe and Company, architect.

Despite the work of students, alumnae, faculty, and friends, the building fund was still too small, and the sisters of the college joined in, holding the first Fontbonne Fair on November 16-17, 1953. Sister Marie James was general chair, and the other sisters contributed craft items, food, baby clothing, novelties, and toys and served dinner in Fontbonne Hall each evening. Drama teacher Donald Stubbs directed a marionette show. Faculty and student volunteers staffed the booths, moved furniture, and washed dishes. A *Wheel* editorial pointed out that the project "has given us a good chance to work together, to laugh together, to display our skills, to develop and to demonstrate our school spirit, and most important of all, it has given us an infinite amount of appreciation for this new hall . . . We thank the sisters and lay faculty for spending many a hot summer night making aprons and kitties . . . But most of all, we thank them for being interested enough to see the need for, and enough courage to undertake so large a project." Proceeds amounted to about $10,000, and the sisters hosted the Fontbonne Fair for three more years.

In 1953, the sisters put on the first Fontbonne Fair, to raise funds for a new building for food service and social activities.

Construction proceeded on schedule until April 1954, when a five-week strike by ironworkers brought progress to a standstill. In September 1954, when the building had been scheduled to open, the college had to find temporary housing for forty-six students who had reserved dormitory space on the fourth floor of St. Joseph Hall. Guest rooms, classrooms, and music practice rooms in other buildings were quickly remodeled for temporary residence. The first and second floors of St. Joseph Hall neared completion as school started. The fourth floor was almost ready too, but the third floor, intended for home economics, was still in a rough state. After camping out in makeshift quarters during September, fourth-floor residents had to pick their way through plaster dust and paint cans in St. Joseph Hall for another month.

On December 5, faculty and students celebrated a prededication dinner in St. Joseph Hall. The spaciousness of the new dining room, the newness of the furnishings, and the glow of candles and Christmas decorations made arriving teachers and students think that they had moved into fairyland. Kitchen staff members were ecstatic with their new facility, which included a new dishwasher. Sister Stella Marie and chef Frank Trojan were busy adapting the food production routine to new quarters; Sister Adrianna Ouellette was beset with the problems of retraining student workers during the grand celebration.

The official dedication of St. Joseph Hall took place on January 4, 1955, as part of the college's year-long celebration of the golden jubilee of its founding. Archbishop John Gregory Murray celebrated Mass in Our Lady of Victory

The traditional family-style dinners continued in the dining room at St. Joseph Hall into the 1960s.

Chapel, with Bishop James J. Byrne and about thirty priests of the archdiocese attending. Archbishop Murray spoke of the long Catholic tradition of educating women. He also spoke of pioneers in the education of women in the United States, exemplified by the Sisters of St. Joseph at the college.

After Mass, the archbishop, attending clergy, and congregation marched in procession to St. Joseph Hall for its formal dedication. A choir of sisters sang responses and furnished music for the ceremony. Open houses were held for sisters, alumnae, friends, and benefactors, all of whom praised the new facility, its lobby graced by a large mahogany statue of St. Joseph, sculpted by Peter Lupori. Cherry-paneled walls in lobby and lounges made them feel welcome.

Sister James Agnes Fogarty was especially happy to be teaching her home management course in the new home economics suite in St. Joseph Hall, rather than in the guest house attached to the chapel. There the enrollees practiced skills from cooking to cleaning, budgeting, and grocery shopping. The 1949 catalog had expressed the mission of the college as one enabling women to live "spiritual lives that demonstrate that their religion is not merely a doctrine to be learned, but a life to be lived, responsible lives . . . keenly conscious of their duties as members of a modern society, keenly conscious of the problems of that society, and prepared to assume a position of responsibility." Through the 1950s, motherhood was one of few "positions of responsibility" considered wholly acceptable for women, and Sister James Agnes, reflecting later, said: "I was lucky to be teaching home economics in those days. All the departments thought of all our students as future wives and mothers; so I was in a perfect setting to teach them the connection between the liberal arts and the home."

Continuing the pioneer theme and as part of the golden jubilee of the college, the drama department produced and presented on April 24-25, 1955, the play *Early Candlelight* by Maud Hart Lovelace (of *Betsy, Tacy, and Tib* fame), set in old Fort Snelling in 1840. Students from St. Thomas were recruited for the roles of Indians. Because of the limited backstage space in Jeanne d'Arc Auditorium, a birch-bark canoe had to be moved from the east side of the auditorium to the west through the first floor of Whitby Hall. Residents of Whitby were startled at times to see loin-clothed "Indians" carrying a canoe through the hall.

Meanwhile, the French department was planning to enter the electronic age by opening a language laboratory in the basement of Whitby Hall. The year before, its faculty members had met under the direction of Sister Marie Philip Haley, to plan the lab. They had no models since few language departments in the United States had even tried to incorporate an electronic laboratory into teaching. Georgetown University supplied a few ideas, but otherwise the faculty had to improvise.

Sister Marie Philip solicited funds for the lab from alumnae who had majored in French and a few other friends. They responded generously, and a major gift from Alice O'Brien of Marine on St. Croix, Minnesota, allowed renovation of the old Whitby home economics quarters, vacated upon the opening of St. Joseph Hall. In the large room were twenty-nine booths and five offices; in the smaller room, sixteen booths. Two recording rooms and a control room rounded out the facility. Each booth was fitted with earphones and channel selector, enabling students to listen to and study a recorded lesson for the day. Slides and filmstrips showing French art, history, and culture were used with the tapes, at first produced by department faculty as no others were available. All the language departments were able to use the lab by September 1955.

Her tenure as president ended, Sister Antonine served as director of the juniorate (recently professed Sisters of St. Joseph) from 1955 to 1958, was province director from 1958 to 1964, and was religious superior of the College of St. Catherine from 1964 to 1970. Then she moved to the provincial house, to start a province archives. She retired in 1978 and died at Bethany Convent on October 24, 1987.

More than subject matter

Sister Antonine was succeeded by Sister Mary William Brady, who was born in Fall River, Massachusetts, and attended Bridgewater State Normal School for two years before teaching another two years. At the suggestion of her brother, the Reverend William O. Brady, then teaching at the St. Paul Seminary and the College of St. Catherine, she traveled west to finish her college work, receiving a bachelor's degree in English from the College of St. Catherine in 1931, before entering the novitiate. While teaching French at St. Joseph's Academy, she began work on a master's degree in American literature at the University of Minnesota, which she completed in 1941. In 1937 she was transferred to teach at Derham Hall High School on the St. Catherine campus. She continued graduate study at the University of Chicago and received her doctorate in American literature in 1947. Living by her belief that teachers set the standards of scholarship, she continued some work in the classroom during the time she was president—from 1955 to 1974 teaching Chinese and Japanese literature in translation in the East Asian section of the four-college Area Studies program. She had studied East Asian literature at Ohio State University during the summer of 1955, knowing she would return to the College of St. Catherine that fall as president.

By that time, regular enrollment stood at 1,014 with total enrollment including regular, evening, Saturday, summer, and special classes at 2,254. The college had six buildings with students housed in four of them, and the administrative arrangement that had served earlier no longer met the college's needs. After much discussion, a new structure was adopted to include Sister Mary William as president, Sister Annette as academic dean, Sister Mary Edward

Sister Mary William Brady held high ideals for her students, in the belief that teachers set the standards of scholarship. The teacher should teach children more than subject matter, she told prospective teachers: "Keep yourself professionally alive by keeping professionally alert."

as dean of students, Sister Barbara Ann Mitsch as business manager, Sister Helen Margaret as registrar, Sister Rosalie Ryan as director of admissions, and Sister Catherine Ann Tauer as assistant registrar and director of placement.

During her presidency, Sister Mary William would again enjoy the counsel of her brother William Brady, who succeeded John Gregory Murray as archbishop in the fall of 1956. Archbishop Brady helped the college in many ways, advising and encouraging Sister Mary William, consecrating the chapel, and strengthening ties between the college and the St. Paul Seminary. As chairman of the Board of Trustees, he urged her to establish a lay board of advisers. Her report for 1958-59 noted: "In November . . . the Board of Trustees urged me to gather approximately twenty good men interested in education, and Catholic education in particular, and men interested in St. Catherine's. I had no trouble in doing so. Twenty invitations were readily accepted."

Setting the standards

Given her belief in the role of teachers, Sister Mary William was especially pleased to announce on December 15, 1955, that the college would receive a grant of $538,100 from the Ford Foundation allotment of $210 million for aid to the 615 private colleges and universities in the United States. For ten years, interest from the grant funds was to be used for raising faculty salaries. After that time, the principal could be used for any educational purpose.

The college also received one of only two surprise "accomplishment grants" to Minnesota colleges (the other was Carleton) of $57,000, for its pioneer work in raising faculty salaries. In 1957 Sister Mary William reported raises of 7 percent in 1955-56, 7 percent in 1956-57, with another substantial raise possible in 1957-58. Faculty, staff, and students rejoiced at the generous grant and honor. Sister Mary William noted: "It is indicative that industry is conscious of the contribution of the liberal arts colleges to the well-being of our nation. It is significant that in designating the fund for faculty salaries, the Foundation recognizes that only the best prepared people should be teaching and should be enabled to pursue further study."

Other programs for the development of faculty and students were already in progress. From 1921 to 1956, the Institute of International Education, founded in the United States in 1919, awarded twenty-eight fellowships to faculty members, chiefly for study in France, with a few for Germany. From 1950 to 1960, thirty-seven Fulbright scholarships, established in 1946 through the sale of World War II equipment overseas, were awarded to faculty, seniors, and alumnae through the institute. Most were for study in France, but there were some for England, the Netherlands, Belgium, and Italy. Sister Marie Philip, chair of the French department, was Fulbright adviser for many years. Her intense interest and high standards helped many applicants obtain scholarships.

The Institute of International Education, which screened the credentials of potential exchange students and circulated notices about them to colleges, also brought many students to the college, especially from France. The institute did not give money but obtained tuition scholarships for students, who usually worked in the library or other campus services for room and board. Sister Marie Philip composed a series of guidelines for those teaching conversation in foreign language departments.

One of the best known French students was Françoise Seidenstein (Duchâteau) '59, who was born in Czechoslovakia and moved to Paris with her family

Local resident Marie-Thérèse Caniaux-Reed and student Christiane Picard-Destelan, both from France, recorded for the language lab so that students could hear conversation by native French speakers.

as a child. She came to the college after completing her first examinations for the Licentiate in English and American literature, taking a year off to improve her English before going on for the rest of the course. Later she taught English in a school in La Rochelle, France.

In 1957, the family of Robert Butler, St. Paul contractor and trustee of the college for over twenty-five years, established a unique scholarship program enabling two sister faculty members each year to enrich their teaching backgrounds by travel and study in Europe. Sisters Mary Davida Wood and Catherine Ann Tauer, the first recipients, spent six weeks studying in a summer session at Oxford University devoted to seventeenth-century British art, literature, history, and politics. They also had time for two weeks in Paris, ten days in Rome, and two days in Florence, where they were entertained by the family of a St. Catherine exchange student, Anna Maria Nati '57. They then attended the Salzburg and Munich music festivals. Their enrichment carried over to their work on campus. One student remarked, "Oh, sister, you make it sound so wonderful and so real. I can hardly wait to find these things for myself." Sisters Mary Edward and Marie Inez, Helen Joseph Sanschagrin and Lucina, Stella Marie and Mary Jane Linn, Christina and Seraphim Gibbons, Elise Marie (Catherine) Palan and Mary Therese Dahm, and St. Mark and James Agnes received Butler scholarships thereafter.

Faculty members faced other challenges as well. In 1957 the College of St. Catherine agreed with St. Thomas that each student might register for one course at the other institution without tuition beyond that paid at the original campus. Requirements were strict: each student needed permission from the dean, and only courses not offered on the home campus or courses that would cause scheduling difficulty for students on the home campus were eligible. Eventually, a joint academic calendar was adopted, along with a uniform hourly schedule allowing fifteen minutes for transportation between classes.

Teaching efforts took on another new dimension with the opening of KTCA-TV, the Twin Cities educational television station, in September 1957. Sister Mary William, chair of the Minnesota Private College Council, which solicited funds for the use of all the colleges, spoke at the dedication. She hailed the new development, pledging the support of the fourteen private colleges of the council, which began to televise the "Private College Hour" that year. A Russian Area Studies course (provided through a grant from the Hill Family Foundation) was among its first programs, running for two half-hours a week for thirty weeks from September to May.

Other early television classes included Sister M. Inez Hilger, OSB, of St. Benedict's College in St. Joseph, Minnesota, teaching Anthropology of the Americas, and Sister Annette teaching the Psychology of Mental Health. The latter was offered on campus, with television sets in Mendel and residence halls. Sister Mary Davida taught Music Literature, or Helps to Effective Listening, for the nonspecialist interested in serious music. Faculty members also delivered a series of lectures, The Living City, during vacation periods.

Not practiced television performers, teachers approached the new medium (live broadcasts) with some trepidation. Mishaps abounded. Richard Leeman of the English department ran out of material ten minutes before the end of the period, *ad libbing* about the town mouse and the country mouse. Sister Mary Edmund dropped her notes on the floor and had to call on student panelists to help her fill in the time. Faculty sisters had to wear bright blue guimpes, which prevented glare while appearing to be white on the television screen. But re-

Sister James Agnes Fogarty had entered the Sisters of St. Joseph in 1927. She received a bachelor's degree in home economics and biology from the college in 1932 and a master's degree in foods and nutrition from the University of Minnesota in 1934, then taught at the college until 1974. In 1959 she received a Butler scholarship for study at the Ecole de Cordon Bleu in Paris.

East Asia Area studies faculty Scott Johnston of Hamline, Hildegard Johnson of Macalester, G.W.C. Ross of St. Thomas, and Sisters Mary William Brady and Mary Davida Wood of the College of St. Catherine on one of the earliest local public educational telecasts.

action was positive, and after the 1962-63 televised presentation of the Area Studies course, coordinator Scott Johnston reported "considerable audience response . . . in the form of telephone calls and correspondence."

Accreditation or not

Evaluation by the Board of American Library Association of the master's program in library science started during Sister Antonine's tenure was set for June 1957 at the latest. The college invited the North Central Association of Colleges and Universities to visit in January of that year, hoping to benefit from its advice and suggestions. Edward F. Pothof and the Reverend Thomas C. Donahue spent time in the registrar's office, the business office, the office of admissions, and the library, interviewing administrators, faculty, and students. They examined the faculty constitution, which had been developed over a period of years and adopted for one year beginning in May 1956. They seemed satisfied with the general requirements for graduation but noted twice a lack of specific requirements for the education of women. They noticed and criticized the several departments offering advanced courses with small enrollments.

Among the college's strengths they listed an experienced, devoted faculty, a tradition of excellence in student achievement, provision for a wide variety of professional and technical fields, good use of the library by students and faculty, competent administrators, and reasonably good financial condition. Among listed weaknesses were the low percentage of faculty members with doctorates, lack of a long-range development plan, and need of physical plant additions, especially a new library. They praised the new master's program in general, but they thought its underlying philosophy had been neither spelled out nor completely applied and noted that none of its faculty members held doctoral degrees, though two members were working on them. They emphasized the low enrollment in the program.

Administrators and faculty members received the examiners' report with shock, particularly because the faculty had not reached complete agreement about offering a master's degree to begin with and because so many professionals in library science outside the college were unhappy with the regulations. In fact, the requirements had resulted in more than four thousand unfilled library positions in the country the year before.

"As a result of both the visitation and a meeting of the Provincial Council of the Sisters of St. Joseph in the St. Paul Province," wrote Sister Mary William in her president's report for 1956-57, "we decided not to invite the Board of Librarianship to come for an evaluation. Instead we agreed to remain an undergraduate college even in this field and to continue to offer to students the same type of curriculum which had, before 1953, prepared numbers of students as librarians to serve many communities. This decision was made public to the American Library Association and to the press early in April. It was applauded as a courageous and fortunate step in the right direction." St. Catherine library science graduates continued to find important positions across the country.

The following school year, 1957-58, brought the visits of other accrediting agencies including the National Council of Accrediting for Teacher Education (NCATE), and the attendant need for a new self-study of curriculum. Sister Mary William noted in her report for that year: "We began as so many colleges did with self-analysis and self-criticism. Secure in the knowledge that our academic standards were high, and firmly grounded in the wise decisions of our predecessors, we decided to take another look at our general education curriculum. Substantially both satisfied us. We are still after fifty years educating Catholic women in the liberal arts tradition. We are still helping them to do a modern woman's work in a modern world. But we also found that the statement of our general objectives needed clarification and revision. In like manner we discovered our general education curriculum would benefit by a new look."

The Educational Policies Committee formulated a new statement of general objectives of the college while the Curriculum Committee worked on a revised schedule of general education requirements, partly the result of the liberal arts curriculum study begun in 1952. On March 31, 1958, the new general education requirements were presented to the department chairs for approval. Subsequently they were adopted by the faculty for two years. Sister Fides (Alberta) Huber, chair of the Educational Policies Committee, presented the new statement of general objectives to the faculty on April 24, 1958, and it was unanimously adopted.

The education department spent several years preparing for a visit by the National Council for the Accreditation of Teacher Education (NCATE). In 1959, a Teacher Education Committee appointed by Sister Mary William studied the current program with a view toward strengthening it in preparation for national accreditation. Agnes Keenan was chair. As work progressed, it became clear that the position of the committee itself must be strengthened. According to NCATE standards, the committee was to be given sole responsibility for working out the policies and program of teacher education. With the consent of the administration and of the Curriculum Committee, the Teacher Education Committee assumed that responsibility, working into the summer.

A seven-member examining committee, consisting mostly of education specialists, visited campus November 16-18, 1960. They met with faculty members, with the Teacher Education Committee, and with the administration. They visited the office of the registrar, the business office, the library, and the curriculum library. Their advice leaned toward the development of more education courses and fewer general education requirements. The Reverend Allan Farrell, SJ, representative of the North Central Association, gave invaluable

The North Central Association of Colleges and Universities found the library plant (beneath the chapel) inadequate for the high student use of its resources.

The visits of several excellent writers enriched the humanities curriculum for all students at the college. Allen Tate, above, visited in the early 1950s, and Flannery O'Connor, below, in 1961.

help in explaining the liberal arts point of view to his colleagues on the visiting team. Earl Armstrong of NCATE wrote later that the council had granted provisional accreditation to the college for a maximum of three years, with five areas for improvement:

1. The functions of the Teacher Education Committee were to be reviewed and clarified.
2. Procedures for admission to Teacher Education were acceptable but criteria were to be strengthened.
3. The number of part-time faculty members was too great in relation to full-time faculty members.
4. Teaching majors for secondary school teachers should be developed.
5. The college was to work out an arrangement for student teachers so that they could spend larger blocks of time teaching each day.

The decision for provisional accreditation was a blow, but the faculty was determined to improve the program, and three years later, in November 1963, David Bowman, a member of the original examining team, revisited the college. His review and a report by Sister Victoria Houle (elementary supervisor for the Sisters of St. Joseph) resulted in full accreditation in May 1964.

New curriculum

Meanwhile several experimental courses were being prepared. The Hill Family Foundation made a grant of $20,000 to finance an integrated program in the humanities. Fifteen faculty members from various departments attended a six-week summer workshop, coordinated by the Reverend Thomas Shanahan of the St. Paul Seminary. The original idea for an integrated course for freshmen in history, literature, art, and music taught by faculty members from these departments developed into "an over-all view of western culture" in 1956-57.

Divided into five sections—Greco-Roman, Middle Ages, Renaissance, Eighteenth Century, Modern—the course included lectures by experts to the whole group and class discussions for ten smaller discussion groups, each with its own leader. The original leaders were Sisters Mary Davida, Cecilia, Fides, Angele, Mary Virginia, and Marie David, plus Peter Lupori, Glen Glasow, Lawrence McCaffrey, and George Poletes. The first year of the course was difficult for the instructors, who found it hard to teach in fields other than their own. They needed a great amount of time to prepare lessons for classes meeting four days a week. The problem of how to integrate knowledge was never fully solved, and at the end of two semesters the faculty was dissatisfied and discouraged though student reaction was positive. One student said: "It has given me enough of an idea of Western culture so that I can appreciate what I see, hear and read. It has given a firm foundation for more study as well as a basis for judging what is good and for deciding what I like." And a faculty member wrote: "Every year the instructors note the real distress [of students] at the lack of neatly outlined textbooks with all of the important ideas in bold-face type, but as the year progresses they watch the students gain real confidence in expressing an honest opinion about the various masterpieces of art, literature, music, and drama chosen for study . . . even when that opinion differs from that held by the majority of the class, or even that of the instructor."

The course was offered until 1963, by which time many humanities faculty members had left the college or begun other work.

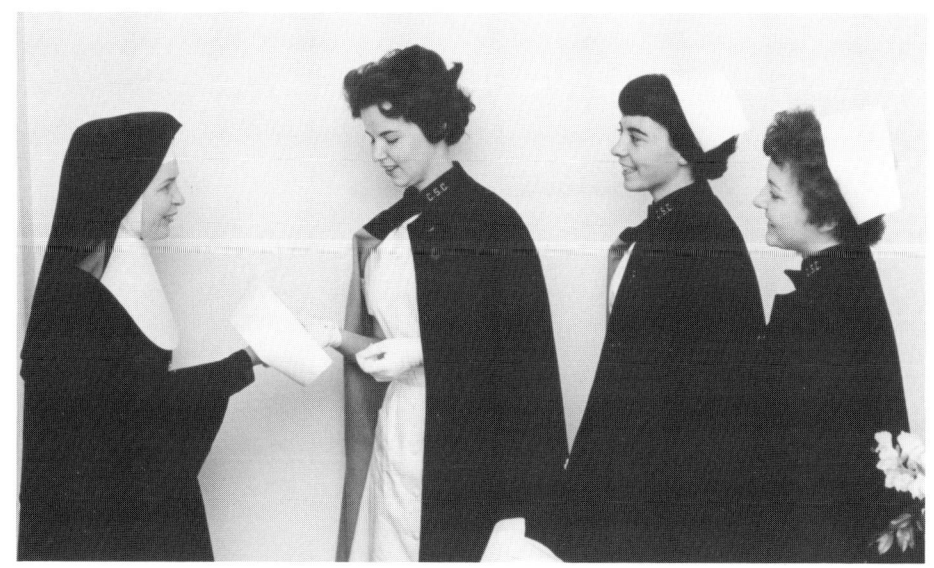

Sister Mary Jane Linn, director of the nursing department, presented caps to juniors Mary Jo Lamb (Burns), Jacqueline Kavaney (Kapsner), and Bonnie Brink (Moosbrugger), all Class of '61.

There were changes in other programs and departments as well. In 1956 Sister Mary Jane Linn succeeded Sister Agnes Leon Mahowald as director of the nursing department, and the next year, at the request of the two hospitals, the college returned one nursing diploma program to St. Mary's Hospital in Minneapolis, retaining the four-year program that used St. Joseph's Hospital for clinical experience. After 1960, the college offered only the latter program.

Sister Jeanne Marie's sudden death in 1958 left the occupational therapy department in a precarious condition. The courageous and generous work of Catherine Daniewicz '52 and other alumnae held the department together until Sister Miriam Joseph (Genevieve) Cummings was was able to take over, in 1961. Sister Miriam Joseph had earned a bachelor's degree in occupational therapy and sociology at the college in 1949, and she completed a master's degree in child development at the University of Minnesota in 1961. Under her direction, the occupational therapy department continued to grow.

The chemistry department was enrolling large numbers of students, especially from the nursing and natural science majors. Its faculty aimed to show students the relationship of science to the mission of the college. Sister Marie James Gibbons wrote in her report for 1957-58: "The chemistry department agrees . . . that a college exists primarily for the *intellectual development of its students.* There are other ways of intellectual development than the scientific method, but the logic of conclusions drawn from reliable data, of the theorizing about phenomenal behavior, can be and is practiced in the chemistry courses at the college . . . The *living tradition of our culture* is largely a scientific tradition and the influence of our 'scientific revolution' is strongly felt . . . No student who follows the course in chemistry with any degree of attention can fail to appreciate the achievement of human culture, gain an orderly notion of human truth and its relation to Divine truth, and develop on the basis of this knowledge the ability to judge with maturity and responsibility; as well as have a reverence for God and all creation."

The launching of the space satellite *Sputnik* by the Russians brought an upsurge of interest in the natural sciences. As early as 1956, Sister Marie James had recommended undergraduate research in chemistry: "That an undergraduate research program is not only desirable but necessary is generally conceded by heads of chemistry departments in liberal arts colleges."

Joann Kvasnicka (Hynnek), Mary Tester (Cullen), and Nancy Ploncinsky (Minahan), all '59, worked on a chemistry problem.

Sister Marie James Gibbons had recommended undergraduate research in chemistry in 1956: "This year it seems feasible to begin a three-year program of research with the sophomores. They have ability and can be motivated. They probably do not have time for an extra course but could be introduced to research through their regular course in analytical chemistry."

By 1959 the department had received a grant for undergraduate research from the National Science Foundation. Three seniors, one junior, and one freshman participated. According to Sister Marie James: "The juniors and freshman were more active . . . it would seem that the time to begin research is below the senior level." From 1960 to 1964 the student research continued. During summers, the students worked full time on projects like studying by polarograph the half-wave potentials of ferrocene derivatives.

Special courses and challenges for students with high academic records became a topic of heavy discussion in the late 1950s. The faculty, much interested in providing opportunities for high-achieving students, was inspired by Sister Mary William's address to the 1958 National Catholic Education Conference, in which she said: "If we as Catholic educators are convinced that the intellectual life is the good life, that in this day we wage a war of ideologies, that the students on our campus, gifted intellectually, are a challenge to the whole campus to cultivate another intellect to see and speak the truth—then we must give some thought toward the proper education of such a student."

Soon the college offered Honors at Entrance to gifted freshmen. Upperclassmen could attain departmental honors, recognition on the dean's list published at the end of each semester, and election to honor societies, Phi Beta Kappa being the highest honor. The Curriculum Committee provided a more concentrated option for the gifted in the program known as Honors Reading.

The Honors Reading program was inaugurated in September 1960, after three years of discussion. From the freshman class, fifty-one students were selected as potential honors students, and twenty-one completed the Honors Reading taught by Sisters Fides and Mary Edmund. The class was organized into two discussion groups, each with a faculty member and a student discussion leader. Gradually, students took leadership to work out their own ideas. The theme was "Human Freedom and Responsibility," with discussion based on great writings of Western culture. One instructor remarked: "Every effort was made to keep the students' originality and freshness of approach unspoiled and at the same time to lead them further under the discipline of critical thinking, careful reading, and logical expression of ideas."

Our Lady of Victory Chapel reflected in the Dew Drop—St. Catherine Campus

In the cloisters—St. Catherine Campus

Fontbonne Hall—St. Catherine Campus

Fencing—St. Catherine Campus

Zerogee by Paul Granlund—St. Catherine Campus

Beneath the cloisters—St. Catherine Campus

O'Shaughnessy Auditorium, Mother Antonia McHugh Fine Arts Complex—St. Catherine Campus

Perch near the Dew Drop—St. Catherine Campus

Volleyball—St. Catherine Campus

St. Joseph Hall—St. Catherine Campus

English Garden near Whitby Hall—St. Catherine Campus

In class—St. Catherine Campus

Graduation—St. Catherine Campus

Getting acquainted—St. Mary's Campus

Running the Mississippi—St. Mary's Campus

Old Main—St. Mary's Campus

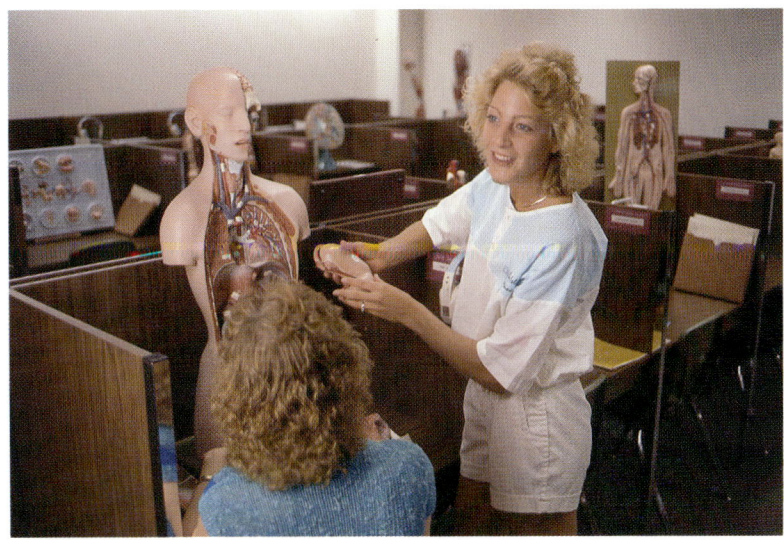
In class—St. Mary's Campus

In the library—St. Mary's Campus

Working out—St. Catherine Campus

Inside Our Lady of Victory Chapel—St. Catherine Campus

In the second year Honors Reading I was offered again, and Honors Reading II, entitled "Man and His World," was initiated with eight students taught by Sister Paul and Eldon Talley. Readings dealt with the growth of modern science and its influence on the contemporary world. Honors Reading II and III attracted few students as upperclassmen occupied with their major fields had little time for electives. Honors Reading I continued for several years until faculty changes made the offering impractical.

The theology curriculum in use from 1947 was revised as a response to a lack of student interest in the courses offered. New teachers with less enthusiasm for the Thomistic curriculum had replaced the veterans, and students began to complain about the abstractness of the courses, their lack of relevance to contemporary programs and the lack of options among courses. Forty-four students (78 percent) responding to a questionnaire distributed to fifty-six Honors at Entrance freshmen in 1959 indicated less interest in theology than in any other courses and voted them the most repetitious of high school courses. After discussions among the faculty and especially with the theology department, the academic dean reported in 1959-60: "The greatest need seems to be a more vital theology program . . . There was a plea for more discussion in theology classes and making the study of theology more meaningful in their lives." The resulting new program recommended courses in Scripture for entering students and in dogmatic and moral theology for upperclasswomen. Electives would be available in apologetics and Christian marriage. But an even more thorough revision was advised.

Additions to faculty enriched the offerings of other departments. George Poletes, who earned a bachelor's degree at Augustana College in Sioux Falls, South Dakota, in 1956, a master's degree at North Dakota State University in Fargo, and continued graduate work at the University of Minnesota, joined the drama department in 1958. He developed a popular annual play performance for children and occasionally took roles in other student performances. He was outstanding as the king in *The King and I* in 1962, as was Margaret Lange (Semans) '63 as Mrs. Anna.

Art professor and sculptor Peter Lupori and Catherine Pribyl, who had joined the English faculty in 1951, decided to marry, in the first intrafaculty wedding at the college. Catherine Lupori later said that student reaction was "really wild . . . There were very few men on the campus at the time." Lupori had proposed after she helped him host a party at the University Club in November 1957. He said, "I wonder if you'd like to marry me?" "Wonderful," she replied. "Everyone told me that I couldn't possibly live with Peter Lupori without seeing the Museum of Modern Art," she remembered. So, after their wedding on April 12, 1958, the Luporis spent their honeymoon in New York City.

In 1959-60, Allayne Daves joined the history department full time. She had a master's degree from the University of Minnesota and was working toward a doctorate at Ohio State University. Before her work at the college, she taught at Morgan State College in Maryland and at Fisk University in Nashville. Several years after Daves left the college for a position in Rochester, New York, Sister Fides wrote: "Allayne Daves was one of the most loved teachers we have ever had on our staff. She was a splendid teacher—organized, clear, interesting, patient, and fair. Her students admired her as a person as well as an instructor, and her colleagues . . . loved her dearly. By her marvelous gentility and her gracious manner she did more to eradicate prejudice and educate our students to right attitudes than any number of courses could have done."

Peter and Catherine Pribyl Lupori stepped off the elevator for a campus reception after their wedding (the first for two faculty members) on April 12, 1958.

Delighted with her soft, clear voice and gentle manner, students signed up quickly for Allayne Daves's History of Civilization and political science courses.

One formerly popular program saw its demise. The academic dean's report for 1959-60 recommended "in view of the constant friction and disagreement" among sponsoring departments, the discontinuation of the Fine Arts Festival "in favor of a creative arts series during the year." The departments continued to offer their spring performances without the framework of a festival.

To live among books

All students and faculty members had to contend with crowded library facilities, by this time spread among four buildings: the main library beneath the chapel, the reserve library in the former power house, the depository library in Derham Hall, and the music library in Caecilian. The opening of St. Joseph Hall in 1955 had provided some relief, as kitchen and dining room space on the ground floor of Derham Hall was turned over to the library. The librarian's report for 1955-56 noted: "Through this expansion three significant areas have been developed: the depository library, the rare book room, and the archives collection. The depository library was made ready for use by painting, repairing the floor, and the installing of 5,512 linear shelving, with 420 feet of wide shelving. This gave us an increased stack capacity for about 13,000 volumes."

Around that time, Georgiana Slade Reny, daughter of Charlotte Hill Slade, gave to the library her mother's collection of first editions and fine bindings, early printing, and Orientalia. These 483 books were added to the library's earlier collection of rare books and fine bindings, and the whole was named in honor of Charlotte Hill Slade. Another part of the collection, consisting of autographed works of literary merit, was named for Sister Antonia McHugh in honor of her concern that students have contact with great people as well as with their works. She had made available the books of visiting authors, and many authors sent copies of new publications to the college. Works of local authors and others connected with the college were added over the years.

The largest special collection was the Ruth Sawyer collection of children's books. In 1942 Ruth Sawyer Durand taught a popular course in storytelling at the college. Afterwards the library collected letters, pictures, autographed editions of her books including *The Least One* and *Blueberries for Sal* as well as a book written and illustrated by her son-in-law, Robert McClosky, who designed the collection bookplate. The Ruth Sawyer Collection was dedicated on April 16, 1958, and Sawyer responded with a story. She told another at a tea given in her honor by the campus library science club, Readers' Round Table.

In addition to increasing its regular holdings and rare book collection, the library had more than doubled its music library with 500 recordings and much sheet music from the Carnegie Corporation in 1948. Housed on first-floor Caecilian Hall and attended some hours by student assistants, the library found it difficult to keep track of records or to know which had been damaged or lost.

The visit of the North Central Association in 1957 had indicated by a 92-percent rating that the library gave excellent service in spite of the cramped quarters. But the problem of room for expansion did not go away; as Sister Mary William noted in the March 12, 1959, *Wheel:* "The library reveals more about an institution of higher education than any other aspect observable. Almost every new college has to decide between a new building and a good collection of books. Sister Antonia believed that an excellent collection of books was essential to the work of a college and that a building to house them would eventually come. That 'eventually' has now come."

Sister Mary William Brady and Ruth Sawyer Durand examined a book in the Ruth Sawyer Collection, dedicated on April 16, 1958, at a convocation in Jeanne d'Arc Auditorium. The library has since expanded the collection with others on the history and art of storytelling, including Sawyer's The Way of the Story-teller. *Children's books in the collection include an eighteenth-century chapbook of* Jack the Giant Killer, *a book measuring less than two inches, and a complete set of the Newbery and Caldecott award books.*

The librarians had already begun, in November 1958, a series of weekly meetings to plan for a new library. According to the librarian's report: "Preliminary discussions centered around the concept of good, functional library planning . . . The second major step in the building program was to inquire of the faculty what services they expected of the library . . . At the time of writing their report, the library staff could say that every service which had been asked for had been incorporated in the sketches and plans in one way or another."

In March 1959, Lang and Raugland, a Minneapolis architectural firm, was commissioned to start planning for a million-dollar library of Mankato stone (again a gift of the Coughlans), to please the aesthetic sense as well as to serve the needs of the college. It was to have a capacity of 300,000 volumes and seating for 500 students. Its special features would include space for the library science department, a rare book room, an archives room, a listening room for records and tapes, a viewing room, a typing room, and a photocopy room.

College Association president Colleen Donahue (Thompson) '60, provincial superior Sister Antonine O'Brien, architect Austin Lange, assistant librarian Sister Christina Varner, Sister Mary William Brady, and Archbishop William O. Brady celebrated with attending faculty and students, the groundbreaking for a new library, November 2, 1959.

The construction contract was awarded to Rauenhorst Construction Company of Minneapolis, with Joseph Woodman, retired building supervisor for the City of Minneapolis, supervisor for the college. Construction moved rapidly, and ceremonies for the laying of the cornerstone took place on May 20, 1960. Monsignor Louis McCarthy, rector of the St. Paul Seminary, blessed the cornerstone, and Sister Mary William placed a copper box filled with archival material, laying on the first trowel of mortar. Construction was completed early in October, with moving day set for October 11.

"Operation Booklift" began shortly after 8:00 A.M. on a crisp sunny day. Action started outside the Reserve Library where faculty, staff, and students formed single file lines. According to the next library report: "At a given signal the first books were handed to Sister Mary William, and to the deans, Sister Mary Edward and Sister Rosalie. As the phonograph played, 'O what a beautiful morning,' the lines began to move in the front door and out the back. In less

Sister Marie Inez Johnson greeted students Mary Martin and Jane Schroeder (Lawrence) '62, part of Operation Booklift on October 11, 1960. Each carrier received one of Sister Stella Marie's brownies for each armful of books transported. In two and one-half days, students and faculty members took 95,000 books from the old buildings to the new St. Catherine Library.

than an hour the old reserve stacks were bare. The workmen moved in and began to unbolt the shelves, for they too were moving to the new location. Librarians and staff members were posted in the new library to point out the place in the stacks for each armful of books. Thus the books were in perfect order as they arrived in the new library . . . One student was heard to say, 'Now I know why the people in the Middle Ages loved their cathedrals so much. It is because they built them.'"

Library service began on October 13, just two days after the closing of the old library. Many visitors arrived to inspect the new building, and tributes came from many sources. Doran Hurley wrote in the January 1961 issue of *St. Joseph Magazine:* "An inspired feature . . . particularly delights me. The Sisters of St. Joseph . . . have installed a large stone pedestal rising out of the very structure of the building on which a beautifully printed English language version of the Bible is to be permanently placed. The sisters' purpose is twofold: to dramatize the importance of Holy Scripture as the cornerstone of knowledge and, since the Bible will be open to anyone's use, to fulfill the main point of having a Bible, which is to enable people to read it. Thus the students at St. Catherine's will have before them physical acknowledgment of [John Henry] Cardinal Newman's great saying, 'It is our duty to live among books; especially to live by one Book and a very old one.'" Hannis Smith, director of libraries for the State of Minnesota, wrote to Sister Marie Inez: "Your new library building goes just far enough beyond the practical to make it a serenely beautiful thing which should serve as an inspiration to learning and intellectual and spiritual development for your college in the years to come."

The faculty study, overlooking the woods and the Dew Drop, was made doubly attractive to faculty members when new books were placed there for browsing. The students especially appreciated the study carrels, where they could shut out distractions and accomplish more work in a shorter time. One student said: "I can't tell you what a difference the library has made in my life." Students from other colleges would soon appreciate the new library, too. Librarians participating in the library cooperation program with the Hill Reference Library had begun to meet regularly in 1959 in an effort to discover new and better modes of interaction. One benefit was the opening of the individual libraries to students of other cooperating institutions.

The library was formally dedicated with a symposium held October 27-30, at which distinguished scholars spoke on developments in Biblical study. On October 27, the Reverend Barnabas Ahern, CP, addressed "St. Paul and Church Unity," speaking of Catherine of Siena, Teresa of Avila, and Yvonne Poncelet, whose Scripture studies "inflamed them with zeal so that they devoted their lives to the work of Christ and his Church." The Reverend John M. McConnell, MM, spoke on "The Bible and Christian Unity," saying "It isn't enough to read the Scriptures if you spend the rest of your life without living the Scriptures . . . meant to give life, hope, courage, and joy." The Reverend Roland Murphy, O. CARM, spoke on the study of the Old Testament, stressing an approach recognizing literary forms such as the epic, short story, love song, state annals, and practical philosophy. On Sunday, October 30, Archbishop Brady blessed the library and installed a gold gesso crucifix, gift of Peter and Catherine Pribyl Lupori, on the walnut wall of the lobby.

After the new library opened, the St. Catherine Alumnae Association renovated the space beneath the chapel for use by alumnae and other groups. The finished Alumnae Center included a small auditorium seating 200, a dining room for 120, and a small kitchen.

Sister Mary William had also secured a $1,000,000 National Defense Loan to construct a new residence building, St. Mary Hall. She remembered a feeling of awe at holding the loan check for a million dollars "just for a minute" before it went into the bank. Ground was broken for the new dormitory in the summer of 1960, with construction complete during the following year.

Her tenure ended in August 1961, Sister Mary William traveled to Rome for study that year, then taught in a faculty exchange with Mount St. Mary's College in Los Angeles in 1962-63. The next year she rejoined the St. Catherine English faculty, continuing her work for the Area Studies program with study in Japan in 1965. She retired from teaching in 1976 and prepared for archival work in Salt Lake City. She has since supplemented her continuing work as an archivist with occasional teaching for programs such as Elderhostel and with travel and speaking engagements for the alumnae association.

Sister Mary Edward Healy, named president of the college in 1961, pledged to uphold its characteristic "high standard of spiritual and intellectual excellence."

A high standard

Sister Mary Edward Healy became president of the college in 1961. She had received a bachelor's degree in Latin and history from the University of Minnesota in 1928, before entering the novitiate. She taught at St. Margaret's Academy and St. Anthony High School in Minneapolis and at Derham Hall in St. Paul. She studied sociology at Catholic University, receiving a master's degree (thesis title: "Man and the Large-Scale Production in the Automobile Industry") in 1940 and a doctorate in 1948. She began teaching at the college in 1941, became chair of the sociology department in 1948, was named dean of students in 1955, and held both positions until she became president.

Maintaining all the other administrators, Sister Mary Edward (to fill the position she had vacated) named Marie Corrigan as the college's first lay dean of students. Corrigan had received a bachelor's degree from the college in 1926 and a master's degree in English and psychology from the University of Minnesota in 1940. She taught English in several public high schools in Minnesota and coordinated the guidance programs of eight Catholic schools. In 1945 she began teaching graduate classes at Catholic University and in 1947 became the dean of women there. In 1952 she returned to St. Paul to care for her father after her mother's death. She continued working in Catholic high school guidance programs until she began teaching psychology at the college in 1955.

St. Mary Hall was completed and dedicated on August 22, 1961, one year after groundbreaking and within a week of Sister Mary Edward being named president. The Reverends William Bullock and Stephen Otis, Sister Rosalie Ryan, and a student watched as Sister Antonine O'Brien, provincial superior of the Sisters of St. Joseph, applied mortar to the cornerstone.

Just a few weeks after the dedication of St. Mary Hall, on October 1, 1961, news arrived of the death of the college's old friend Archbishop Brady, of a heart attack in Rome, where he had been preparing for the opening of Vatican II. Greatly saddened, the college mourned his death with its new president. Archbishop Leo Binz succeeded Brady as *ex officio* chairman of the Board of Trustees of the college.

A blending of cultures

Even with a new library and dormitory, both the college and high school, on campus since its opening in 1905, needed more room. The school known as Derham Hall (in 1986 it became part of Cretin-Derham Hall) moved to a new building on Randolph and Warwick avenues in the fall of 1962. Then, with stable housing and programs for the development of faculty in place, the renewal and expansion of current programs, many of them international in scope, was the order of the day.

By the spring of 1962, Area Studies had progressed through a third three-year cycle of the study of Russia (with 59 students enrolled), the Middle East, and the Far East. Student reaction to the program had been generally positive. Coordinator Scott Johnston of Hamline reported for 1958-59: "We have done important educational and interfaith work on a frontier area of the American college world." The next year, James Colwell of St. Thomas College wrote: "Many students openly stated that it was the best course they ever had in college. As a result . . . many students decided to go to graduate school to study with emphasis on international relations or area studies." In the 1962 evaluation presented to the Hill Family Foundation, students and faculty concluded generally that world harmony could be achieved only through knowledge and blending of the cultures of many. All agreed that the program gave "vital awareness" of areas studied and provided an important opportunity to share their views with students of other colleges. The Hill Family Foundation renewed its grant to support the program for five more years (and then for another five), with African Area Studies added in 1963-64, when the program began to hold classes on alternating campuses rather than downtown. Latin American Studies were to be added to the program in 1964-65.

Stimulated by the enthusiasm of Julio Castaneda of the Spanish department, the college had already begun to hold its own Latin American Institute with Castaneda, Charlotte Millis, Sister Angele, and Sister Lucina as faculty. Jose Maria Chaves, educator and expert on international law, spoke on "The Church and Social Change" and on cultural and educational problems at the first one, in 1961. He had helped to establish the first public high school in Bogota, Colombia, in 1941, and he was a founder and first dean of the University of the Andes, the first private university in Colombia, in 1958. The second Latin American Institute, held in 1962, emphasized "Brazil, a Giant in Transition." The chief speaker was Armando Pacheco, head of the division of philosophy and letters of the Pan American Union, who was directing preparation of the *Dictionary of Latin American Literature*. He spoke on "Brazilian Literature: An Introduction." The third Latin American Institute, in 1963, focused on "Social Change in Latin America," with Jaime Fonseca of the National Catholic Welfare Conference speaking on "Challenges in Latin America" and "Social Change and the Alliance for Progress." An exhibit of Latin American books and newspapers was displayed in the library and in the lobby of St. Joseph Hall.

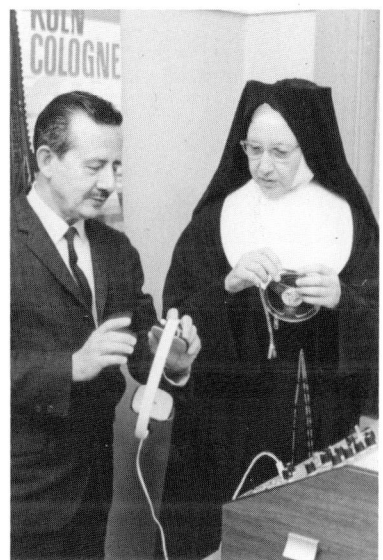

Julio Castaneda of the Spanish department inspired the Latin American Institute first held on campus in 1961. Above, he and Sister Agnes Rita Lingl of the German department examine tapes in the language laboratory.

The college hosted a Far East Area Institute sponsored by the Area Studies program in 1962, with Sister Mary Davida as chair. Lectures on literature and the arts and a library exhibit of scroll painting, carvings in jade and ivory, and fine editions of rare books on Oriental art and literature from the Slade Collection were featured. Speakers included Joseph Yamagiwa of the University of Michigan, Bernard Phillips of Temple University, and John Bennett of Washington University.

For the Africa Area Studies first offered in September 1963, Sister Marie David taught African art, and Sister Nathaniel (Mary Ann) Hanley taught African music. An African Area Studies Institute was held on campus in September 1964. Frederick C. Patterson, president of the Phelps-Stokes Foundation, spoke on education in East Africa. "The big need in African education," he said, "is to relate it to the community and national development, and the United States has this kind of education to offer."

While the Area Studies program expanded, the French department began to reach across the sea in a new way by offering institutes for secondary school teachers of French under the National Defense Education Act (NDEA) Language Development Program of the U.S. Department of Health, Education, and Welfare. The institutes were to increase proficiency in the language, familiarize participants with the culture of contemporary France, and acquaint them with new methods, techniques, and materials for teaching.

Any college hoping to offer an institute abroad was required first to offer a summer institute on the home campus. Sister Marie Philip, longtime chair of the French department, was director of the 1962 summer institute at the college. Administrative assistant Dolores Schaefer '58 taught one conversation class, Sister Marie Ursule taught phonetics and writing, and Sister Mary Henry Nachtsheim conducted a seminar in cultural materials and conversation. Former faculty member Anne Condon Collopy (McKeown) '28 taught a class of twenty-five ninth-graders for five weeks, demonstrating new teaching materials and techniques.

The institute, open to French teachers from both public and private schools, required that each participant hold a bachelor's degree, be teaching French in a public or private secondary school, and have superior or good audio-lingual competencies. From 155 applications, 41 teachers from public schools and 19 from private schools were admitted. A staff composed of native French speakers prepared an excellent curriculum on language and linguistics, culture, and teaching methods. Dinners prepared by staff and participants, excursions to St. John's University in Collegeville and St. Teresa's College in Winona, music, films, and lectures made up the informal program. Although the institute required seven weeks of intense study, the evaluations of participants were enthusiastic, describing it as "well-organized" and "very comprehensive." They mentioned "the atmosphere of cooperation and friendliness among participants regardless of nationality, race, or creed," and "the excellent rapport between participants and staff, who were together for all activities." Staff and participants agreed the institute was a rich professional and personal experience.

The next great challenge was to hold a similar NDEA summer language institute in France. Besides improving language competency the program was to offer immersion in the culture of contemporary France, opportunities for conversation with French people, and a deeper understanding of the French spirit. Accordingly, Sister Marie Philip and the institute staff prepared to offer a language institute at the University of Rennes in Brittany. Early in 1963, the program distributed 5,400 brochures to high school teachers of French and administrators, and 433 completed applications were returned by March 1. On the basis of a stringent set of criteria, 60 participants were selected from all over the United States. The program consisted of a week of orientation and study of urbanism, art, music, and theater in Paris, a bus trip from Paris to Rennes, via the Chateaux of the Loire, and six weeks of study at a building leased from the University of Rennes.

Although the curriculum remained much the same as in the institute on campus, greater emphasis was made on the culture of Brittany and the action and reaction of tradition and change. The report to NDEA read: "Emphasis was placed, not on general information and statistics, which could be procured without going to France, but rather on concrete situations . . . Throughout the course instructors endeavored to relate questions, not only to the past, present, and future of France but also to European, Atlantic, and world communities." After the six weeks of classes at Rennes, participants made a ten-day study tour through Poitou, Auvergne, the Midi, and Lyons, with return to Paris through Burgundy.

The friendliness and hospitality shown to the participants by the people of Rennes was extraordinary. Michel Le Roux, editor of *Ouest-France,* procured

Sister Marie Philip Haley reported of the first NDEA French institutes: "We had our own program, and hired our own professors—many of them the best authorities in their fields. Besides we had a fine staff of wonderful men and women to assist in field research, travel, conversation, planning daily living together. I consider the quality of the staff and their presence—meals, travels, other recreational programs—one of the main features."

for participants invitations to about ninety homes. Many of these resulted in further invitations to dinner or family events. There were two formal receptions, one given by the institute staff and participants for the people of Rennes, the other by the mayor of Rennes with representatives of the university, the Chamber of Commerce, the military, and the press, to honor members of the institute. The mingling of classes of society and types of people was unique.

Some participants found the curriculum too heavy and free time too restricted, but approval of the informal program—especially the meals, the films, and the family contacts—was almost universal. One participant said: "The variety of entertainment and experiences was truly exceptional. It seems that through conferences, visits, trips, and personal contacts with the people, we have learned more in nine weeks than we would be able to do in a year in any other program."

After the first successful institute in Rennes, applications multiplied. Five more were given in France under NDEA grants, and three more in France under St. Catherine sponsorship without NDEA funding. Altogether five hundred American high school teachers of French were personally enriched by intensive study of the French language and immersion in the culture of France. Marie-Thérèse Caniaux-Reed '71, a Frenchwoman and former teacher at the college, continued the French connection by establishing a graduate summer program with the University of Rennes. For more than ten years, she brought business majors in law, marketing, and business administration from the university—to do a month's internship in a Twin Cities business while living at the college. The program has continued in a slightly altered form since her retirement.

The outreach of the college was extended by the enrollment of outstanding students from around the world. Martha D'Costa, from Africa, for instance, graduated in 1962. Her family originated from Goa in the southern part of India but moved to Tanzania when she was very young. She received credit for some courses taken in Tanzania to earn her bachelor's degree from the College of St. Catherine with a major in English and psychology. After graduation, she returned to Tanzania to teach and wrestle with the problem of whether to remain there or to marry the young doctor she met while studying at the college. She decided to return to the United States and marry Dr. Michael Koch.

The Polga family of Hastings, Minnesota, was instrumental in bringing more African students to the college. Ben Polga, superintendent of schools in Hastings, was so impressed with the college and its high scholastic standards that he encouraged all three daughters to attend. After graduation, the oldest, Margaret Rose Polga (Hinkle) '61, decided to join Teachers for East Africa, a precursor of the Peace Corps. While teaching at Marian College, staffed by the Maryknoll Sisters at Morogoro in Tanzania, she met Daria Pana (Tesha) '66, an intelligent young African student. Margaret Rose arranged for Daria to attend the College of St. Catherine, which supplied a tuition scholarship. The Polga family helped with other expenses. After graduating with a bachelor's degree in English, Daria earned a master's degree in education from Columbia University. She then returned to Morogoro to teach in a girls' high school. Eventually she became its headmistress.

When Catherine Murray (Mamer) '61, a friend and classmate of Margaret Rose Polga, joined her in teaching at Marian College, she became interested in Mary Rose Ryan '67, who had been left with the Maryknoll Sisters by her Caucasian-American mother. Her African father's identity never became known. When Murray returned to the United States the next year, she arranged

In 1963, Daria Pana (Tesha) '66 from Tanzania, Christiane Houglet from France, and Germana Portesan (Nijim) '63 from Brazil watched Laura Ines Bracamonte of Peru dance at a party for international students.

for Ryan to accompany her. Murray eventually adopted Mary Rose Ryan and arranged for her to attend the college. At a gathering of Twin Cities international students, Ryan met Kjell Bergh of Norway, who attended Macalester College. Shortly after graduation, Ryan and Bergh were married. They continued to live in Minneapolis, where she eventually wrote a book on physical fitness and started a fitness center based on African music and dances.

Mie Nakatsu (Arntson) '65 and Yukiko Hamaya, two exchange students from Kyoto, Japan, arrived in the United States in 1963. Mie Nakatsu was the youngest of three girls in the family. Her older sister, who became known as Sister Madeline Marie, entered the novitiate of the Sisters of St. Joseph and eventually became principal of the high school in Tsu, Japan. The Japanese students noticed many differences between life in the United States and that in their native country. Mie was amazed at the amount of meat consumed by the average American: "In Japan we have meat once or twice a week—fish the rest of the time. In America you even have meat for breakfast." Yukiko observed: "Americans are naturally friendly. Also here you talk to any teachers. In Japan we do not."

Nadia Saad (Bettendorf) '65, an Arab student from Israel, arrived at the college in 1962. Through the Institute of International Education she received a tuition scholarship for study in the United States. She was the first Arab to receive a scholarship in the thirteen years the institute had been receiving applications from Israel.

Finding solutions

Preparing leaders for religious organizations and movements had continued as a part of the Catholic mission of the college, with the daily routine including opportunities for Mass and Compline or the rosary in chapel or dormitory. A retreat, May crowning of Our Lady, Eucharistic Day, and other devotions con-

Auxiliary Archbishop James J. Byrne led the Eucharistic Day procession on May 21, 1954.

tinued as annual campus events. The words of Sister Mary Judith Stoughton quoted in the May 10, 1951, *Wheel* still applied: "The Christian cannot escape the obligation to let the face of Christ shine out in his whole life and work. Although there is no blueprint ready for the lay apostolate there are possible solutions for its problems. Some of these solutions opened up by pathbreakers have taken form as the family apostolate, the liturgical movement, the Grail, Designs for Christian Living, the Catholic Rural Life movement."

In 1961 a lay mission group was organized to recruit teachers for summer Bible schools in the southern dioceses. The group sponsored various money-making activities to help pay bus fares south. The missions visited provide board for three to four weeks. Thirteen students went to Powhaten in Virginia, Birmingham in Alabama, and Austin in Texas. They prepared for teaching religion with a Confraternity of Christian Doctrine course and for working in recreational programs with a class in physical education.

The small number of Catholics in southern states—only 2 percent in Alabama, and 7 percent in Virginia—meant the work of the students would be difficult. Many Southerners mistrusted Catholics or were afraid of them, so the students' first task was to convince people that Catholics are human. The students could not accomplish a great deal in such a short time, but they believed their example of enthusiastic Catholic life influenced some of those they met.

Some faculty-student apostolate ventures were conducted cooperatively. The Lay Mission Group, the Sodality, and the Confraternity of Christian Doctrine sponsored a Lay Apostolate fundraising week in 1962. The climax was a faculty talent show featuring Julio Castaneda and Imogene De Smedt dancing the tango, George Poletes singing "The Road to Mandalay," and a student swinging from a high trapeze. Sister faculty members sang parodies of Gilbert and Sullivan songs. Richmond Kingman and the Reverend Joseph Angers, OP, arrived as astronauts landing on the moon to find the College of St. Catherine. The audience hoped for a repeat performance, but faculty performers declared it a once-in-a-lifetime event.

The Heavenly Brothers—Angelus Boyd, OP, and Raymond Marieb, OP— first appeared at a college hootenanny in 1963-64. The duo played "vibra-tubs" and sang songs like "When" and "I'll Do My Crying in the Rain." Boyd explained his instrument in the February 19, 1964, *Wheel* as "really just a laundry tub, but vibra-tub sounds better." The brothers later performed with Pamela Ahern of the English department as "the answer to [popular folksingers] Peter, Paul, and Mary" in a benefit performance for the lay missions.

"Heavenly Brothers" Angelus Boyd, OP, and Raymond Marieb, OP, performed with English professor Pamela Ahern at a benefit for the lay missions in 1963-64. The trio billed itself as "Peter, Paul, and Almond Joy."

Reflection and hope

In 1963 the St. Catherine chapter of Phi Beta Kappa observed the twenty-fifth anniversary of its installation on the campus in 1938, sponsoring a series of lectures: The Right Reverend Monsignor James Shannon, president of St. Thomas, spoke on "American Catholic Education Today," provincial superior Sister Antonine on "The Impact of a Liberal Arts Tradition," and Hildegarde Stielow, secretary of the North Central district of Phi Beta Kappa, on "The History of Phi Beta Kappa." By the end of the year, 296 had been inducted in all.

The silver anniversary was a time for reflection on the past and hope for the future. Sister Antonine, former student, teacher, dean, and president, spoke at the anniversary dinner in May 1963, describing the early years of Phi Beta Kappa on campus: "Those twenty-five years have been years of change, and if we can assess them with some objectivity, years of progress. They have been years of rigorous discipline and genuinely hard work. The compensations have been largely found in the superior achievements of students, the fidelity and courage with which they encountered life in these difficult times. Students have been most certainly true to their Catholic heritage."

Two years earlier, James W. Armsey had announced that the Ford Foundation's "Special Program in Education," begun in 1960, would soon become available to private colleges. In *News from the Ford Foundation*, he explained the program's intent: "To give each college wider freedom in which to develop its own program, and to encourage the colleges to assume fuller responsibility for reaching and maintaining higher levels of educational excellence. The matching terms were designed to help each institution elevate its fundraising level, develop its own natural constituency and push its financial goals." When the college expressed interest, evaluator G. H. Griffiths visited campus in October 1962, reporting "a rich and delightful experience from beginning to end . . . I continue to think back a good deal on the people I met, the ideas encountered, the programs discussed, and the buildings, grounds, and facilities seen."

As a result of his visit, on June 24, 1963, the Ford Foundation awarded the college one of thirteen private liberal arts college grants, with Smith the only other women's college among them. The challenge grant of $1,000,000 was to be matched by $2,000,000 raised by the college between July 1, 1963, and June 30, 1966. The foundation immediately presented the college a check of $300,000, designating $225,000 for debt retirement and the rest for curriculum, faculty salary increases, and library acquisitions. Use of the remainder of the grant and matching funds could be decided by the college.

Sister Mary Edward Healy, above, announced the Ford Foundation $1,000,000 match grant at a press conference in 1963. Valerie Nash (Glarner) '67, below, washed cars as part of a five-day campaign by students to help make the $2,000,000 match. Students also used traditional events like the Maypole dance during May Fete to raise money for the grant.

All potential donors—alumnae, parents, friends, businesspeople, parishes, and others—were contacted for gifts in the college's first "capital campaign." Students as well as faculty and staff members went to work on the project. From April 30 to May 6, 1964, for example, students conducted Ford Week, beginning with a convocation and continuing with films, a program of African dances by students Daria Pana and Mary Rose Ryan, and dancers from the

Temple of Aaron. The students put on a Saturday workday, hiring themselves out for typing, housecleaning, babysitting, and carwashing services. The week concluded with the traditional May Fete, and the students raised $1,100.

Shortly thereafter, Sister Mary Edward was chosen provincial superior of the sisters. She said: "I just can't become provincial now because the Ford Foundation grant is here and we have to match it. We have to work so hard." Nevertheless, she left the college as provincial. She served in that capacity until 1970, then taught at Mount St. Mary's College and the University of California, Los Angeles, for one year. She taught again at the College of St. Catherine from 1971 until 1974. Known for her love of people, she continued working as a telephone operator and receptionist at the college until 1981. She died at Bethany Convent on September 27, 1991.

The breadth of programs, collections, plant, professions, methods, and perspectives of the college had expanded during her presidency, as it had during the terms of the presidents before her. During the 1950s and early 1960s, the college had gained three new buildings including an extraordinary library, as well as new courses with an international view. But it had also taken steps toward cooperative problem-solving and a larger place in the world—without losing sight of the values and traditions of the past.

Freshmen of the late 1960s, dressed within the bounds of a relaxing dress code, celebrated the end of initiation with the release of their beanies. The tradition gave way to other college practices and ideas during the decade that followed.

A college trying to embrace and disseminate truth must include a variety of ideas and of persons who do not necessarily reach consensus easily on any issues.

A variety of ideas

Sister Alberta (Fides) Huber became president of the college in 1964, less than a year after the assassination of President John F. Kennedy in Dallas had stunned the American people. Discouraged at the death of the liberal president, black Americans were continuing their fight for civil rights amid growing unrest. Under President Lyndon Baines Johnson, U.S. military involvement in Vietnam was escalating. Betty Friedan's book *The Feminine Mystique,* published in 1963, was beginning to reach women with the message that they had too long been trapped as subservient housekeepers and childbearers.

St. Catherine students had worked and studied with people of color both on and off campus; their relatives and friends were being drafted for service in an apparently unwise military action. They were women of conscience and growing consciousness. Like other Americans, they would struggle with questions about Vietnam and equal civil rights. And they would act. The straightforward new president of the college, the first who was not also the college's religious superior, had a warm sense of humor and close contact with students. Her ability to welcome change would serve the college well during a time of national and international strife.

Chair of the English department from 1959 to 1963 and academic dean in 1963-64, Sister Alberta began a fifteen-year tenure as president in 1964. She formed a new administration with Sister Helen Margaret as academic dean (followed in 1970 by the first lay and first male dean, Dwight Culver) and Sister Marie James as dean of students, in charge of services incuding housing, recruiting, admissions, and student loans, service contracts, and publications.

Sister Alberta knew her first task even before she started, as she vigorously took up the challenge of raising funds to meet the 1963 Ford Foundation challenge, which continued until March 1966. By then the campaign had raised $2,600,000, somewhat in excess of the grant provision that the college raise $2,000,000—and three months ahead of the deadline. She wrote to the Ford Foundation on February 14, 1965: "We will never be the same again, and we are happy about it." Faculty members had received raises of about 7 percent and grants for study, financial aid to students was increased, a new office of counseling and guidance was established, and curriculum was expanded in mathematics, chemistry, foreign languages, and humanities. Administrators, faculty members, and students were excited by plans for a new fine arts building and auditorium.

Sister Alberta (FIdes) Huber, named president of the college in 1964, was born in Rock Island, Illinois, and attended the college for two years before entering the novitiate. She received a bachelor's degree in English from the college in 1939 while teaching at St. Anthony High School. She joined the faculty in 1940, receiving a master's degree in English from the University of Minnesota in 1945 and a doctorate in English from the University of Notre Dame in 1954.

That all will be one

For Catholic women, events of the 1960s and 1970s took place against the background of the Second Vatican Council, or Vatican II. Pope John XXIII had called for an ecumenical council in 1960, inviting all Catholic bishops, "that all will be one fold and one shepherd" (John 10:16). The American bishops called it "the internal renewal of the Church in the spirit of the gospel." They came to know each other in Rome, working on topics such as poverty, modern warfare, missionary work, the lay apostolate, and religious liberty, eventually brought together in *Schema 13, The Church in the Modern World.* The council met annually for four years and produced sixteen documents to bring Church teaching abreast of the needs of the modern world.

Faculty members and students discussing the first document, on the subject of liturgy and available in translation in 1963, profited from the work on liturgy done by the Benedictine monks at St. John's University. On October 10, 1964, the *Wheel* printed questions about the council with answers from students and faculty: "Will Catholics be affected by changes in the liturgy?" Sister Mary William said: "God's word is a living word . . . The service of the word is designed to enable us to hear his word, to understand its meaning, and to allow it to take root in us so that our response in love will always be faith, which according to St. Paul, 'comes from hearing.'" Student Jean Goerdt said: "The new liturgy will convince Catholics that liturgy is not something one writes about or talks about, so much as something one does." The Reverend Russan Cole, OFM, a theology instructor, said: "The new liturgy is one of the Church's many massive efforts to talk to her people and to enable her people to talk to God more coherently and intensely."

Professor of systematic theology at Luther-Northwestern Seminary Warren Quanbeck, one of eight Lutheran observers of the council, spoke at the college in May 1966. He had attended weekly meetings of the Secretariat for Christian Unity and participated in the second, third, and fourth sessions. According to the *Wheel,* he noted that "the theological outspokenness and openness of the bishops and theologians grew as they moved into the third and fourth sessions." He mentioned five council documents of special interest to Protestants—*The Constitution on the Church, The Constitution on the Liturgy, the Church in the Modern World, The Decree on Ecumenism,* and *The Decree on Religious Freedom*—saying the latter was a must for the Church, at least on the American scene. In September 1966, Sister Mary Luke Tobin, SL, the only American nun among the eight religious and eight laywomen observers at the council and an adviser on *Schema 13,* spoke at the student-faculty institute. She said: "Our reception by the Council Fathers was gracious if somewhat skeptical about what women might find of interest at an ecumenical council. They should have known that everything interests women." She hoped the defensiveness and isolationism of the Church would become a thing of the past.

In the meantime, faculty and students worked together for renewal. Sister Mary Davida composed music for a Mass in English, *Mass in Honor of the Tower of David.* She used Byzantine-style music to create a Mass that would not be difficult for untrained voices. The Mass was used both at the college and at several parishes in the area.

Although Jewish people were not invited to sessions of the Vatican II, they were very much interested in cooperation with Christians. On May 3 and 4, 1967, members of the congregations at the college and at the Temple of Aaron

St. Catherine and St. Thomas students formed a fifty-voice chorus, and Jacob Goldstein of the Temple of Aaron was the cantor for two performances of "Love Songs." Dancers were choreographed by Loyce Houlton of the Minnesota Dance Theater, who also taught modern dance classes on campus.

in St. Paul cooperated in presenting "Love Songs for Sabbath" written by Jewish composer Jack Gottlieb and directed by Sister Catherine (Lucina) Kessler. She had heard the composition, which he wrote for the Park Avenue Synagogue in New York City, at that temple. When they met at a summer session in New Orleans, Gottlieb gave her permission to perform "Love Songs" in the chapel on campus.

Members of the Temple of Aaron expressed great concern about texts from their Sabbath Eve service, part of the "Love Songs" theme of welcoming the Sabbath as the Sabbath bride, being sung in a church, by Gentiles. Slowly they came to understand that the texts were being used in prayer and with respect. Later Rabbi Arnold Goodman invited the chorus to perform the songs at Adath Jeshurun Synagogue in Minneapolis. According to a *Wheel* editorial on May 12, 1967, "It was an experience that touched on what gives life its meaning—love, human relations, the beauty of the world and man's ties with God. An experience of this magnitude is tremendous in itself. But when it is shared with a people from whom we have traditionally been separated, and when it is a sharing in the life and thoughts of this people, the experience becomes profound."

Certain inalienable rights

More than fifty years before the founding of the College of St. Catherine, Elizabeth Cady Stanton (in 1848) had proclaimed: "All men and women are created equal and are endowed by their Creator with certain inalienable rights." The college had dedicated itself to the education of women: only women were admitted; only women graduated. No students worried that young men might receive more attention in class. All students benefited from daily contact with strong female role models, and many St. Catherine graduates were professionally prominent.

Abigail Quigley McCarthy had written in *Integrity* in September 1953: "In the century in which the Providence of God has placed us, woman is in public life. It is futile, then, to say that she should not be. Or . . . that Catholic women do not participate in public life because they are at home with their children. As a matter of accuracy they are not." And the *Wheel* reported in April 1954 that according to Sister Annette Walters, "Our own college psychology department, established in 1942, provides for three types of students: those women who will specialize in psychology and go on to graduate school; those who study psychology to help them with such professional work as medicine, teaching, social work, nursing, and business; and lastly, that majority of students who will not use it professionally but will use it in their everyday life as homemakers and mothers. The psychology field is wide open to women since it has been found that women have qualities which aid greatly in this work."

Still, women wishing to participate in public life faced many closed doors. Many professions were entirely closed to them; nursing, teaching, and secretarial jobs were the norm; pay in all three fields was low. Women participating in civil rights work for others had found a vocabulary to effect change for themselves. Discussing the work of Betty Friedan, Gloria Steinem, Bella Abzug, and others, they began to claim their rightful place in business, the professions, government, and anywhere else their abilities and interests took them. In keeping with growing ecumenism, social awareness, and recognition that women might contribute more, the college instituted several new majors and opportunities for research and service for both students and faculty.

In 1964, Sister Mary (Kevin) O'Hara, chair of the philosophy department, announced that a major in philosophy would be offered in the fall term. Institution of the major had been considered for some time. Charles De Koninck, dean of the school of philosophy at Laval University in Quebec, had spoken at a convocation at the college in 1950. Asked by the *Wheel* whether women should study philosophy, he said that they should and that they would make good philosophers: "Women are close to nature, and so have a grip on reality. Besides, fewer and fewer men are studying philosophy, and someone must carry on." For some years, the college's general requirements had called for several philosophy courses (Logic, The Nature of Man, Metaphysics, Ethics) for every graduate. The new philosophy majors were required to take a philosophy seminar and attend a series of philosophy colloquia. The Reverend Hilary Freeman, OP, gave the first colloquium on the topic "Change." Sister Mary gave the second, on "Normality," and Ulric Scott presented the third, on "Historical Theories."

In 1965, French philosopher, novelist, playwright, and journalist Gabriel Marcel spent March 11-12 on campus. Sister Mary heralded his arrival in the March 10 *Wheel:* "Everywhere he has lectured he has drawn crowds, eager to see this champion of the rights of the individual person, this defender of the sacred against the overweening pretensions of technical efficiency. M. Marcel has brought to the philosophy of our time a sense of mystery, a reverence for the spiritual and an appreciation of the dignity of every human being." Marcel gave two public lectures, "The Myth of God in Contemporary Thought" and "Wisdom in a Technological Age," and conducted two informal discussions with students. At one of the latter sessions he read part of one of his plays, *The Funeral Pyre,* which showed the idolatry of a mother for her dead son. Gabriel Marcel loved the students and they loved him; he welcomed their questions as one learning something important from them.

Students followed visitor Gabriel Marcel from place to place, hanging onto his words. Some even considered changing their majors to philosophy.

By 1965 Sister Mary (Gertrude) Thompson was directing chemistry research projects at the college. She had earned a bachelor's degree in chemistry at the college in 1953, a master's degree in physical chemistry at the University of Minnesota in 1958, and a doctorate in chemistry from the University of California-Berkeley in 1964. While combining her interest in science and research with music and literature, she led the faculty in obtaining grants for her work and that of her department. She spent several summers doing research at the Argonne National Laboratory, then shared what she learned with students; she spent a sabbatical year, 1979-80, doing research there with J. C. Sullivan of the Heavy Metals and Radiation Chemistry Groups on the chemistry of plutonium and neptunium in solutions resembling natural water. This work led to an understanding of what can happen during nuclear testing and to ground water near leaking reactors.

Also in 1965, members of the senior class became highly critical of the theology department. They complained of outdated texts, poor teaching, a number of fragmented courses, lack of electives, rigid Thomistic viewpoint, and a lack of relevance to contemporary thought. The faculty, with no former experience of protest at the college, discussed the concerns at department meetings and informally. The theology department added a few elective courses, including Christianity and Culture, Comparative Religions, and Contemporary Theological Problems, but a more comprehensive change was in order.

Toward the end of March 1966, Sister Rosalie Ryan, chair of the theology department, announced a new curriculum in theology, offering a choice of classes and three-credit courses, to be initiated the next fall. She had received a bachelor's degree at the college in Latin and English in 1936 and master's and doctoral degrees in English from Catholic University in 1948 and 1952. She told the March 18 *Wheel*: "We hope to provide the orientation proper to a Catholic college by the solid Biblical and theological bases of the new courses, and by including contemporary material."

In 1966-67, Donald Byrne, a graduate of Marquette University in theology and one of the first laypersons educated to receive a doctorate in the field, became the first layperson hired to teach theology at the college. Students immediately liked his question-and-answer method of teaching, which made them feel a part of the course. He was enthusiastic about the changes in liturgy, telling the March 17, 1967, *Wheel:* "The Church won't regret its new liturgy. The problem now is to increase the awareness of the people, especially adults, as to why the changes are taking place."

Several years earlier, on October 9, 1964, the *Wheel* had carried an editorial stating that: "Many students and faculty members would like to see St. Catherine's offer a major in theology. The major would be helpful to those teaching in Catholic high schools and elementary schools. Lay people are taking over more and more positions in schools and parishes, and their need for background in theology is great." The new theology curriculum was so popular that talk of a major became serious. Members of the department pointed to expansion in religious education, the development of lay leadership, and the need of an informed laity. In April 1967, the faculty approved a major in theology to begin the next fall.

Joan Timmerman, the Reverend Peter Esterka, Larry Goodwin, Thomas West, and Thomas Loome joined the theology faculty in the twenty years following. Sister Vera Chester, who had joined the faculty in 1959, had earned a bachelor's degree in English at the college in 1954 and a master's degree in

Professor Larry Goodwin, teaching above in 1981, was one of several new professors hired to carry forth the college's major in theology, initiated in 1964.

theology at Marquette in 1962. She received a Schmitt Fellowship for graduate study at Marquette in 1963 and a Fulbright-Hayes Fellowship for research on the writings of John Henry Newman in England in 1966. She earned a doctorate in theology from Marquette in 1971 and continued her teaching in the St. Catherine theology department.

In 1969 Sister Catherine (Paul) Litecky began to study theology at St. John's University, her thesis entitled "The Influence of the Mercersburg Theologians on Liturgical Renewal in the Reformed Church in America." Meanwhile she taught introductory courses in theology at the College of St. Catherine. She served as chair of the theology department from 1970 to 1977 and from 1982 to 1985. In 1973 she joined a world religion tour studying in Thailand, India, Turkey, Israel, Greece, Hong Kong, and Japan. On sabbatical in 1977, she attended the Religious Leaders Program at the University of Notre Dame. In an article published in the Fall 1974 *SCAN*, she wrote: "The foundation for all traditional Catholic theology is built on God's revelation to us in the Sacred Scriptures. As a college we are aware of the importance of religion in the general objectives . . . What we try to present in our classes and in our talks to other groups is the Catholic theology of Vatican II."

Some faculty members were reaching other groups in new ways. After hearing an appeal of the National Catholic Conference for Interracial Justice for Teachers in Southern States, Sister Marie Philip, for instance, volunteered to teach intermediate French for a summer at a black college in Augusta, Georgia, during the summer of 1969. She found the students at Paine College weak in language skills but very friendly and much interested in France. She was impressed by the concern about religion on the part of students, faculty, and staff.

Sister Teresita Judd took a sabbatical leave in 1969-70 to teach anatomy and bacteriology in the nursing program at Harlem Hospital in New York. As the only white person in an African-American community, she learned much about the culture, especially about racial issues and black militancy. She wrote home about a strike against the nursing program there: "Classes this week have been very difficult. The students were sullen, unfriendly and doing little things as if to goad me into saying or doing something which they could pick up. You know how fond I was of these youngsters . . . I held my own but the tension was making it almost impossible to teach. This afternoon I was giving them a make-up test, and after about ten minutes I stopped teaching and told them just how I felt about them, about what nice students they were before, how I enjoyed teaching them, and somehow now they had been taught to hate and be mean, and that when you hate you get hate back, and if they loved they would get love in return . . . Quite a speech from me, but it seemed to work a miracle. The second hour, the class came to life. They responded to everything."

By the end of the decade, the desire for professional social service was great enough to warrant a separate major in social work. Degrees in sociology had been available earlier, but even that larger discipline had evolved slowly. The college's 1932-33 catalog listed "Sociology and Social Service" for the first time. The next year's catalog described its aims as "to contribute to general education and to foster scholarly attitudes toward social problems." The subject area first appeared under philosophy (ethics), then under education, then psychology, and finally as a department in its own right, with some social work as a part of the larger discipline. Reflecting later, Sister Mary Edward said that during her presidency (1961-64): "We were teaching some social work courses because that is what the girls wanted to go into. In their junior

Sister Catherine (Paul) Litecky's years as chair of the theology department (1970-77 and 1982-85) were marked by growth in the numbers of both students and faculty.

year they took a course in group work . . . and they did their field work at the Jewish Community Center, the Christ Child Center, and several other community centers. As seniors they took a course in case work, and during that time they did their field work in case work agencies." Finally, in 1969, social work was established as a separate major.

In 1970 Sister Ellen (Agnes) Murphy '53 began to teach in the education department. Already known as a specialist in preschool and kindergarten teaching, she had received a master's degree from the University of Notre Dame and a certificate from the Midwest Montessori Teacher Training Institute in Chicago, and she had served a year of internship in Montessori methods at Marywood College in Grand Rapids, Michigan. Sister Ellen then began to teach early childhood education at the college and to develop courses for a sequence in that field. She was instrumental in establishing a program for prekindergarten teacher licensing approved by the Minnesota Department of Education in 1972. The first private school with such a program, the college developed its laboratory preschool as a model site for observation and for student teaching by students in the program. Student majors later had the option of taking Montessori methods in addition to state department certification.

From the late 1920s until 1966, the college offered a secretarial studies major that prepared students for jobs in business but not for administration or management. Major requirements included intermediate shorthand and typing, business machines, introduction to business, and office procedures. The catalog listed courses in accounting, marketing, management, and law as "Offered at the College of St. Thomas."

Sister Barbara Ann Mitsch, head of the secretarial studies department for many years, had begun to teach at the college in 1928 while working on a bachelor's degree in history and secretarial studies completed in 1935. She continued teaching secretarial studies full time, with remarkable influence towards the ideals of responsibility, honesty, and workmanship. In 1948 she assumed responsibility for the college accounting office, cutting her teaching to half time but also completing a master's degree in business education at Columbia University in 1954 and serving as treasurer of the college and secretary of the Board of Trustees.

By 1966 the number of students majoring in secretarial studies was so low that some thought of discontinuing the offering altogether. As women's interest in greater participation in the workplace grew, however, enrollment in business courses began to increase dramatically. Over the next several years, the department made a transition in name and content from secretarial and business education to business administration, and by 1969 it offered the latter major through an exchange arrangement with St. Thomas.

In 1970 Lucille (Bettenburg) Laughlin '36 became chair of the business administration department. She had majored in secretarial studies and French, then obtained a master's degree in business education from the University of Minnesota before first teaching with Sister Barbara Ann in 1958. The number of senior business administration majors grew from 5 in 1970 to 44 in 1977, when she was adviser to all the senior majors and to 136 junior majors as well. In 1976 she started evening classes for adult women in a program called Women Expand, which encouraged women in secretarial jobs to grow towards management positions.

Though Vatican II had encouraged greater involvement by the laity and suggested that the sisters wear modern dress (begun by some sisters at the col-

Sister Barbara Ann Mitsch taught secretarial studies for many years, then also served as treasurer of the college and secretary for the Board of Trustees. Many benefactors and trustees of the college received beautiful table linens as a "perk" of working with her on the board.

lege in 1966; some began using their family names in 1968), officials of the Church were not enthusiastic about women's growing consciousness. Nevertheless, by April 15, 1970, a teach-in on the women's movement, sponsored by a developing campus group, attracted more than 150 students and teachers, male and female. A panel composed of Monica Carle (Johnson) '72, Sister Mary O'Hara, Sister Helen Coughlan, Susan Woulfe Plaster '70, Judy Heimel (of the Women's Counseling Service, speaking for the Twin Cities-area Women's Lib Group), and others addressed the meeting. According to the *Wheel,* Monica Carle referred to Betty Friedan's book, claiming: "Now women are rising up, rejecting the status forced on them by our society . . . They have been taught to think that they are inferior to men; that their body is their best asset; that they must compete for men, not with men on an intellectual level; that they are ruled by their emotions, not by reason; that they must have a career or marriage; that their personal identity vanishes with marriage."

Discussion of women's issues continued on campus and nationally through the decade and beyond. Those pleased at the passage of specific national legislation regarding women's rights were greatly disappointed when state ratification of the Equal Rights Amendment (that no one be denied equal rights on the basis of sex) failed despite a two-year extension of the deadline. They discovered that unless more women could be elected to state legislatures and to Congress, laws related to sexual discrimination (the "glass ceiling" and harassment) might never make it on the books. Others might be overturned or simply unenforced. Nevertheless, the feminist struggles of the 1970s opened new windows on women's lives. This meant new programs at the college as elsewhere.

By 1973 new possibilities for women were evident in the curriculum, especially in art and interdisciplinary courses. Women in Art was introduced as an optional core program. Women in America presented women from the point of view of the social sciences, literature, theology, and history. Students were enthusiastic about the new thinking, and on November 12-22, 1974, the CAGB sponsored "Women's Week," with a program including films, lectures, and dramatic presentations. Vivica Lindfors gave a dramatic series of portraits of thirty-six women prominent in history. On November 17, Jeanette Ridlon Piccard, aviator and scientist, spoke on her efforts to be ordained an Episcopal priest. She criticized the hypocrisy of a church that refers to women as "sons of God" and denies them the right to act as priests. Ordained without the consent of her church in July 1974, she was forbidden to celebrate Mass until a national convention approved her ordination and that of ten other women (in 1977).

The interests of administrators, faculty and staff members, and students in women's issues coalesced into what became known as the Women's Interest Group or WIG. The student handbook for 1976-77 said WIG's "main goals are to facilitate campus activities, programs, and policies that are of interest to or concern to women." Norma Rowe (of the Continuing Education staff), an early leader of the group, gave a more trenchant description: "WIG is and always has been, primarily a political action group, that is, WIG works as a special interest group to assure that St. Catherine's fulfills its mission as a women's college."

In 1977, "to assure language usage consistent with the college's commitment to women," WIG recommended that the faculty follow the National Council of Teachers of English guidelines for nonsexist use of language where appropriate for college communications, that it ask administrators and staff members to use the NCTE guidelines, and that it establish an *ad hoc* committee of volunteers to review and revise, if necessary, existing publications according

Student events like this old-time fashion show in 1978 mirrored the current concerns of women in some of their accomplishments of the past.

to NCTE guidelines. The faculty voted yes to the recommendations in 1977. That year WIG also sponsored an author's party for current and former St. Catherine faculty members contributing essays to *Women in Minnesota: Selected Biographical Essays*, published by the Minnesota Historical Society Press. Gretchen Kreuter of Macalester College and Barbara Stuhler of the University of Minnesota were editors. Contributors included Abigail Quigley McCarthy on Jane Grey Swisshelm, Eileen Manning Michels on Alice O'Brien, and Sister Karen Kennelly on Mary Molloy.

On September 28, 1977, WIG sponsored an outside Dawn-to-Dusk Read-a-Thon. Students and faculty members from 8:00 A.M. to 8:00 P.M. read selections from the writings of Virginia Woolf, including *A Room of One's Own, To the Lighthouse,* and *Orlando,* and from her biography. A ten-minute film was shown throughout the day. According to reader Colleen Mlecoch '78, the event was meant to raise consciousness and elicit concern for the status of the college as a women's institution. The work continued.

Growing cooperation

The new business administration major made available in 1969 was one result of widening opportunities for cross-campus participation. By 1965-66, more than eighty Katies and sixty Tommies were taking at least one class at the other college; many more students were showing interest in the exchange. Students suggested using vans with volunteer student drivers between campuses that year, but the idea didn't work well in practice; a more permanent driving arrangement was needed. Early in 1966, the presidents of the College of St. Catherine and St. Thomas, Sister Alberta and the Very Reverend Monsignor Terence Murphy, proposed to the Hill Family Foundation a study towards increased cooperation. In July the two colleges received word of support from the foundation. By the fall of 1966, they had arranged for the use of a shuttle bus between the two colleges with a regular driver and schedule of trips.

Longtime employee Wes Brown took on the job of driving an old bus called the "Purple Arrow" or "Blue Bomber" between the St. Catherine and St. Thomas campuses. He became both friend and counselor to its passengers.

In January 1967, the two college presidents chose a coordinator-director for academic aspects of the exchange. Lawrence Barrett of Kalamazoo College, who had worked with the Ford Foundation and the North Central Association, was to develop cooperation over an eight-to-ten-year period. He told the *Wheel* on May 5, 1967: "They want, through cooperation, to produce a better education for students, and to make their schools more attractive to students and instructors." An additional grant enabled Sister Seraphim Gibbons, St. Catherine chair of mathematics, and Roman Sevenich, St. Thomas chair of business administration, each to take a year's leave of absence from teaching to help plan the program. They formed a staff committee of six and an advisory committee of more than thirty teachers and administrators from the two colleges.

The advisory committee urged that the faculties become better acquainted to facilitate cooperation in curricular matters. At several combined faculty meetings (followed by dinner) and department meetings, members of both faculties tended to stay within their own groups rather than mingle with others. But some progress was made, and a few departments like music and speech-theatre held joint sessions, leading to some class exchanges. Some years later, the colleges formed several joint departments with shared faculty members (speech-theatre and social work).

Meanwhile Barrett had continued his study with interviews and an examination of library resources. In a report to the faculties in March 1968, he said:

"Three things are changing very rapidly around us. For one, our traditional financial resources are proving inadequate to our needs, and no new and viable way of financing private higher education has yet been devised. For another, the demands made upon the liberal arts colleges, the services they must render their students, the needs of society, are shifting so fast that the traditional liberal arts college is already obsolete . . . Finally, the political structure and the planning procedures built into the traditional college tend to make for stasis rather than for adaptation [when] adaptation is essential to healthy life." Faculty task forces gave their findings to Barrett, who submitted his report, *Institutional Cooperation, (1968)* with recommendations including these (verbatim):

- I would like to see St. Catherine's and St. Thomas eliminate the general education requirements for graduation and the [major] requirements . . . to see them identify the interests and abilities of every individual student when he enters and then tailor a program to meet his needs.
- I recommend that the many duties of departmental chairmen be divided among a number of men in each department, and that the chairmanships be rotated biannually among these men. I also recommend that chairmanships of key committees be rotated among faculty members.
- I recommend two or three appointments made each year be at the rank of associate or full professor . . . joint appointments. Salaries for appointments must be high enough, regardless of existing scales, to assure top-quality people, even at the cost of creating inequities.

Long before the move for the exchange of academics, the College of St. Catherine had conducted a social exchange with St. Thomas students. Above, Sheryl Akes was one of seven cheerleaders rooting for the Tigers at a Tommy football game in 1963.

Some recommendations, including those listed above, were not acceptable to one college or the other; some were acceptable to neither. But the process continued. Each college agreed to honor for its own degree majors available only at the other. St. Catherine students could for the first time earn degrees in journalism, geology, physics, and business administration; St. Thomas students in art, library science, elementary education, and occupational therapy.

While the exchange program enriched its offerings, the College of St. Catherine remained open to ideas for keeping its own program dynamic and relevant. Many colleges in the 1960s considered adopting an interim term for January, an awkward month in a two-semester schedule. Should examinations be held before Christmas, cutting short the first semester? Or should they be left until January, with students facing finals soon after Christmas vacation? The Interim or 4-1-4 program (providing four courses in the fall semester, four in the spring, and one in January, during which students could study subjects not in the regular program, do intense study of a subject in their major fields, do independent study, travel abroad, or take an internship) was one answer.

A St. Catherine-St. Thomas institutional committee, formed to explore cooperation in offering interim courses, collected the opinions of students and faculty in a questionnaire, then held open meetings to answer questions before recommending in October 1968 that Interim be adopted in 1969-70. The St. Catherine faculty voted immediately in favor of the recommendation as did the students. They could choose independent study, internship, or a course at St. Thomas, St. John's University, or any college offering Interim. The St. Thomas faculty voted to stick with its old schedule, complicating the effort, but the students adapted, and several years later, in 1975-76, St. Thomas adopted the Interim, granting academic credit though the College of St. Catherine did not.

Conversion to the course system and two semesters plus Interim was initiated at the College of St. Catherine by the fall of 1970. Once everyone became used to the change, it proceeded smoothly without an increase in faculty. The one-month Interim seemed to meet its objectives—to provide a change of pace, a variety of educational experience, and greater opportunity for independent study. Adverse comments came from only a few students unable to register for their first choices or required by their majors to take courses at St. Thomas.

At first some faculty members thought students might not be able to handle the concentrated study of Interim. Others thought that the variety of courses might increase to a point where the faculty could not handle them all. Some feared mixed motives for students going to California, Florida, or Hawaii, for Interim. Would student effort and faculty standards be up to par? In practice most students chose subjects they liked and studied hard, but providing enough slots in Interim courses in a time of growing enrollment was difficult. In fact, there were more Interim courses in 1970 when enrollment stood at 1,230 than in 1978 with enrollment over 2,000. Eight courses enrolled 40-plus students each that year, and two had over 100, accounting for 42 percent of students.

Faculty members such as Sister Mary Davida Wood, who taught a popular music appreciation course, carried a disproportionate share of the Interim load. A favorite of students, she had graduated from the college with a bachelor's degree in music and French in 1933, received a master's degree in music from Columbia University in 1941, and studied at the Eastman School of Music in New York in 1948-49. The daughter of politically active parents in whose North Dakota farmhouse the Nonpartisan League began, she led a band called "Peggy Wood and the Splinters" before she entered the novitiate.

While the Colleges of St. Catherine and St. Thomas worked to find common ground, cooperation among the several libraries and colleges also grew. Legal and insurance matters necessitated the acquisition of legal status for the library consortium established in the early 1950s. And on April 16, 1969, the libraries (now including those of Augsburg, Bethel, and Concordia as well as those of the College of St. Catherine, Hamline, Macalester, St. Thomas, and the Hill Reference Library) incorporated as Cooperating Libraries in Consortium (CLIC), financed in part by an annual contribution from each. The formation of CLIC made more than a million volumes available to students and faculties

While interfaculty cooperation was not entirely successful, intrafaculty relations seemed just fine. Albert Biales, music, and Barbara Boyce, psychology, attended concerts, plays, and lectures, married on June 14, 1965, and taught an interim course—on the psychology of music—together.

The formation of CLIC and then MINITEX gave Katies access to millions of volumes beyond those in their own substantial library. At right is the reference room.

of the cooperating colleges. Services could be secured by walk-in or courier. Periodicals could not be borrowed, but photocopies of articles could be sent. In just one year, the St. Catherine Library provided 1,964 pages of photocopy for exchange. During the next two years, the resources of the University of Minnesota and the St. Paul Public Library became available through the Minnesota Library Information Network (MINITEX), increasing the number of available volumes to about three million. The librarians have continued to meet and develop new means of cooperation for the computer age.

The use of computers and computer education developed slowly at the college. The 1969 catalog announced: "Computer instruction is available at St. Catherine's at two data processing facilities at a large new installation adjacent to the campus [the Administration Center of the Sisters of St. Joseph] and at St. Thomas for students enrolled in business or related courses, or in the Quantitative Methods major." In 1973-74 the Minnesota Educational Computing Consortium (MECC) was organized by the University of Minnesota to provide computer capability for schools throughout the state. When private colleges were invited to join the consortium, the College of St. Catherine did so at once. Sister Seraphim, in charge of the development of computer capability, was already working toward establishing a center. Computer education became possible when on-line access opened through CLIC.

The mathematics department, chaired by Sister Seraphim, and the library science department were those most interested in computers at the time. Gradually the math department introduced several courses: Introduction to Computers, COBOL Programming and Applications, and Computer Science I and II. The library science department offered a course in Information Science and Technology and used a telephone hook-up with Dialogue for database search. Sister Seraphim supervised the installation of several terminals on the ground floor of Mendel Hall, with a telephone link to a mainframe at Control Data. The company had donated terminals, microcomputers, a Plato software course, and several other courses to introduce faculty and students to computers.

As the libraries were incorporating, the joint Area Studies committee was beginning in 1969 to plan for the continuance of Area Studies at the end of grant funding in 1972. The committee decided to offer two areas of study a year for the next three years, then to implement an interdisciplinary major in East Asian studies with faculty from all four colleges. The Hill Family Foundation granted funds for the following three years with the understanding that Augsburg College in Minneapolis be included.

In 1971, the Hill Family Foundation granted the four-college St. Paul consortium $10,000 to plan cooperation beyond the library and area studies programs. Jack Armstrong of Macalester College was appointed half-time coordinator of the project. The four college presidents began to hold biweekly meetings in October 1971 to develop a further proposal to fund a four-year cooperative experiment in five areas—admissions, transportation, urban affairs, minority education, and planning. Funds were also requested for a coordinator's office. The proposal was accepted, and the Hill Family Foundation granted $600,000, also with the stipulation that Augsburg College be included. Andrew Helmich was chosen coordinator and Evangeline Burton, administrative secretary. The consortium became known as the "Five College Program." One recruiting brochure urged the prospective student "Take Five."

In 1974-75 plans were made for a formal organization of the five-college consortium that might more easily deal with outside groups and legal questions. The consortium became the Associated Colleges of the Twin Cities (ACTC) in 1975-76. Cooperation extended to joint purchasing and a joint course description brochure, though different copy deadlines caused some difficulties and the latter project was soon dropped.

After expiration of the five-year grant from the Northwest Area Foundation (formerly the Hill Family Foundation), the costs of the program—administrative salaries, office rent, and office expenses—became the responsibility of the administrators of the five colleges. The presidents, finding the costs too great, directed that the budget be cut by 50 percent. The assistant director's position was terminated, and the executive director's position was cut in half. In reviewing progress for the February 1978 *Journal of the Associated Colleges of the Twin Cities,* the consortium wrote: "Many projects have been successful beyond our expectations, some have not been for a variety of reasons. We have reached the conclusion that it is not possible at the present time . . . to increase the possibilities of cooperation or to continue to fund an administrative office at the level it has now reached." Nevertheless, the May journal noted that the presidents had reaffirmed their commitment to cooperation: "New ideas will continue to be explored and additional efforts will be made to remove obstacles to the exchange process."

The speech-theatre department continued to put on plays at the college regardless of other changes in campus life. An annual play for children, directed and often written by George Poletes, became a favorite tradition in the 1960s. Students took all the roles for Hansel and Gretel, *above, in 1965.*

Taking a stand

Extracurricular life continued through the 1960s as it had earlier, with freshman orientation through a Big Sister program, Winter Carnival, May Fete, father-daughter dance and mother-daughter luncheon, college plays and concerts, dances (sometimes with a blind-date service) sponsored by the student government (College Association Governing Board or CAGB), and a variety of campus publications and clubs. Political clubs like the Young Republicans and Young Democrats flourished during and faded between presidential election years. By the late 1960s, however, students were beginning to take an active stand on the rules and customs of the college as well as on larger issues.

Kristine Smyth (Gorrilla) '71 remembered how quickly the milieu of the college changed in her four years on campus. Wearing dress slacks to take finals in December 1968 was the first step to a quick abolishment of any dress code. By the time she graduated, the family-style dinner was reserved for special occasions, and academic dress for convocations was a thing of the distant past. Residents could come and go at will, and male visitors were allowed in the dorms during certain hours. Retreats were not required, and students of legal age could drink without being expelled. But what she remembered most was listening on the radio to lottery numbers being drawn for the military draft.

Many students had begun to consider more thoughtfully the issue of American involvement in Vietnam after the Reverend Daniel Berrigan, SJ, theologian, priest, poet, playwright, and nuclear pacifist, spoke at the college on "Exploring Our Freedom" on March 25, 1965. Just returned from travel and study in developing countries including Russia, Egypt, and others in Africa, he could not reconcile the poverty of some nations with "rich America." But he believed peace was the issue of the time: "Catholics are cringing away from it, making a bourgeois identification with Pentagon policy and an automatic assumption that our military policy is identical with morality."

In 1966, student Minh Han Vu told the April 28 *Wheel* that the Communists "promised many wonderful changes . . . but when we actually lived under the Viet Cong government, we found out what they are really like. They took away property, forbade the practice of religion, and caused much suffering." Her family and thousands of other North Vietnamese had responded by emigrating south. Anyone who heard her would want to help. But should the United States participate in Vietnam's civil war? By June 1967 the government had said yes to 387,000 American troops fighting for South Vietnam.

During the months of unrest preceding the 1968 election, Senator Eugene McCarthy of Minnesota challenged President Johnson on his stance in Vietnam, and Senator Robert F. Kennedy of New York quickly followed with a similar bid for the Democratic nomination. In a series of incredible events, the president decided not to run, Martin Luther King was shot in April, and Kennedy was killed the night he won the California primary. Another Minnesotan, Vice President Hubert H. Humphrey, was nominated at a troubled Democratic convention; he lost a close election to Republican Richard Nixon that fall. Nixon began a slow withdrawal of troops but escalated the bombing.

On October 19, 1969, during a national Moratorium Day, students at the college held a prayer service, a Mass for Peace, and two teach-ins, and participated in a march on the Capitol. Vicki Sellner '70 told the December 12, 1969, *Wheel* why she demonstrated: "I went to Washington because I . . . needed to know that more people wanted peace and were willing to work for it . . . for my brother Chuck, who had ended his life marching into battle . . . for my other brothers, in hope of not seeing their flag-draped coffins."

In April 1970, the New Mobilization Committee asked students and faculty to fast for peace for several days each month until U.S. involvement in Vietnam ended. Then U.S. entry into Cambodia and the deaths of Kent State students at the hands of National Guardsmen escalated the protest, attracting many who had not spoken before. Three hundred attended a College Association meeting to discuss how students might make their views known. They decided not to strike classes but to abstain from social events. They canceled May Fete and set up booths to help students write their representatives in Congress. They canvassed for neighborhood opinion during free hours rather than during class time. At the end of the school year, seven students traveled to Washington to interview their own representatives and several from other states. Nixon was elected again in 1972, signed a peace agreement in 1973, and resigned the presidency in disgrace in 1974—after a campaign tactics cover-up that further disillusioned most Americans. South Vietnam surrendered unconditionally to North Vietnam in 1975.

The Reverend Daniel Berrigan, SJ, spoke at the college on March 25, 1965: "We cannot allow ourselves to be sucked into war and preparations for war. The prophets have always purified society by refusing to be swallowed up by it."

Three years later, the St. Catherine community responded to the pleas of an old friend from Southeast Asia. Ngo Pham, called "Angie" by classmates, had studied at the college from 1952 to 1956, graduating with a major in social sciences. She earned a master's degree at Loyola University in Chicago, then returned to Vietnam and married Dinh Van Tran, also a former exchange student. She became a director of the National Bank of Vietnam, but after several years Communists taking over South Vietnam sent her to prison for three months, allowing no contact with her family. After she was released, she and her husband decided to leave Vietnam. They abandoned all they owned, fleeing at night in a Chinese boat for a fee of $3,000 for each member of their family, including five children and four other relatives. After ten days at sea, the small fishing boat with 280 passengers arrived at a refugee camp in Malaysia in December 1978. The family wrote to Sister Mary Edward, one of Angie's professors, and the St. Catherine Alumnae Association for help.

Many alumnae—especially Patricia O'Connor Myser '56, president of the association, and Marguerite Loftus '40, the coordinator of Archbishop John Roach's Commission on Migration and Refugee Affairs of Catholic Social Service, arranged for transfer of the family to the United States. Sandra Kamman Butler '56 and Kay Sullivan Bendel '56 mobilized other members of Angie's class, who worked with Sister Mary Edward to secure and furnish a house in West St. Paul and provide clothing and toys. Angie and her husband, Dinh, soon obtained positions in the St. Paul Department of Education and registered the children in public schools. All five children eventually completed postsecondary education; Ngoc Tran, the only daughter, graduated from the College of St. Catherine in 1974.

Bricks for the arts

The way the college looked from the outside also changed during Sister Alberta's tenure. In 1968 the trustees authorized the building of a fine arts complex and application to the U.S. Department of Health, Education, and Welfare for a loan to help finance construction. Work originally scheduled to begin in the spring of 1967, a year after the Ford Foundation challenge was met, had been delayed partly because of problems with fundraising. Students, faculty, and alumnae continued their benefit events, with students sponsoring a series of three concerts featuring cello, violin, and vocal artists. Marguerite Gignac Hedges of the music department faculty was vocal soloist for one.

With funding complete, construction of a fine arts complex began in 1968. The architect was Curtis Green of Hammel, Green and Abrahamson, and the contractor was Gunnar Johnson. Much discussion centered on what would be the best location for the complex. A site on Cleveland Avenue near the Dew Drop was considered too marshy for a substantial foundation. Another favorite site, between Mendel and Fontbonne, seemed too small to accommodate all the departments needing space. Finally a compromise was reached. A new auditorium and the music and speech-theatre departments would be housed in a building between Mendel and Fontbonne. A visual arts building would be situated between Mendel and Caecilian. The complex would be known as the Mother Antonia McHugh Fine Arts Center.

Construction of the new buildings was complete in 1970. The music department moved in that summer; the art department moved to its new building the following January. By the time the auditorium was finished, requests for

Huge northern window walls provided the light for work at one of a line of potter's wheels in the new visual arts building, part of the Mother Antonia McHugh Fine Arts Center completed in 1970. The Catherine G. Murphy Galleries in the same building provided fine exhibit space for both resident and visiting artists.

space for concerts had been received from the Minnesota Orchestra, the St. Paul Chamber Orchestra, and the Schubert Club. Formal dedication of the Fine Arts Complex took place October 1-4, 1970. A series of events made evident the great possibilities for a fine arts education offered by the new facilities:

October 1   The Minnesota Orchestra, conducted by Stanislas Skrowaczewski played works of Beethoven, Skrowaczewski, Berio, and Sibelius. The work by Berio was specially commissioned for the opening of O'Shaughnessy Auditorium.

October 2   The Dublin Players from Ireland presented Brian Friel's play *Lovers: Winners* and *Losers,* with notable performances by Anna Manahan and Niall Toibin.

October 3   The Minnesota Dance Theater, directed by Loyce Houlton, presented three new contemporary ballets.

October 4   Helen Vanni '46, former member of the Metropolitan Opera, performed Julia Perry's "Stabat Mater" and Vivaldi's "Gloria" with the St. Paul Chamber Orchestra, assisted by Marguerite Gignac Hedges and the St. Catherine and St. Thomas choruses.

October 6-9   Otto Piene, kinetic sculptor, showed his inflatable sculptures in the Visual Arts Building galleries. Present to assist visitors in creating their own sculptures in soft material, he also erected wind sculptures outdoors to lend festival color to the campus.

Major music groups including the St. Paul Chamber Orchestra and the Minnesota Orchestra (the latter above, directed by Stanislaw Skrowaczewski) requested concert schedules before O'Shaughnessy Auditorium was even finished.

The opening of the Fine Arts Center colored most of the events of the year. Students ushered at concerts; the music department sponsored more events with its own hall; and speech-theatre students were inspired by having their own space for experimental theater. Other local groups—the Twin Cities Youth Orchestras, dance groups, and the St. Paul Opera Company—began to request time for performances in the new space. At first there were rock concerts, patronized not so much by St. Catherine and St. Thomas students as by other young people from the Twin Cities. Parking at such events became a huge problem handled as well as could be expected, but the destructiveness of the rock audiences led the auditorium management to dispense with these events. I. A. O'Shaughnessy, St. Paul businessman and philanthropist for whom the auditorium was named, later contributed for the construction of a parking lot, to accommodate audiences at the auditorium. Staffing, finance, and maintenance problems at the auditorium, however, became a persistent concern.

Another continuing concern was the increased demand and need for flexibility in on-campus housing. In 1964 there were 501 places for residents, with 11 more if the home management and chapel house beds were counted. In 1967, for instance, 80 more students enrolled than could be accommodated. When other alternatives proved impractical, the college decided to install mobile homes on campus, obtaining a special permit, granted reluctantly and for one year only by the St. Paul City Council. Sister Seraphim undertook the installation and supervision of the trailers, shopping to find the best deal and arranging for sewer, electrical, and water connections. Inspectors approved the equipment, and the mobile homes were ready just as the freshmen moved in. They found living in the mobile homes a unique experience occasionally enlivened by St. Thomas students serenading outside their windows.

In 1968-69 temporary housing was provided on the second and third floors of 1890 Randolph Street, the former novitiate, while two small dormitories were constructed, each housing 54 students. The buildings eventually came to be known as Crandall Hall (for Prudence Crandall, a white woman who opened a school for black students in 1803) and Stanton Hall (for Elizabeth Cady Stanton, abolitionist and supporter of women's education and the eight-hour workday). While esthetically pleasing, they were hastily constructed without basements and later suffered leaks in spring.

With still more students wanting housing than could be accommodated, overflow students were housed in Mary Hall, the nurses' residence at St. Joseph Hospital, with 41 of the 44 available beds occupied during the first semester of 1972. Problems of transportation and meals and concern about students living downtown limited the use of Mary Hall to 18 beds during the second semester. The next stratagem, taken first in September 1974, was to rent space in an unused residence hall at Hamline University. The hall, suitable for college women, would house 96. There were some problems with transportation and meals, but the women living at Hamline said the food was better there.

Finally, in 1975, an apartment building of 36 units (the "Georgia" in honor of Sister Georgia Morrison), where student residents kept their own kitchens, was constructed along Fairview Avenue. Built with a loan from the Higher Education Facilities Authority, the apartments were so popular that an identical building (the "Alberta" in honor of Sister Alberta Huber) was constructed on a site to the south in 1976, stabilizing the balance of students and housing.

Around the same time Jeanne d'Arc Auditorium, which could accommodate an audience of about six hundred, underwent some badly needed renovation. Grants from the Kresge Foundation and the St. Paul Foundation helped with new plaster, paint, drapes, and floor coverings. New seats and new ceiling lights were installed, and the electrical and sound systems were overhauled. A formal opening of the renovated auditorium in October 1976 featured speeches of dedication and a woodwind concert by a St. Paul Chamber Orchestra ensemble. Besides space for lectures and recitals, the auditorium would provide an audio-visual supplement for classrooms, meeting space, and a home for the regular Tuesday evening film series directed by George Poletes.

Jeanne d'Arc Auditorium was almost completely gutted during its renovation in 1976.

Students continued to climb onto buses shuttling them between the College of St. Catherine and College of St. Thomas both during and after the controversy about whether the two colleges should go coed.

To be or not to be . . . coed

The question "Will St. Thomas go coeducational?" had been asked before, but in 1974, the faculties, students, and staffs of the College of St. Catherine and of St. Thomas began to argue about it. That year St. Thomas conducted several studies among its students and alumni, who mostly recommended that the college become coeducational. Late in 1975, a "joint" committee, consisting of four St. Thomas members and one from the College of St. Catherine, concluded that "the available evidence, admittedly empirical, indicates strongly that enrollment would increase as a result of coeducation. The increase might result in as much as $150,000 the first year. It should eventually reach five times that . . . St. Thomas should pursue its coeducational ventures in cooperation with the College of St. Catherine, whether or not St. Catherine's becomes coeducational."

In November 1975, the St. Catherine faculty sent a resolution asking the St. Thomas faculty, administration, and board of trustees to reconsider. The St. Catherine Board of Trustees resolved that "the present cooperative relationship between the two colleges should not be altered and that St. Catherine's should not go coeducational, and we respectfully urge that St. Thomas not act to become coeducational." But St. Thomas had already hired an outside team of consultants—the Reverend John P. Daly, SJ (former president of Sogang University in Korea), Sally Furay, RSCJ (provost of the University of San Diego), and Edward Henry (former president of St. Mary's College in Notre Dame, Indiana)—to study the matter again. After four months of research, they submitted a report in January, released for publication by the St. Thomas board of trustees at the end of March. It urged consideration of a merger (though it hesitated to use the word); in lieu of that, it recommended "that St. Thomas adopt the program [of coeducation] unilaterally."

In April 1976, Sister Alberta advised students to wait and see, that decisions about going coed were distant, but: "If St. Thomas were to become a coeducational institution, St. Catherine's future enrollment could be affected." Meetings between representatives of the two colleges continued through summer. Rumors flew again when school opened in the fall. Alan Graebner of the

St. Catherine history department read a position paper at a September 1976 faculty meeting, saying: "Our deliberations ought, I believe, to begin with the question, what do we at St. Catherine's want to be?" He suggested that if St. Thomas went coed the College of St. Catherine might be strengthened in its role as an institution especially for women.

On October 19, 1976, Monsignor Murphy announced that the College of St. Thomas would become coeducational, moving to meet the demand for a four-year Catholic coeducational college in the Twin Cities. About one hundred women would be admitted as undergraduates in September 1977. Many people reached the conclusion that St. Thomas had decided months earlier to become coeducational. The only question now was what the College of St. Catherine would do. Alumnae answered two-to-one in favor of keeping the college for women only. Sister Alberta reported to a joint meeting of the boards of trustees of the two colleges that the vote (almost unanimous) of the College of St. Catherine was to remain a women's institution.

Since that time, many all-men's and all-women's colleges have opened their doors to students of the other gender as coeducation seemed the preference of most entering students. Other colleges have had to close their doors entirely. Ten years after St. Thomas began admitting women, Monsignor Murphy wrote in his October 22, 1987, *Aquin* column: "The delay in making the decision came because of a concern that it might have an adverse effect on St. Catherine's. This has not proven to be the case." But the College of St. Catherine had to take bold steps to maintain its identity and enrollment.

While the colleges decided about coeducation, the students continued the exchange, and by 1975-76 Katies were taking 2,602 classes at St. Thomas. Tommies were taking only 1,769 classes on the St. Catherine campus. With the imbalance desirable to neither institution, the two faculties began an intense study of the problem in 1977. A liaison committee recommended a long-term goal of balanced exchange, defined as a difference in the number of courses taken by students at either college of less than 10 percent of the total exchange.

The St. Catherine faculty approved recommendations including that the college expand its course offerings in certain areas, that students be required to take liberal arts core requirements on the home campus with the exception of one such course at each of the ACTC colleges, that all freshmen be required to take courses during the first year on the home campus except for majors not offered there, and that sequence courses be completed on the same campus.

Everyone worked hard to make the change. In the business department, for example, 69 majors took courses at St. Thomas in 1978. Gary Seiler, on the faculty from 1972, had succeeded Lucille Laughlin as chair of the department when she died in an automobile accident in May 1977. In 1978 Seiler hired more business administration faculty, and the college reinstated the economics and political science departments. Though the balance would swing from one college to the other, the academic dean reported a balanced exchange at the end of 1978-79. By 1980-81, the 500-plus St. Catherine business majors could take all required courses on their home campus.

Gary Seiler, above left, earned bachelor's and master's degrees in business education in 1972 and 1975 and a master's degree in business administration in 1978 from the University of Minnesota. He expanded the St. Catherine business department while working on his doctorate, received in 1988.

Other cultures, other views

The college's breadth of vision also widened through Sister Alberta's tenure. Students and teachers from other lands and cultures by their presence and views made St. Catherine students eager to learn about other countries.

Named coordinator of the Office of Intercultural Student Affairs established in 1978, June Noronha worked as a resource for anyone at the college dealing with cultural differences.

Sister Mary Henry Nachtsheim, above with students, had a vast file of international study programs and extensive experience abroad, which facilitated her work as director of the Office of International Studies, established in 1978.

Sister Mary of the Angels Stuart Otarola, RMM, from Chimbote, Peru, and Madre Elena de la Cruz Vincente (Sister Helen of the Cross) Alonso, RMM, from Santander, Spain, attended the college in 1963-64. They belonged to an international missionary order. American culture was especially fascinating to Sister Mary of the Angels, a young and lively art major who delighted in playing children's games in the snow, the first she had ever seen. She wrote later: "Today [Dec. 31, 1967] is a sunny day in Bordentown, New Jersey. We have no snow, therefore I cannot make my angels. I hope that those I made are still there. They will give you an opportunity to think of me. I need nothing to think of you; you are in my mind and in my heart."

Establishment of the Office of Intercultural Student Affairs in 1978 affirmed the presence of international students on campus. June Noronha, the child of Indian immigrant parents who had lived in Kenya, was named its coordinator. After she studied in the United States, Kenya refused to admit her because she was Indian, and India did not admit her because she was carrying a passport from Kenya; Britain refused her entrance because she was not British. Finally she was admitted to the United States for study at Macalester College. She then advised international students at the College of St. Catherine, eventually counseling minority students including African, Spanish, and Oriental Americans and American Indians.

To make international exchange easier, the college also established in 1978 the Office of International Studies, first directed by Sister Mary Henry Nachtsheim, who had graduated with a bachelor's degree from the college in 1937 and master's and doctoral degrees (all in French) from Laval University in Quebec, Canada, in 1951 and 1962. She taught French at Derham Hall (high school) for several years and began teaching for the college in 1958. She had told the *Wheel* in September 1977: "It is advantageous to the student to get experience in foreign study while she is in college, since the time is available, she is in a learning situation and has the opportunity of association with teachers and fellow students . . . Such an experience is an opening of new horizons and frequently lasting friendships across cultures."

The Minnesota intercollegiate association known as Student Project for Amity among Nations (SPAN) helped American students arrange study in Brazil, Japan, Czechoslovakia, and other countries. Under the general supervision of the University of Minnesota, it was financed by student work and by donations from Minnesota business people and others. Expenses for the trip were kept at a minimum with SPAN paying for transportation and living costs very low. The advisers of SPAN announced topics a year before each two-month visit so that students could learn the language and research the background of the country to be visited. Professors could apply to be teachers and leaders of student groups.

Linda Burgess, a St. Catherine student from Oronoco, Minnesota, spent June and July of 1972 in Cairo, Egypt. She reported in the September 24, 1973, *Wheel*: "My interest in international relations and the Middle East led me to study the changing world of the Egyptian woman . . . The roles in the city and those in the rural places are completely different. The village women have held the same traditional roles for thousands of years. They're secluded and are content to be wives and mothers, while the city women are more aware of the real world and some have even begun to go out and get jobs."

Problems for international students in a new country were to be expected, but minorities within the United States experienced tension as a way of life.

The college had faced difficulty in recruiting African-American students, since most were not Catholic and many did not have enough money for tuition. A more active recruiting program helped bring in more African-American students, some of them very talented young women. In the 1940s Ikalina Moore Savoy '42 (Spanish and sociology), Rita Rhodes Spellman '45 (nursing), and Emma Mae Blackwell Hill '47 (sociology and education) graduated from the college; in the 1950s, Therese Bailey Britts '50 (biology), Louverne Noble Williams '55 (education), and Sybil Murray Denis '58 (French).

St. Catherine students interested in psychology and sociology were able by the 1960s to take part in an in-country exchange program with Xavier University in New Orleans, which in 1962 had only four Caucasian students of about eight hundred. Dorothy McBean and Sheila Krueger Lesterson '67 were the first St. Catherine students to study at Xavier in the fall of 1965. They found it much like other liberal arts colleges, though the pace of life was slower and social life more relaxed. Two students from Xavier University, Patricia Hand and Cosette Weatherspoon, both residents of New Orleans and both English majors, began study at St. Catherine in the fall of 1965. By the 1970s up to fourteen African-American women were graduating from the college annually.

Eldridge Cleaver, former Black Panther member and author of *Soul on Ice*, spoke to a packed house in O'Shaughnessy Auditorium on October 15, 1970, giving a new perspective on American life. He had left the country in 1958 to evade arrest on a charge of parole violation in connection with charges of attempted murder and assault. During exile, he visited Cuba, Algeria, France, North Vietnam, North Korea, and China. He voluntarily returned to the United States to be arrested and stand trial but eventually was released on bail. Seeing the repression of peoples under Communism and the abuse of power in military dictatorships had changed his mind about the need for government regulation to restrain violence. The process led him to believe the United States the most free country in the world.

Three years later, Jacqueline Bowman Bledsoe '70 (sociology), a Twin Cities resident working towards her doctorate in educational administration at the University of Minnesota, was hired as a counselor for African-American and African students at the college. Bledsoe gave high priority to the fight against sexism and racism. Counselor and coordinator from 1973 to 1977, she tried to influence students toward higher academic achievement. Earlier the associate director of the metro-urban internship program at Augsburg College, she wanted to help bridge the gaps between peoples of different cultures: "We have not been taught to deal with people who are different from ourselves. There is need for training in cultural diversity." In cooperation with students and professors from the University of Minnesota, Bledsoe guided St. Catherine students in the observance of Black History Month, planning speakers and social events well accepted by the larger black community.

Though not as many, American Indian students of the early 1970s also clamored for recognition. The college responded by offering two courses—Indian Art and Ojibway Language. Gertrude Buckanaga was coordinator of Indian activities from 1972 to 1977. A member of the Ojibway White Earth Reservation, she received a bachelor's degree in education from Concordia College and a master's degree in educational psychology at St. Thomas in 1971. While at the College of St. Catherine, she worked on an education specialist degree at the University of Minnesota. She had held positions in teaching, data processing, bookkeeping, and counseling.

Sandy Schuck (Reynolds) '67, above, presided over the CAGB in 1966-67.

The speech-theatre department produced a Carson McCullers play, The Member of the Wedding.

In interpreting Indian customs to students Buckanaga said: "Historically the Native American Indian culture provided for special events in the life of a female person, whether it was at birth, the reaching of womanhood, marriage, giving birth or death—certain ceremonials were for the community to give recognition to the members. At these times it was important to instill that their standards in child care, homemaking, and relationships will affect the whole community. Therefore, usually a male elder would speak to remind the female member honored that 'the future of the people lies in the trail of the woman.'" With Buckanaga's help, some Native American students were able to see greater possibilities for remaining in college and graduating.

Buckanaga brought Ed McGaa, a Pine Ridge, South Dakota, Sioux to teach North American Indian Culture and the Sioux language at the college. He had negotiated with the U.S. government for the American Indian Movement (AIM) when it occupied Wounded Knee, an Oglala Sioux community in western South Dakota that had been the site of a massacre of more than two hundred Indians by the U.S. Seventh Cavalry in 1890. AIM declared that Wounded Knee had seceded from the United States and become a new Oglala nation. It requested a full investigation of the Bureau of Indian Affairs, run by the U.S. Department of the Interior. According to McGaa in the April 2, 1973, *Wheel,* a treaty made in 1868 gave the Sioux all of western South Dakota, so that legally they were on their own land: "We want the Bureau of Indian Affairs and the Department of the Interior to quit wasting government money, and spend it on appropriate things, like projects for the Indian people." But even the St. Catherine programs for American Indians ended when Buckanaga left for another position in 1978.

Faculty members acted on issues of justice related to other groups as well. Sister Annabelle (Aloise) Raiche, professor of education who had received a bachelor's degree in history from the college in 1960, a master's degree in educational administration from Boston College in 1962, and a doctorate in education from the University of Minnesota in 1965, wanted justice for migrant workers. While attending a symposium on Ignatian spirituality at the University of San Francisco, she filled out a form for participation in a day of solidarity with the United Farm Workers (UFW) in Fresno. The UFW wanted to provide labor to growers without using contractors, who charged the workers 10 percent. The workers also had been denied the right to choose a union.

The group from San Francisco set out at 11:00 P.M. on July 30, 1973. Its members were to meet the workers at dawn at a park in Parlier, near Fresno. There they planned to talk, work with, and celebrate Mass with the workers. But when they arrived, they learned that the harvest had started and the workers would not be able to come to town. The group was then invited to join a picket line at one of the growers' ranches with the warning that some might be arrested because of a court injunction allowing only two pickets per hundred feet and use of a bullhorn only one hour a day. Sister Annabelle decided to join the picket line.

After a short Mass, the demonstrators set out for the Sun Ranch. They were met by sheriff's deputies and growers. At about noon a sheriff's bus arrived, and the demonstrators were arrested and taken to the Industrial Camp Barracks. There they were treated without brutality but were taunted by the guards. The religious men and women of the group refused to post bail and finally were granted permission to leave under their own recognizance. They refused to leave unless others with the same charges were also released. This was eventu-

Gertrude Buckanaga served as coordinator of Indian activities at the college from 1972 to 1977. A member of the Ojibway White Earth Reservation, she served on the Governor's Minnesota Crime Commission, United Fund, and Minnesota State Vocational Advisory Committee. In 1977 she received from Minnesota Secretary of State Joan Anderson Growe a citation of honor for her work in Indian education.

ally granted. In the process, the sisters and priests who took part in the protest learned more of the plight of the farm workers than they expected.

Sister James Agnes was invited by Eva Wilson, a nutrition consultant with the United Nations, to work in Brazil from November 1975 until the summer of 1976 with sisters teaching domestic science and rural education in a "superior school" in Sao Paulo. They needed help in setting up a curriculum in home economics like those in the United States. She quickly studied Portuguese before her journey, speaking well enough upon arrival to assist the sisters with their plans. She visited Brasilia and Rio de Janeiro and arranged for Brazilian Joseph Ferreira to study at St. Thomas College.

The primary, indispensable source

Religious ministry by various people and organizations had always been a part of campus life, but in the fall of 1972 the chaplain, the Reverend Camillus Gott, OFM, and Sister Maxine Eckes agreed that "there's more to campus ministry than arranging liturgies and planning penance services." With the support of the president and the dean of students, they began to explore areas of need and interest. With no space easily set aside for a ministry center, they conducted meetings, retreats, and prayer groups in the Katycombs (a lounge in Fontbonne for day students), the smoker, and the basement of Whitby. As they searched for space, they were assisted by the National Campus Ministry Guidelines, which defined campus ministry as: "a pastoral apostolate of service to the entire college community, through care and concern for persons, the proclamation of the Gospel and the celebration of the liturgy."

Father Gott and Sister Maxine continued the planning of liturgies, gave retreats, and organized a series of talks on understanding sexuality. They met with campus ministers of the college consortium to plan ecumenical services. Two weekend retreats were held at Timberlee, a lake camp on Big Fish Lake, near Cold Spring, Minnesota. The requirement for an annual student retreat had been dropped a few years earlier, so the weekend was for many a first retreat.

For the first time, in 1972, students and sisters served the community as Eucharistic ministers, lectors, and musicians. These offices were in accord with the Constitution on the Sacred Liturgy promulgated during Vatican II: "Mother Church earnestly desires that all the faithful should be led to the full, conscious, and active participation in liturgical celebrations which is demanded by the very nature of the liturgy . . . In the restoration and promotion of the sacred liturgy this full and active participation by all the people is the aim to be considered before all else, for it is the primary and indispensable source from which all the faithful are to derive the true Christian spirit."

In 1972, students and sisters served the community as Eucharistic ministers, lectors, and musicians.

The Eucharistic ministry was to be a continuing concern for Campus Ministry. In 1973-74, Father Gott was transferred to Mount St. Francis College in Indiana, and Sister Maxine was left to carry on alone. With no priest on staff, Sister Maxine spent much of her time on the telephone, locating celebrants for Mass, making little progress on a stable program for Campus Ministry. The next year (1974-75) the Reverends Thomas Hill and Gavin Brandt, OFM CAP, were hired. Full of youth and energy, they used the chapel house as a center for Campus Ministry, attracting many students to the program's work. Sister Maxine spent the year studying at the University of San Francisco.

During the next few years many staff changes slowed the ministry. Hill left the team; Sister Maxine and Father Brandt returned. When in 1975 the Reverend Edward Foley, OFM CAP, joined the Campus Ministry staff along with students Mary O'Connor (Brandt) '78 and Ann Thompson '78, the future seemed bright. Before his ordination in May 1975, Father Foley had been a deacon at St. Veronica Parish in Milwaukee. He already had a master's degree in music and liturgy from the University of Notre Dame. Especially enthusiastic about the new rite described in Vatican II's *Constitution on the Liturgy,* he soon began to call for volunteers to participate in the liturgy and social action.

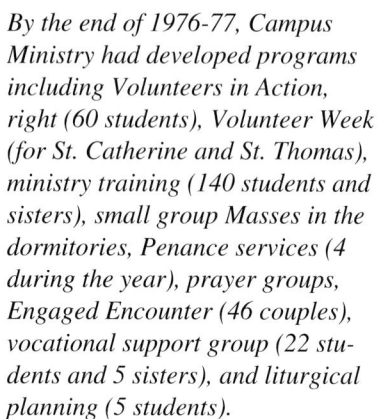

By the end of 1976-77, Campus Ministry had developed programs including Volunteers in Action, right (60 students), Volunteer Week (for St. Catherine and St. Thomas), ministry training (140 students and sisters), small group Masses in the dormitories, Penance services (4 during the year), prayer groups, Engaged Encounter (46 couples), vocational support group (22 students and 5 sisters), and liturgical planning (5 students).

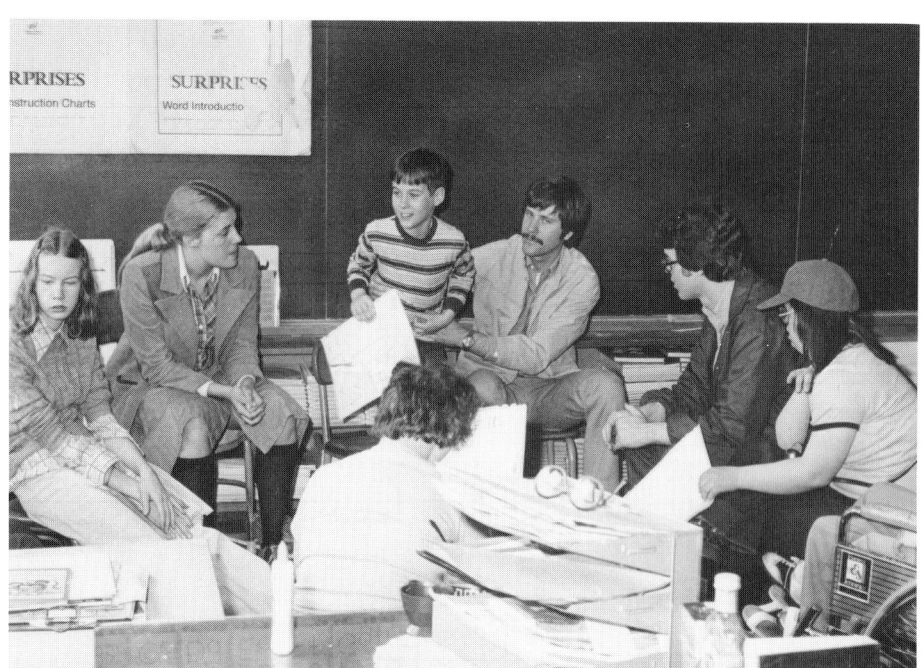

Foley's call brought in many volunteers for the liturgy—Eucharistic ministers, lectors, music ministers, and "ministers of hospitality" (ushers). His training program impressed the new ministers with the importance of their work through the words of St. Augustine: "Would you understand the body of Christ? Hear the Apostle saying to the faithful, 'If then you are Christ's body and his members, it is your own mystery which you receive.' It is to what you are that you reply 'Amen.'" The program flourished, and students and faculty members took part in a Lenten series called "Ashes to Easter" in 1975-76. Sister Maxine became assistant province director of the Sisters of St. Joseph, and Sister Marian Walstrom '60 succeeded her.

On November 8, 1977, at a Mass culminating a month of training, 108 women were commissioned as ministers to the St. Catherine community, bringing the number actively participating in celebration of the Eucharist to 226. The Reverend Kevin Fane, OP, joined the Campus Ministry in 1977 after serving at Holy Rosary Parish in Minneapolis, and during his first semester was in charge of Engaged Encounter, in which couples discussed being and becoming married, with special emphasis on communication and spirituality.

Social Justice ministry had become prominent by 1978, and its team members led observance of World Hunger Day on November 13 that year. Events on campus included the Social Action Fair, a collection of food, clothing, and money for several local service agencies. St. Catherine students also cooperated with St. Thomas in Volunteers in Action (VIA), a group committed to outreach for the needy of the community. Each member gave at least one hour a week to help the mentally and physically handicapped, senior citizens, or youth through tutoring or other services. Social Justice ministry grew so large that the Campus Ministry had to appeal to other groups for help. In 1978-79 "peer ministers" were chosen from the student body to help fellow students be active in various aspects of the ministry and to lead some programs. The first peer ministers included Mary (Molly) Hauser (Natwick) '79, Doris (Kathy) Kathryn Long '79, and Mary Patricia Wollan (Quigley) '81.

Weekend legacy

Sister Alberta Huber ended her long tenure as president on July 1, 1979. During difficult times, she had brought the college from an enrollment of 1,300 to 2,000, adding new programs and expanding others while maintaining academic excellence and completing major construction. Her vision included "some graduate programs, certainly some post-baccalaureate programs . . . education of women beyond the age of twenty-five—either actually continuing or getting hold of that vast number of women out there who have never had exposure to college. I see that as a great need for the whole nation—an immense resource of talent that's left untapped, and we have a lot to give them." She had already begun. In the 1970s, women whose roles as mothers and homemakers had prevented them from completing or beginning education beyond high school became especially interested in continuing education courses. Women returning to the job market became more aware of their need for further education.

Marie Corrigan, who had returned to her teaching in 1965-66 and been influential in setting up the new counseling program at the college, took the adult education program forward in leaps and bounds when in 1971 she first offered a noncredit seminar for adult women exploring the possibility of beginning or returning to college work for a bachelor's degree. Sixty women attended her first open house. The seminar, repeated several times, gave participants information, skills, and confidence in their ability to complete their college work. Through her warm, encouraging personality and nonthreatening approach, she persuaded several women to enroll in regular college courses. These first Reentry Adult Program (REAP) students were delighted at their success in classes with much younger women, and they persuaded others to try, too.

In 1974, after two decades of offering informal adult education, the college established the Office of Continuing Education. A task force had been named a year earlier to draw up a list of past and current offerings for "older women" and to form a three-year plan. The task force defined continuing education: "Educational opportunities offered to women who have previously considered their formal education terminated, or who are over twenty-five and have interrupted their formal education for a period of time." It recommended immediate appointment of a director of continuing education "to consider expansion of existing courses to become a program of 'life-long learning.'" It noted the potential for the program to make a financially useful contribution to the college during a time of projected enrollment decline. And it recommended consideration of day care for preschool children, adjustment of residency requirements for unconventional students, equalization of tuition and fees including fees for Interim, and credit for life experience. In the summer of 1973, seventy people including four men enrolled for five three-week "mini-courses" offered in addition to the regular summer sessions. The following summer, ten such courses met with equal success.

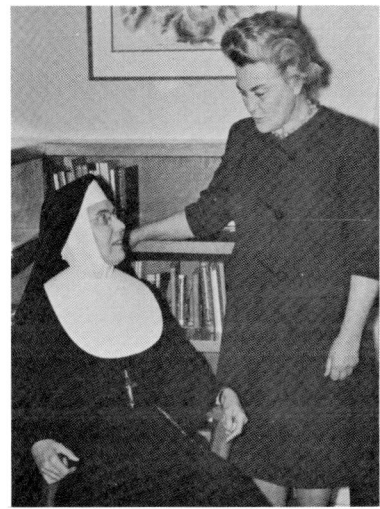

Word of the death of Sister Annette Walters, left, arrived at the college as Marie Corrigan, right, worked to encourage women to return to school. Sister Annette's dedication to justice inspired accolades from many organizations she had supported: the Leadership Conference of Women Religious, Church Women United, the National Federation of Temple Sisterhoods, the American Jewish Committee on Women, the Women of the AFL-CIO, and the National Council of Black Women. She was academic dean at the college from 1955 to 1957 and executive secretary of the Sister Formation Conference in Washington, D.C., from 1960 to 1964.

In 1974 Sister Therese Sherlock became full-time director of the Office of Continuing Education. Norma Rowe became assistant director, and two others were added to the staff. The office was to plan noncredit seminars, provide publicity, develop child-care facilities, and develop policies encouraging study by older women. The office continued to add programs to its roster—REAP and Credit for Academically Relevant Learning (CARL)—and to update programs for professionals, particularly in library science, occupational therapy, social work, education, and nursing. Many workshops offering the Continuing Education Credits (CEUs) required for teaching and nursing became available. Women in Management, a certificate program that evolved from the Women Expand program in business administration, became part of Continuing Education in 1978-79, with Jacqueline Crawford its director. She began working to develop a bachelor-degree track for the program.

Weekend College provided new educational opportunities for women, and as Larry Goodwin predicted in the February 23, 1979, Wheel, *"a hedge against a possible decline in enrollment."*

During long-range planning in the late 1970s, Sister Alberta wrote to Sister Therese: "What are the possibilities of a weekend college here? Commuters only—on Saturdays—for one or two specific programs? Degree programs? Non-degree programs?" A task force formed to assess the potential for a weekend degree program studied the issue, then recommended setting up a weekend college, primarily for motivated women whose other responsibilities prevented their attendance at day or evening classes during the week.

Plans were made for classes to meet for three and one-half hours every other weekend for fourteen weeks, with much work done through independent study. At first there would be four majors: business, social work, communications, and theology. Courses would be taught by regular faculty, so as to integrate weekend courses with the day program and assure quality. The plans prompted the usual question among faculty members: Would the classes meet for enough hours to merit full credit? Catherine Lupori, chair of the English department, explained that Weekend College would offer majors only in fields lending themselves to nontraditional teaching methods. Sister Eleanor (Mary Edmund) Lincoln, said: "The program would also allow a student to take responsibility for her own learning." Others emphasized the independent study, saying only those with the greatest potential for the work would be admitted.

With the wrinkles ironed out, Weekend College won approval, and Mary Alice (Sister St. Alfred) Muellerleile was named its first director. She had received a bachelor's degree from the college in 1961 and master's and doctoral degrees in English from the University of Chicago in 1967. Danforth and Kent fellowships enabled a year's study in England before she began teaching in the English department.

Shortly after Sister Alberta's tenure ended, Weekend College opened. On September 7, 1979, 127 students recruited through advertising and "information days" began classes. By spring 1980, courses had tripled from the original six offerings, and the total number of students was 322. Muellerleile had told the *Wheel* in May 1979 that "we have to be very creative and also very orderly and organized." The college did everything possible to make the weekend students comfortable, providing coffee and doughnuts between classes, assigning a post office box and faculty advisor for each student. There were some kinks: The hours of the bursar, bookstore, and registrar were adjusted. Students from a distance were provided overnight housing. Soon the excellent teaching and prompt concern for their problems made weekend students feel at home.

Nurturing the challenge of futurists, Sister Alberta had encouraged many new ideas like the Weekend College, as well as independence and responsibility within the departments of the college. For her work, she received honors including the Certificate Palmes Academiques from France, an honorary doctorate of letters and the first St. Thomas Aquinas Medallion from the College of St. Thomas, an award from the City of St. Paul, and later, an Outstanding Achievement Award from the University of Minnesota. After her presidency, she served as grants coordinator for the college development office, then studied in Rome before resuming her teaching. She remains on the faculty today.

Sister Alberta Huber, above, steered the College of St. Catherine for fifteen years, through a tumult of challenge and change. At left, a new idea in art— Sky Ballet, *a kinetic sculpture by Otto Piene, October 10, 1970.*

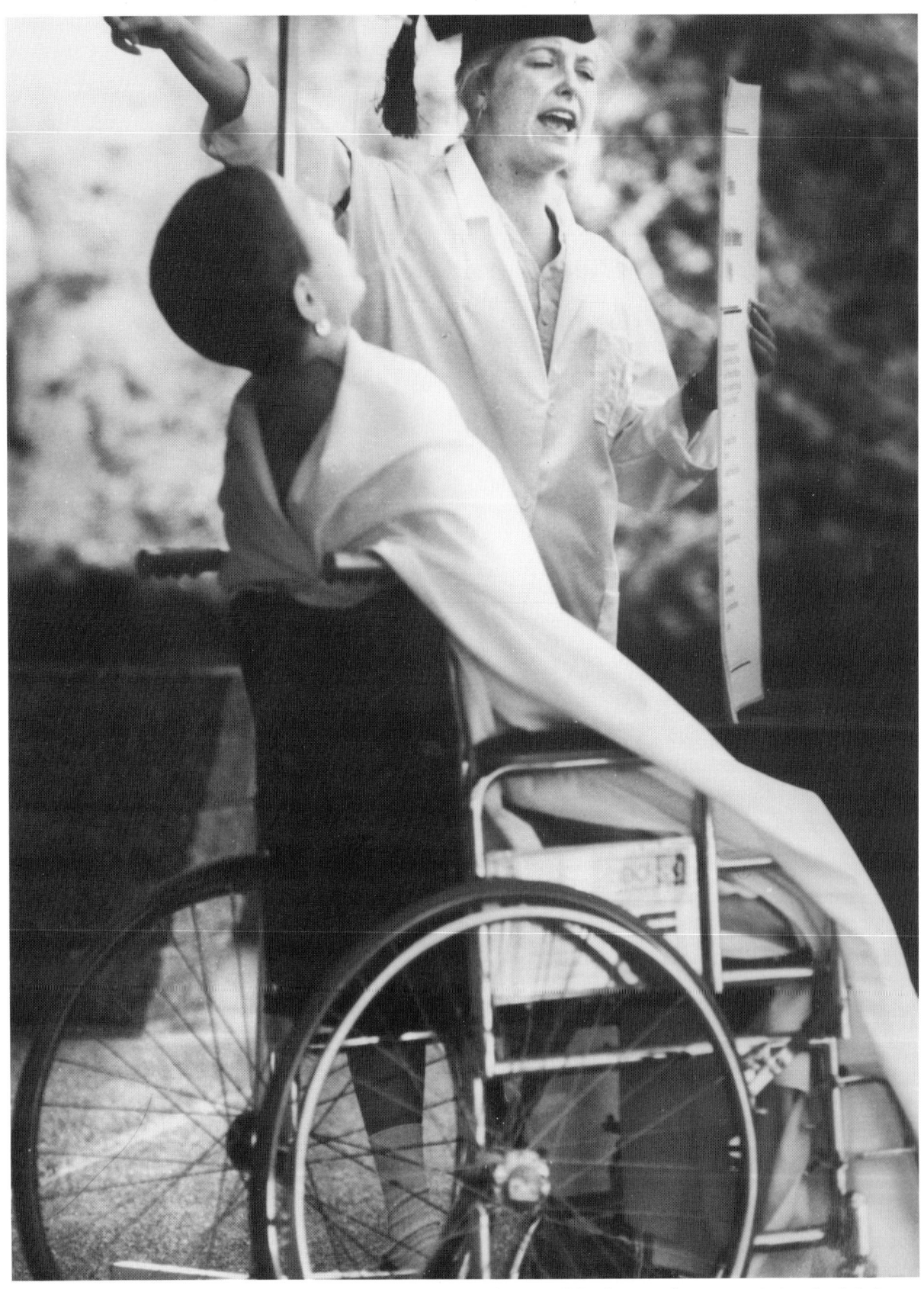

"We are not the patients; we are the doctors!" shouted Muriel Quinn '90, above with mannequin in wheelchair at a St. Catherine rally on May 7, 1990, supporting students who wanted Mills College (Oakland, California) to reverse its decision to admit men. The cry responded to media suggestions that women's colleges were irrelevant.

It is important for us to create our own traditions and to live out the values and spirit of the college in a contemporary way.

In a contemporary way

Upon Sister Alberta's retirement, a special committee of the Board of Trustees conducted a national search for a new president. In 1971 amendments to the articles of incorporation and bylaws had called for fifteen but not more than twenty-one trustees with a majority of them Sisters of St. Joseph. Amendments in 1979 reduced the requirement for a majority of sisters to one-third. Qualifications required for the president of the college included that she be a Sister of St. Joseph with a doctoral degree and administrative experience.

Sister Catherine McNamee, from the Albany (New York) Province of the Sisters of St. Joseph, was the choice. She taught Spanish and education at the College of St. Rose before becoming vice president for academic affairs at that college. Later she served as director of liberal arts programs at Thomas Edison College, the New Jersey State College for External Degrees. In 1975 she became president of Trinity College in Burlington, Vermont. She relinquished that position to assume the presidency of the College of St. Catherine. She was the first president from outside the St. Paul Province.

On September 6, 1979, chaplains Kevin Fane, OP, and Edward Foley, OFM CAP, officiated at the outdoor Mass opening the academic year. Afterwards, students, staff, faculty members, and administrators marched in academic dress from St. Joseph Hall to O'Shaughnessy Auditorium behind the college banner. Festivities continued in the auditorium with welcoming speeches by Sister Eleanor Lincoln, professor of English, for the faculty; Sara Dillon, College Association president, for the students; and Thomas Carlin, chairman of the board, for the trustees. Sister Catherine in her first address at the college, called "Beginnings," responded in part: "During the few weeks which have transpired since I have assumed the presidency, I have been vividly impressed by several strengths of our fine institution . . . immediately evident to a newcomer is the physical setting . . . Other positive impressions include the high-quality academic program, the commitment of the students, faculty, administrators, trustees, and members of our sponsoring body, the Sisters of St. Joseph of Carondelet; the sense of pride in a strong religious heritage; the emphasis upon preparing women to assume new roles in society and preparing society to welcome women in these new roles."

Sister Catherine's leadership style was reflected in her comments in the September 7, 1979, *Wheel:* "I think the president's job is mainly to set the pace for the institution, to provide a focus for the vision of the college from the

Sister Catherine McNamee made her first official appearance as president of the college in attire from the University of Madrid. She earned a bachelor's degree in Spanish from the College of St. Rose in Albany in 1953, master's degrees in elementary education (1955) and Spanish (1958) from Boston College, and a doctorate in Hispanic literature from the University of Madrid in 1967.

point of view of the faculty, students, and the alumnae." Her administration was blessed with capable assistants who knew well the tradition of the college and the competitive parameters in higher education with which it would have to cope. Anita (Sister Mary Gabriel) Pampusch became academic dean, Rosemary Hart dean of students, and Albert Vonhof continued as business manager. Charles Dougherty was the director of development.

After her formal inauguration, Sister Catherine would list three priorities for her administration:

1. making the college more visible on a national level
2. working toward refining the long-range plan
3. completing the study made by the space committee.

Her first duty, however, was to enjoy the seventy-fifth anniversary of the college's founding—to look back on what it had accomplished and dream for the future. In 1978 several committees had begun planning for the 1980 observance. The motto chosen—The Past Is the Present Is the Future—stressed the forward movement of development and change. Focusing on the interests and achievements of women everywhere, programs including some of the most prominent women in the world were in place by September 1979. In a threefold celebration, the past was to be honored February 7-March 25, the present April 27-May 1, and the future December 2-4.

Alumnae, in charge of the first session, presented a slide-narration program, a sort of a St. Catherine family scrapbook including humor, sentiment, and history. Sunny Bach Wicka '55 narrated a dialog between the Past (played by Patricia Connolly Durkin '55), the Present (Judith Galloway '81), and Future (Sister Mary Virginia Micka). Pat Durkin wrote the script and original music, including a song. The refrain, taken up by other committees, became a kind of theme song for the year:

> Once there was a place where people cared
> A place where people grew because they shared.
> And all the places I have been, have never quite compared.
> Once there was a place where people cared.

A scrapbook of slides celebrating the seventy-fifth anniversary of the founding of the college showed that though some things changed, others stayed the same. Residents were as eager to get mail in 1978 as were Helen Miller (Richard), Mary Wall (Tegatz) and Mary Ellen Foley (Porwoll), all seniors in 1948.

The slides pictured college life from the days when Sister Antonia was dean. The older buildings and classes, as well as the former dress of students, annual events like Winter Carnival, May Fete, Eucharistic Day, and student programs like the Varsity Show, evoked laughter, wonder, and nostalgia.

The Very Reverend Monsignor William Baumgartner, rector of the St. Paul Seminary, celebrated Mass in Our Lady of Victory Chapel. Sister Mary William commented on the Scriptures for the day. She noted: "Resourcefulness implies that there are resources. In the early days the prime and only resource was the presence and dedication of the Sisters of St. Joseph. This . . . was the living endowment that ensured the continuity of the college and satisfied accrediting bodies in lieu of dollars and cents, of which there were very few. Today there may be a few more dollars and cents, but without the presence and dedication of the entire college community, today would certainly betray the building of our past . . . So built in the past the college has continued for seventy-five years to welcome 'living stones,' fellow workers inside and outside classrooms, for everyone, as St. Paul says, is doing the building of God's temple—hundreds who have spread to east and west, to north and south, remembering St. Catherine's and grateful for its existence and gifts."

The celebration took an unexpected turn when Sister Catherine decided to make a pilgrimage to the Monastery of St. Catherine of Alexandria, on Mount Sinai in Egypt. Because the Sinai had recently been returned to Egypt by Israel, she and others believed Anwar Sadat might grant a visa for such a journey. After considerable correspondence with the State Department and the American ambassador to Egypt, Sister Catherine and Catherine Watson, travel editor of the *Minneapolis Tribune*, were allowed the visit.

Maintained by Orthodox monks for more than 1,400 years, the Monastery of St. Catherine is the oldest extant Christian monastery in the world. Catherine of Alexandria, a laywoman philosopher of the fourth century, was sentenced to death. Some two hundred years later, her body was discovered on top of Mount Sinai. According to legend, angels brought her remains to the spot. A monastery was built there to commemorate her faith.

After losing their luggage in a harrowing journey to the Middle East, the two women arrived at the monastery in disheveled traveling clothes. But the monks, one of whom spoke English, expected them, and His Beatitude Archbishop Damianos, Metachion of St. Catherine's Monastery, greeted them warmly. Sister Catherine presented to him a bronze medal of St. Catherine designed by Peter Lupori. She also presented an encomium written by Sister Mary William, head of the college archives, and printed by Judith Duncan, a Twin Cities calligrapher. The tribute read: "Greetings to the Monastery of St. Catherine at Mount Sinai from the College of St. Catherine, St. Paul, Minnesota, U.S.A. On the occasion of the seventy-fifth anniversary of its founding the faculty, staff and students of this college for women which has for its patroness Saint Catherine of Alexandria, wish to thank you for guarding the rich tradition of Saint Catherine, for preserving the precious treasures of your monastery, for sharing both with a world in need of both, wish to promise to cling faithfully to truth and goodness as Catherine did, to preserve the rich treasures of our cultural heritage, to share our inheritance with the courage and generosity of Saint Catherine of Alexandria. January, 1905-March, 1980."

In return, the archbishop presented to Sister Catherine a medal of St. Catherine of Alexandria and pictures of the monastery. The visit included a climb to the top of Mount Sinai and tours of the ancient monastic halls. Catherine Watson gathered material for three full-page stories, which appeared in the travel section of the *Minneapolis Tribune* on three successive Sundays.

The second session of the jubilee featured a symposium, "Women Speaking for Justice" (April 27–May 1). Betty Smyth Williams roused consciousness with her presentation, "Can There Be Peace in Northern Ireland?" She and Mairead Corrigan had been shocked at the death of three children in a 1976 clash between the I.R.A. and English soldiers in Belfast, Northern Ireland. They persuaded ten thousand women, Catholic and Protestant, to march in protest of the killing of children. From this protest grew the organization called the Peace People, and for their work, Williams and Corrigan received the 1977 Nobel Peace Prize. In her address, Williams stressed that peace can come only from those who refuse violent action, not from government or the military.

Estelle Ramey, professor from the Georgetown University School of Medicine, spoke on "Value Judgments in the Ivory Tower of Science." Noting that most research was planned by men, conducted by men, and controlled by masculine perceptions, she pointed to areas of research left untouched because of the few women in research. Science and people in general, she said, are poorer because of sexism in science. Mallica Vajrathon, research officer of the United

The Monastery of St. Catherine at Mount Sinai presented Sister Catherine with this medal of St. Catherine of Alexandria for the college. The panels of a frieze at the main entrance to the chapel depict the St. Catherine legend:

1. *The emperor demanded that Catherine sacrifice to idols, but she refused.*
2. *The emperor declared Catherine exempt from the sacrifice if she could confound the court philosophers. Debate followed.*
3. *When Catherine confronted the emperor with her victory, he threw her in prison.*
4. *An angel (or the empress) comforted her.*
5. *The emperor ordered the court philosophers burned. Catherine comforted them before death.*
6. *Catherine was condemned to torture on the wheel.*
7. *The wheel broke. The emperor promised Catherine everything if she would sacrifice.*
8. *She refused again and was beheaded.*

Nations Food and Population Agency, addressed "Development Issues in the '80s of Concern to Women." Finally, Hanna Gray, president of the University of Chicago, spoke on "Portia Faces Life." Indicating the importance of the liberal arts in higher education of women, she stressed that women must learn leadership not only through intellectual pursuits but also through participation.

The final event in the second anniversary celebration was the inauguration on May 3, 1980, of Sister Catherine McNamee as the eighth president of the college, the first so formally installed. Over two hundred delegates from colleges, universities, and learned societies attended. Archbishop John Roach provided the invocation and Thomas Coughlan, Jr., chairman of the Board of Trustees, presented Sister Catherine with a presidential medallion for wear at ceremonial functions. In her inaugural address Sister Catherine spoke of educating for social justice: "In our colleges and universities we must prepare our students to respond in the realm of politics to social injustice and the denial of human rights . . . It is the role of our educators, as well as activists, to call attention to the moral and religious dimensions of secular issues, to keep alive the values of the Gospel norms for social and political life, to participate in the task of transforming society."

The year-long celebration of the seventy-fifth anniversary of the college came to a close with a look at the future at the end of the year. In a public address on December 4, 1980, Sister Catherine paid tribute both to the founders of the college and to those who had continued: "The entire Church owes much . . . to those generations of sisters who provided higher education to their students, financed by their own labors and often by their own funds . . . We all know the role played by Sister Seraphine Ireland, Sister Antonia McHugh, and the many outstanding women who followed them throughout the seventy-five years of St. Catherine's history. It was they who had the original vision that inspired so many gifted scholars and teachers, both lay and religious, to join them in this important work of 'educating the new women for the new world.'"

Back to business

In her contacts with alumnae throughout the country, Sister Catherine quickly learned that their defining values for the college were intellectual growth, concern for individuals, leadership for women, and Christian community.

In 1979-80, two new interdisciplinary course offerings enhanced awareness of the college's liberal arts tradition. Faculty members from the history, philosophy, and theology departments team-taught a course with one semester devoted to Christian humanistic thought and a second to an investigation of the college's Christian humanistic tradition. Funded by the National Endowment for the Humanities, the curriculum was planned jointly by the College of St. Catherine, St. Olaf College in Northfield, St. John's University in Collegeville, and Luther College in Decorah, Iowa. Funded by the Lilly Foundation, St. Catherine philosophy and English faculty members jointly developed another course, Reasoning and Writing.

That year, the fastest-growing departments on campus were economics and business administration. Business courses became popular in the regular session, evening classes, and the new Weekend College. While the largest numbers of majors in liberal arts were in biology, those in the physical sciences and mathematics grew notably. Top students in the 1980 graduating class were chemistry majors bound for medical school and research.

Mallica Vajrathon spoke of women in developing countries and their concern for the study of food, health, and family issues. Research should address these and other social and economic questions of third-world countries, she said, rather than focus on the political crises of the areas that had been the focus of most research to date.

Several college departments received confirmation of accreditation during the year. The National League for Nursing confirmed the accreditation of the nursing program, directed by Marguerite Hessian '49 since 1972. The National Council for the Accreditation of Teacher Education (NCATE) approved the college's programs in early childhood, elementary, and secondary education. The music department applied to the National Association of Schools of Music and was awarded associate membership for the bachelor of arts.

The theology department began to offer a certificate program in pastoral ministry approved by the faculty early in 1978. Sister Gertrude Foley, SC, of Greensboro, Pennsylvania, a doctoral candidate at Aquinas Institute in Dubuque, Iowa, planned, developed, and directed the certificate program, called Equipping for Ministry. She told the *Wheel* in September 1979: "A lot of people when they hear 'Pastoral Ministry,' think only of parish ministry . . . There are many ways in which people can serve others . . . Whether caring for the sick, working with youth, or serving on a parish council, one can serve with more confidence after being trained." The program included courses in theology and psychology as well as a practical internship.

In July 1980, 127 students completed the first successful year of Weekend College (WEC). In addition to offering business, communications, theology, and social work majors, WEC introduced adult women to the natural sciences, history, humanities, sociology, philosophy, and theology. Regular faculty members taught for WEC, assuring continuity among day, evening, and weekend offerings. Continuing Education addressed the needs of women in surrounding communities, offering 30 noncredit courses in 1979-80. Of special note were institutes on women and religion, advanced cardiac rehabilitation, dimensions of American spirituality, and database searching for librarians.

Polly Penny, formerly of Integro, a Twin Cities management and consulting firm, became director of Women in Management, which shortly became the Management Development Center for Women. Penny had set up a training program for International Multifoods after raising a family and becoming involved in civic activities. She used her Twin Cities business contacts to make the center visible. In the September-October 1979 issue of *Greater Minneapolis Magazine,* she said the program was "company-oriented and geared to the needs of women who wish to advance within their own organizations." Students ranged in age from twenty-eight to fifty-seven, with nearly 95 percent employed full time. Most had children and households to manage. They learned basic theory and methodology, then analyzed their own corporations' annual reports rather than studying abstract models from textbooks. The center offered seminars, conferences, and workshops throughout the year. Jennette Gudgel followed Penny as director in 1981-83, and the center gradually disappeared into the Weekend College.

The college joined the national Elderhostel circuit, beginning a program of week-long on-campus learning experiences for senior citizens, further enhancing the college's reputation as a center for higher learning.

That all these innovations put a strain on resources was evident in the increased difficulty of some departments in providing Interim courses. This prompted serious faculty debate about the wisest use of the Interim and its value as an academic requirement. Even the academic dean speculated that Interim might be a good idea whose time was past. But students, particularly those who highly valued international study programs and internships, and faculty members had mixed feelings about suggestions to discontinue Interim.

This graphic is the symbol of the Pastoral Ministry Certificate Program offered for theology, non-theology and master's of theology students. Its sixteen 1988 graduates were involved in ministries in Episcopal, Congregational, and Roman Catholic churches, providing spiritual direction, evangelization of the alienated, and religious education. They worked in pastoral and grief ministries, in RENEW, as hospital chaplains, in ministries to battered women, the elderly, sick, and shut-in, as well as in prison, Hispanic, and liturgical music ministries.

As the number of students straight out of high school decreased, students with greater experience enriched many of the traditional classes.

Changing times made their mark on the college community. A decline in the number of sister faculty members was augmented by the increasing number of laypersons in significant positions in most departments, academic and administrative. That the tradition of leadership by the sisters was evolving into a lay leadership model seemed appropriate in the light of Vatican II.

The 1980s showed a dramatic change in the student body profile, with a majority of students finding it necessary to work part time. Thus some combination of work and study played a role in many academic programs. The college began to recruit more adult students as there were fewer and fewer students of traditional age (eighteen to twenty-one). At the same time, a dramatic increase in the number of intercultural students resulted from new recruitment and admission programs. Under the leadership of June Noronha, the Office of Intercultural Student Affairs set up support programs to assure high retention of foreign and minority students. With a grant from the St. Paul Foundation, the office organized a Hispanic motivational program—Un Primer Paso—for junior-high-age Latinos. This program brought many interested Hispanics to the campus and had a positive impact on minority enrollment.

Nonetheless, demographic studies predicted a great decline in college-age students in Minnesota during the decade, exacerbated by uncertainty regarding student financial aid from government grants and loans. Indeed, cutbacks in aid posed the deciding factor for students choosing less expensive state colleges. The threat of enrollment decline prompted uneasiness among faculty members, who saw the potential for course curtailments and personnel cutbacks.

The early 1980s presented the College of St. Catherine with financial management challenges—starting with a deficit for the 1980-81 school year and greatly exacerbated by an enrollment decline in the fall of 1982. Any retrenchment, repugnant to the faculties and staffs of all small colleges, was especially likely to depress the morale of the St. Catherine community, already operating within tight financial constraints. Sister Catherine and her administration faced their responsibilities bravely with a judicious cut in course offerings. She told department chairpersons to hold the line on hiring—no new teachers unless extraordinary enrollment trends dictated otherwise. In one year, faculty cuts brought the student-teacher ratio close to fifteen-to-one, and academic areas of the budget were cut by $700,000. The measures were painful for faculty and students; good beginning teachers did not have contracts renewed and popular classes were cut. But the president promised that issues of morale would be a priority in 1983-84, and she noted: "We ended well in the black with a surplus of $86,000, achieved with great effort and personal sacrifice from all parts of the college... Our 1982-83 financial statements... prove we can make hard decisions, set priorities, and re[al]locate resources."

One difficult decision was for the discontinuation of Interim. After much discussion indicated general approval for Interim among faculty and students, the Educational Policies Committee (EPC) voted on February 22, 1982, that the term be retained and a motion to that effect be brought to the faculty. But strain on the budget necessitated further retrenchment, and Interim offered one of few opportunities to cut. On January 6, 1983, Sister Catherine announced to the faculty the findings of the Budget Committee's deliberations and review: "Although it is clear that some things of value do occur during the Interim, the Interim idea does not serve well the needs of the contemporary student population, including as it does, adults, part-time students, and traditional-age students who need to assist with their own educational costs. The conclusion... is inescapable: the educational benefit derived from Interim is no longer sufficient to justify the cost... the Budget Committee has decided that funding for all on-campus Interim courses should be eliminated, beginning in January 1984."

The announcement fell like a bolt from the blue on faculty members, some of whom had expended considerable time and energy to build and publicize Interim courses. But in February 1983, the faculty, too, voted that on-campus Interim courses be eliminated. A note from Interim coordinator Meg Wilkes-Karraker held little solace: "The college continues to offer many opportunities for students during January—internships, foreign travel, skill building, independent study, physical education, study at other colleges, employment and even R & R! I hope we can advise students to consider the variety of programs available and to choose programs that best meet their needs and interests."

Three full-time positions had been eliminated earlier and retrenchment continued to erode faculty morale. Continued cutbacks in government aid at both the federal and state levels forced deep cuts in the operating budget wherever it would not affect the quality of education. Department chairpersons continued working with the vice president and academic dean to reallocate resources rather than request new ones. Inflation, the loss of younger faculty members, and declining enrollments threatened the stability of some smaller departments: Latin had been eliminated as a major in 1981. Questions about retaining German arose, but the major stayed. Cuts in departments and the trend toward annual tuition raises carried the growing negativism to the students. At the same time, earlier trends reversed, and the college received many more students through cross-registration than it exported to others. Of particular concern were the large numbers of St. Thomas students taking St. Catherine theology and education courses: the two institutions negotiated towards exchange agreements beneficial to both.

All these concerns together prompted the Ingersoll Study—"A Market Survey among Traditional-age Potential and Actual College Women in 1982-83." This study found that the composite perception of the college by prospective students was one of a good though not outstanding educational institution and that its single-gender aspect was a negative. In the eyes of most high school girls, the college was a quiet, tranquil, not particularly exciting place. The need for immediate attention to recruitment was clear.

The visits of speakers such as Toni Morrison, above autographing books for students, were a welcome break to students, faculty members, and administrators concerned about budget in 1982.

Student life included strong academic demands but offered many opportunities for other activities. The challenge seemed not to institute new ones but to renew and expand traditional activities and get the word out. In addition to dances for Homecoming, Christmas, and Spring Fling, the student government sponsored Octoberfest and Senior Send-Off, picnic affairs featuring local bands. Sports enthusiasts found satisfaction in the Dolphins, a synchronized swim team presenting an annual aquatic show. The volleyball, and swim teams were competitive. Swim team member Jennifer Bergstrom '83 was named an All-American swimmer in 1980, the first St. Catherine athlete so honored.

Student publications provided opportunities for acquiring and enhancing artistic and journalistic skills. The literary/art magazine *Ariston*, the yearbook *Etos* (formerly *La Concha*), and the newspaper *The Catherine Wheel* provided the community with vehicles for the exchange of ideas and information, for the expression of campus and worldwide concerns, for publication of students' best literary and artistic efforts, for promoting freedom of expression, and simply for sharing the entertaining and challenging concerns of college life.

Student government planned and expanded on-campus activities during the 1980s. At right, banner carriers announced and united the new freshman class during the campus parade for the 1989 Opening Celebration.

In 1982 students were introduced to some marked changes in housing. Renovation of Caecilian Hall, formation of a residents' council, and a restructured summer program resulted in the conversion of nursing classrooms and offices to dormitory space. Students in Whitby Hall had access to a new elevator. In addition to twenty-five resident advisers (RAs) and six apartment advisers (AAs), fifty-five students were employed as daytime receptionists in residence areas during the academic year. Evening receptionists were discontinued for budgeting purposes. Further space reallocation resulted in drastic changes in Derham Hall, and 1983-84 was the first academic year ever in which no students resided there. Since then, all but the fourth floor, where some sisters live, has been given to administrative offices and functions.

There were changes in administrative personnel, too. At the close of the 1980-81 academic year, Rosemary Hart had resigned as dean of students for a position at Willamette University in Oregon. The associate academic dean, Marilou Eldred, had served as acting dean of students through the fall semester of 1981 and, after a nationwide search, become dean in January 1982. During the same year Sister Anita's duties as academic dean had been redefined and her title changed to vice president and academic dean. Michael Murphy was named associate dean for student academic services, and Mary Ann Rehnke became associate dean for faculty personnel and academic programs. Auxiliary Services, with Karen LeBon as director, was defined to include the bookstore, special services, mail services, O'Shaughnessy Auditorium, printing/typing and telephoning services, and aligned to be cost-efficient and to maximize income.

Douglas Lowry had been hired as director of academic computing in 1980. His first task was to develop academic computing objectives and identify hardware and software suitable for faculty and students. In conversations with both, he introduced the possibilities of computer-related courses and potential use of computers in teaching. Some faculty and students who had used computers elsewhere were eager for advanced work. "Computer literacy" became the slogan of the day. Evaluations of computing needs by both staff members and an outside consultant, however, led to the conclusion that the college needed better on-campus computer facilities and capabilities for both academic and administrative computing. So despite financial straits, the college in 1982 purchased hardware and hired an institutional research/management information specialist to make the computer center operative, its planning spearheaded by Sister Anita. She hired Michael Garris as director of computing services in February that year. Plans were formed to move accounting functions from the Sisters of St. Joseph Administration Center computer system to the college system in 1983-84.

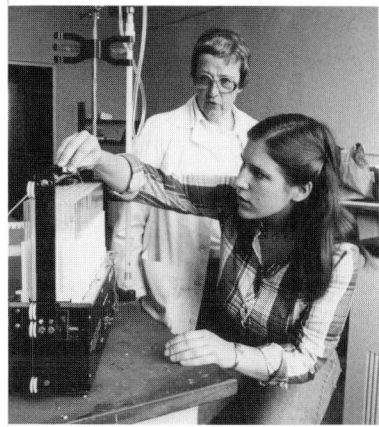

Sister Mary Thompson, chemistry, observed student Rosemary Labin conducting a lab experiment in 1981. In 1984 Sister Mary was named a semifinalist in the "Professor of the Year" competition sponsored by the Council for the Advancement and Support of Education.

Academic life continued despite administrative changes, with faculty productivity at an unusually high level. Research endeavors were aided by grants including the Sister Marie Ursule Grant, the Bremer Grant, and the Dean's Small Grants Fund, to mention just a few. Special grants in 1981-82 included $50,000 from the National Endowment for the Humanities for a "Writing across the Curriculum" program, a $104,000 Bush Foundation grant for faculty development, and a $115,000 Northwest Area Foundation grant for curriculum revision, all enabling the college to pursue its tradition of innovative teaching. That year, too, a plan for developing a program of review for liberal arts programs at the college became possible through a request to the Association of American Colleges. The review process was developed by the Liberal Arts Task Force and the EPC under the guidance of the academic dean.

New academic programs emerged as dictated by need. The traditional library science major was transformed into one of information management. New and advanced courses in computer science appeared on the class schedule. Responses to a questionnaire sent by the theology department to local and regional parishes, colleges, and seminaries verified the need for a master's program not tied to seminary preparation. Approval of a master's theology program (based on texts of theology developed over the centuries) had to come from the EPC, from the general faculty, and since it was to be the first graduate degree program, from the North Central Association of Colleges and Universities. Faculty arguments for and against the establishment of a graduate program echoed those of the 1950s. Sister Anita defended the proposal in the April 30, 1982, *Wheel:* "We envision ourselves as a strong theological center in the Twin Cities. Having a graduate program in that area and not limiting it to a single-sex population would give us greater visibility." The faculty finally approved the master's program in May 1982 by a vote of 57 to 37. Larry Goodwin, of the theology department, said: "The master's program will allow women to achieve leadership roles in ministry . . . Women's values are being kept in mind with this program." The master of arts program in theology opened to both men and women in the fall of 1983.

Collaboration of the college with outside business ventures included a link with the Institute of Technology at the University of Minnesota for a dual degree in engineering; planning internships in international business with the Institut de Gestion at Rennes, France; seeking out exchange possibilities with programs in Mexico City and in Nagasaki, Japan; planning for a business ethics program with Midway National Bank in St. Paul; and approval from the North Central Association for courses at the Fashion Institute of Design and Merchandising in Los Angeles for home economics students.

Through the 1980s, graduating classes reflected a shift from majors in the liberal arts, with a preponderance of majors in professional departments: business administration, education, nursing, social work, and occupational therapy. And, while Weekend College had the same strong liberal arts core as the weekday program, almost all WEC students enrolled in professional majors. During the 1982-83 school year, 60 percent were in business administration. Given the tradition of the college, the administration and Board of Trustees still hoped for a return to the liberal arts as preparation for many entry-level professional positions in business, industry, and government.

Peter Lupori taught a popular evening course in clay sculpture for Continuing Education. Above, he gave a mini-course in the subject for students and their parents on Family Day.

To revitalize its liberal arts programs, the college decided to create a WEC humanities major and minor. Sister Alberta Huber, professor of English, was appointed project director. Planners wanted to explore the academic resources of the college and the cultural resources of the Twin Cities area for unique learning opportunities for nontraditional students. Such a program might well serve REAP students as well as those in WEC. The plan projected the development of seventeen courses, all geared to the nontraditional student, over a three-year period, with the hope that each participant would cultivate a disciplined way of assessing human experience through the study of literature, history, fine arts, ethics, philosophy, and theology. Thinking, reading, writing, and speaking would be the tools of intellectual growth. The student would thus acquire a learning method to use during her lifelong dialog with the world in which she lived and worked. The dream was real but ideal, perhaps premature and grandiose for fiscally sparse times. It simply did not get off the ground, and debate over the role of liberal arts curriculum simmered through the decade.

Continuing Education was also in a state of flux. Originally it had served the needs of adult learners coming to the college for short courses, evolving into a center for REAP students and sponsoring the Women in Management program. In 1980-81, it took on administration of the summer school, and during the next year REAP was transferred to Admissions. The Office of Continuing Education continued to supervise certificate programs and noncredit programs including short courses and conferences, as well as Elderhostel and Seniors Go to College. Continuing Education clearly had become an academic programming unit.

With a changing clientele, the college defined the REAP student as "any woman, age 25 or older, who has interrupted her education after high school or during college for at least a few years and who is now re-entering or seeking to re-enter the day college for the purpose of self-enrichment, career training, or completion of a degree." To help these students adjust to college life, the Administrative Council designated a special REAP lounge, and the college established a REAP scholarship. Over time, the increased number of older students and attention accorded them became a source of contention among traditional students, who feared REAP programs would change the major thrust of the college.

With a vision for program development, the Subcommittee for Long-Range Planning in 1982-83 made recommendations including that the administration:

- develop a professional program at the master's level (whether this would be an MBA or management program, or a leadership institute for women was to be determined by research among professional women and other leaders in education)
- consider development of a center for adult learning that would focus on adult learning methods and address the needs of individual students
- investigate off-campus degree programs, considering sites and content.

Retention of a diverse student body was still a priority. Un Primer Paso had started off well, and the college wanted to continue it. Ten Hispanic peer advisors who attended the college received special training in communication skills, time management and goal-setting, advising and role model techniques, intercultural communication skills, and career and educational exploration. These peers assisted with parent/student workshops, visited prospective students in their homes, participated in activities in their schools, and continued contact with new students. An initial parent meeting held at Our Lady of Guadalupe Catholic Church in St. Paul, on February 9, 1983, attracted twenty-five parents and thirty students. Three additional weekend workshops focused on cultural exchange; these were conducted by an advisory board composed of representatives from the metropolitan Hispanic community. A summer institute for prospective college students of Hispanic background was held in June on campus. Reading, writing, math, and social studies were taught with a view toward helping students hone the skills needed for success in college.

Campus Ministry focused on increasing student involvement in liturgies and on regular offerings of support for students' spiritual needs. Students participated in all phases of liturgical functions, preparing and conducting

Campus Ministry grew in visibility, assuming a role of greater influence as concern about the mission of the college became more crucial to administrative planning.

Many women leaders, including Bella Abzug, above in 1987, and May Sarton, below during an earlier visit in 1963, enriched campus life and inspired students and faculty in the 1980s.

evenings of recollection and coordinating music and prayers for campus functions. Ministry formation nights were organized, and Campus Ministry team members worked with the Office of Student Affairs in examining, representing, and responding to the concerns of students.

Chapel renovation planning began in 1982 with Frank Kacmarcik as consultant. Much went into the study of the history of the chapel as well as of its current and projected use. Relocation of the altar, ambo, and president's chair in the center of the transept, along with elevation of the central space and placement of the organ directly against the wall behind the altar, was considered. Pew chairs were envisioned in a circular configuration around this central space. The dialog concerning renovations surfaced wide differences about contemporary liturgical needs and functions among members of the community. This and the tight financial times meant that most of the plans would not be realized then, but the altar was moved forward to an expanded, elevated space.

Interest in women's issues and scholarship continued. On September 25, 1980, Abigail Quigley McCarthy spoke to a student convocation on "Woman's Quest for Her Future in the Church." She had been a member of a group called to discuss and formulate a response to the Minnesota Bishops' "Papers on Women" issued in March 1979. She said that "to be allowed [their] full biography . . . women need to use their gifts, with the problem not of attaining everything men have but of seeing themselves as they really are . . . Women's unity depends on whether or not they can really focus on the terrible problems of injustice and see that their injustice is totally unchristian."

In January 1980, four students attended a workshop at Augsburg College on sexual harassment. Barbara Appleby '83, Amelia Lindgren '83, Celeste Lasich '82, and Mary Lee Kersten (Day) '84 then met and decided to form a feminist issues group to be known as FIG. In spring 1982 FIG sponsored a lecture, "Nuclear Madness and Denial of Death," funded by departments on campus. This program led to FIG sponsorship of a lecture on "Sexism in the Media" the next fall. More students and some faculty members joined FIG.

Members of FIG attending a battered women's coalition learned of the need for informational centers to which women could turn for help. With the help of Campus Ministry, Amy Lindgren and Barbara Appleby '83 procured the use of Room 204 in the chapel house and gathered books, tapes, catalogs, and magazines to stock its shelves. They furnished it with a table, chairs, and a bulletin board from the housing office and other places on campus. On March 13, 1983, the staff hosted a reception to announce the center's opening. Susan Bowers was its first faculty adviser; Geri Chavis followed. Staff members (both students and faculty members) began to look for ways to work on issues such as violence against women, child abuse, and world peace, but the immediate concern was for funds. Folksinger Carrie Gerendasy performed two benefit concerts, with 75 percent of proceeds going to the center. Staff members conferred with a subcommittee of the college's Strategic Long-Range Planning Committee (SLRP), which agreed to cooperate in providing a center that would facilitate, conduct, and implement research by and about women. What had been called the Women's Resource Center became the "Women's Research and Resource Center."

Support for the center grew. Dean of Students Marilou Eldred donated a telephone. Student Activities donated furniture from Marian Lounge. Denise Oehlers '85 facilitated the first research project sponsored by the center. Working with Eldred, she began writing *Profiles: Twin Cities Women's Honor List,* selecting from a list of innovators nominated by their peers. The staff of the center worked with the campus chapter of MPIRG (Minnesota Public Interest Research Group) to conduct Women's Issues Week, a series of programs on peace encampments, self-defense, pornography, and sexual offense.

Educational aspects of the women's movement gained greater prominence when Sister Anita, academic dean, established by a memo on September 23, 1983, an ad hoc Committee on Women's Studies. The committee included faculty members Catherine Lupori, Meg Wilkes-Karraker, Alan Graebner, Eileen Gavin, Geri Chavis, and Julie Belle White, who jointly recommended courses for a Women's Studies minor. The idea was not to add new courses but to use existing classes in developing an interdisciplinary track. The committee suggested Women in America (sociology), Rhetoric and Sex Roles (speech-theater), Human Sexuality (interdisciplinary), and History of Women in America (history). The minor was approved by the EPC and faculty.

The academic year 1983-84 was Sister Catherine McNamee's last as president of the college. Financial accomplishments included the completion of an $8,000,000 capital campaign, making possible the opening of the computer center. Remodeling of the former reserve room, in the northwest area of the library, resulted in its opening on May 23, 1983, with full use the following fall. The center included two offices, a receptionist area, a small seminar room, a microcomputer lab, space for the mainframe computer, and an area for terminals. Computing capabilities grew rapidly during the first eight months of operation: software was upgraded, new graphics capabilities were added, additional terminals were installed, administrative computing began, and academic computing projects were developed. Jim Jones joined the staff as coordinator of academic computing, and John Walski as coordinator of administrative computing. During a thunderstorm in the summer of 1984, lightning struck a tree near the center, damaging computer ports and shutting down the mainframe for several days. After that, all administrative and most academic services were put on line. The computer quickly became part of daily life on campus, and computer literacy was made a requirement for graduation. The use of computers by both faculty and students increased so much that the microcomputer lab was moved to the Learning Center beneath the chapel in 1987.

Judith Guest, author of Ordinary People, *was the 1984 commencement speaker.*

Another financial innovation was the "per course" tuition policy adopted to assist students attending college part time. The student body continued to draw more re-entry adult women, weekend college women, and certificate students. For the first time, two REAP students, Barbara Elden Larney and Anita Rentz, ranked at the top of the Class of '84. Approximately 40 percent of the top twenty seniors that year were older students.

The faculty brought much honor to the college. Sister Mary O'Hara, philosophy, received a Fulbright grant to study religious women in India. Janice Nadeau, nursing, received a Bush Foundation leadership fellowship. Grace McDonald, nursing, was chosen an extramural associate with the National Institutes of Health in Washington, D.C. David Luedtke, swimming coach, was named an advisor/researcher for the 1984 U.S. Olympic Team.

In addition to launching the master's degree in theology in 1983-84, the college started Evening College, an opportunity for students to earn degrees in communications or business administration exclusively through evening courses. While the former was an outgrowth of the Catholic tradition and a vital liberal art, Evening College addressed the scheduling and role conflicts of modern women. The college was becoming an around-the-clock institution.

More complicated overall offerings called for major administrative changes begun early in 1984 and carried out through the next year. Five areas were added to Student Affairs: Academic Advising, Career Services, Learning Centers, Security, and Child Care. Financial Aid was placed under the dean of admissions. REAP reported to the associate academic dean. The professional staff increased from eighteen to twenty-one. Despite a tight budget, Auxiliary Services got new WATS lines and a COIL telephone system program was installed. The sisters' facilities at Bethany, the Administration Center, and the buildings at 1880 and 1890 Randolph, along with all of the phones on campus, were placed on one system. A new College Center Planning Committee presented three alternative College Center proposals to the Board of Trustees in April. Few of the recommended renovations met fruition, though changes to West Marian Lounge made that area of St. Joseph Hall more functional.

In the summer of 1984, Sister Catherine returned to the East Coast, to become dean of Dexter Hanley College in Pennsylvania. She had brought good repute to the College of St. Catherine through leadership in both national and international areas of Catholic higher education. She had made the college visible to the immediate community by serving on boards of many business institutions. And as the first chair of the Commission on the Role of Women in the Church in the St. Paul-Minneapolis Archdiocese, she had negotiated for several conferences on women in the church to be held on the college campus. Sister Catherine had indeed worked to fulfill the college's threefold mission.

All is possible

The Board of Trustees appointed Vice President and Academic Dean Anita Pampusch, on leave from the Sisters of St. Joseph, to act as president of the college during its year-long national search for a new president. The search committee, with approval from the Board of Trustees, then found her the best candidate and, waiving the requirement for sisterhood, appointed her the ninth president of the college in May 1985.

Anita Pampusch, named the ninth president of the college in May 1985, is a member of St. Edmund's House of Cambridge University in England, where she researched the papers of Sir Isaac Newton in pursuit of her doctorate in the philosophy of science, received from the University of Notre Dame in 1971.

A favorite of students, Anita Pampusch was known for her ability to see the big picture, to set priorities, and to present ideas persuasively. "Enthusiasm is important," she told *SCAN* in Spring 1990. "It generates a feeling that all is possible, that this is a solvable problem." She retained strong bonds with the religious community and was thoroughly committed to the tradition of the college. As Sister Mary Gabriel, she had received a bachelor's degree in math and chemistry from the college in 1962, then earned a master's degree in philosophy from the University of Notre Dame in 1970 and a doctorate in 1971. She was a National Science Foundation trainee from 1966 to 1970, and she conducted research funded by the National Endowment for the Humanities in 1972. She joined the College of St. Catherine as an instructor in 1970, becoming tenured in 1975. In 1976-77 she was an American Council on Education Fellow in Academic Administration at Goucher College in Towson, Maryland. Promoted to associate professor in 1978, she was vice president and academic dean from 1980 to June 1984. She served a five-year term as president from 1985 to 1990, then was appointed for a second term.

President Pampusch wanted to continue the process of reaffirming the goals of the College of St. Catherine that her predecessor had begun, and she focused her first term on redefining the college as a Catholic liberal arts college for women. This prompted work to strengthen the college through improved admission practices, curriculum, and internal administration. The energetic president initiated a thrust to develop a program leading to a master's degree in organizational leadership. She also expressed hope to start a center for ethics, responsibility, and values in which the college could do research and programming on the conflict between personal ethics and organizational ethics. The role of women in this area was to be a major concern of the center.

The Center for Ethics, Responsibilities, and Values became a reality in the summer of 1984 under the leadership of Douglas Wallace. Nationally recognized for his innovative approaches to education, Wallace had earned bachelor's degrees in philosophy from the University of Minnesota in 1958 and in divinity from the Colgate-Rochester Divinity School in 1963 and a doctorate in educational administration from the university in 1973. He was vice president of social policy at Norwest Bank in Minneapolis, had been an adviser for the media, ethics, and law center at the university, and was a member of the Minnesota State Board of Education. In his new position Wallace worked with college departments to develop mechanisms for the inclusion of a focus on ethics across the curriculum. The center was also to provide service to organizations (especially corporations) by way of programs and seminars devoted to the development of ethical awareness and sensitivity, thereby giving the college high visibility and extending its mission through its links with outside agencies.

In 1985 the center officially began its work with a $50,000 grant from the McKnight Foundation. Confirming the mission of the center, the faculty helped solidify a framework for five program levels: Crisis Management, Anticipatory Management, Sharpening Ethical Perspectives, Deepening Ethical Perspectives, and Deepening Moral Courage. Teaching modules were designed for seminars offered to such firms as the Pillsbury Company, Cray Research, Opus Development, Ed Phillips and Sons, Honeywell, and Control Data. Ethics Across the Curriculum workshops were offered to faculty members with a design toward the inclusion of ethics issues in their respective courses.

Concerned about planning for the college, the Board of Trustees in June 1984 directed the administration to examine realistic strategies for moving strongly into the future. This mandate resulted in plans to develop new programs aimed at recruiting traditional-age students and examining existing plans to determine whether they were flexible enough for the challenges of a changing world. The board also advised the administration to begin planning for another fund drive to provide monies for envisioned projects. President Pampusch immediately addressed the revamping of the Office of Institutional Advancement under a new executive director, Kathleen McLaughlin (followed by Janet Miner). Pampusch also began negotiating with the St. Catherine Alumnae Association to move its successful fundraising function to the development office; its integration was realized in the fall of 1985. Steps were taken to increase the effectiveness of the college grants office, and attempts to reach larger supporters of the college were made through increasing the visibility of the President's Council, the Parents' Council, and the Board of Trustees. The president conducted visits, talks, and meetings with local church, civic, and professional groups as well as with alumnae chapters. In 1984-85, all business transactions were transferred to the newly installed college-owned computer, making it easier to implement financial controls and budget reporting.

The changing nature of the student body was a continuing challenge. Forty-five percent of students were over 23 years of age in 1984-85. Nineteen percent of the full-time student equivalent that year was provided by evening, WEC,

Ruth Haag Brombach '60, named executive director of the St. Catherine Alumnae Association in 1973, has seen it grow from 6,000 members to 16,500. The association hosts an annual reunion and provides information, programs, and other services to alumnae around the world. Brombach says that changes in alumnae services have reflected the changes in women's lives and that the challenge of serving women who care deeply about spiritual, philosophical, and professional issues makes her work exciting.

and graduate or special students; 40 percent of the student body was enrolled part time. The associate academic dean, dean of students, and Office of Academic Advising devised a plan to link faculty academic advising with the Student Development Center. The CREATE program aimed to establish a core of faculty advisors especially for first-year students. That year the college added a chapter of Delta Mu Delta, the national honor society in business administration, recognizing the increase in business majors. And the English department sponsored the first contest for prospective high school writers.

To enhance its growing emphasis on excellence, the faculty in January 1985 passed the Academic Integrity Policy, dealing with issues of plagiarism, cheating, and other areas of academic ethics. The new policy provided uniform guidelines for the enforcement of standards informally practiced in the past, stressing excellence in education through the search for truth and justice. These values were to be expected of all chartered organizations on campus. Participation in extracurricular activities was to lead to a commitment to values based on knowledge, familiarity, understanding, association, and respect for individuals regardless of background.

A decision by the Sisters of St. Joseph to support a joining of St. Mary's Junior College in Minneapolis with the College of St. Catherine thrust a substantial administrative task upon the new president. In May 1985, the same month she was inaugurated, the boards of the two institutions endorsed a plan for acquisition. The College of St. Catherine would have two campuses retaining earlier titles, with one board and one president. Plans called for a consolidation of administrative service and an affiliation of departments to produce new programs. Immediate needs included a new catalog that would include changes in the curriculum made to fit the successful two-year programs at St. Mary's into the overall curriculum program. The transfer from a quarter system at St. Mary's to the semester system was imperative. The joint use of faculty members at both campuses was deemed an asset. Mary Broderick, academic dean

On September 1, 1986, St. Mary's Junior College officially became the St. Mary's Campus of the College of St. Catherine. Sister Anne Joachim Moore signed the cession documents as Sister Karen Kennelly, Sister Mary Hasbrouck, and President Anita Pampusch looked on.

of St. Mary's, and Marilou Eldred, dean of students (named vice president for administration for the College of St. Catherine in the following year), worked closely for the coordination and cooperation of the two campuses.

The college continually addressed the needs of its local area community. In a joint venture with the College of St. Thomas (in 1990 it became the University of St. Thomas), the College of St. Catherine sponsored a Center for Senior Citizens' Education. Courses at the two colleges opened to senior citizens, with a special effort towards helping senior citizens to become more secure in addressing the economic problems of the day. Older citizens might share their experiences with younger students in such a setting, and the center could provide a clearinghouse for community education information. The venture became very popular among its Twin Cities constituents.

With its history of challenging young women to achieve their potential through higher education, the College of St. Catherine in the fall of 1985 expanded the high school enrichment program first offered in the late 1970s, by adopting a postsecondary program offering college-level courses to juniors and seniors from Minnesota high schools. Students entering this program had to meet strict requirements, taking only one or two courses a semester. Receiving high school credit and/or college credit for courses not offered at their respective high schools, they tended to register for advanced courses in math and special courses in the liberal arts. The program provided good public relations for the college and brought prospective students to the college campus. It encouraged participating high schools to assess their curricula.

Other new programs also enhanced the mission of the college. The Master of Arts degree in Organizational Leadership (MAOL), approved by the North Central Accrediting Association in August 1985, became operative in January 1986. The college nursing department, in collaboration with St. Olaf College and Gustavus Adolphus College, began implementation of the Minnesota Intercollegiate Nursing Consortium (MINC) in the fall of 1986. Students from all three campuses were to be housed on the St. Catherine campus and take both their nursing and some liberal arts coursework at the college. The Adult Nurse Practitioner Program developed subspecialties in pediatrics and geriatric care. The installation of a telescope and observatory dome in Mendel Tower extended the visibility of the physics department. Recognizing the need to adapt to a changing environment and to provide community confidence building, computerization, and data-gathering, these innovative programs demonstrated the acute global awareness necessary for effective planning.

Since the demise of the Honors Reading program in the 1960s, some faculty members and administrators had dreamed of setting up an honors program to challenge some of its brightest students. Begun in spring 1987, the new Honors Program aimed to deepen students' love of learning and understanding of great issues, past and contemporary. The program helped clarify and emphasize the college's commitment to the liberal arts and academic excellence. Each honor student had to maintain a 3.5 grade-point average (GPA) in her major and overall studies and complete at least six honor courses with a 3.0 GPA. She was to engage in a major research or creative project, documented by a written paper and presented orally in a public forum, with the guidance of a faculty member. The Honors Committee consisted of a coordinator and four faculty members from varying disciplines selected by the academic dean. Sister Margery (Thomas More) Smith of the English department was its first coordinator. She received a bachelor's degree in English from the college in 1949 and

Visually impaired student Bunny (Marlene) Tabatt took a test for the physical therapy assistant program at St. Mary's Campus in 1986 by listening to questions on a tape and typing out her answers. Her seeing-eye dog, Buff, wore a sign saying "I'm working. Hands off."

The new Honors Program set up to challenge the brightest students included a special retreat, here in 1988 at Timberlee on Big Fish Lake, near Cold Spring, Minnesota.

a master's degree in English from Marquette University in 1961. She began teaching at the college in 1968, and received a doctorate from the University of Chicago in 1970 She coordinated the Honors Program until 1990, when history professor Alan Graebner took it on.

Despite, or perhaps because of, the pressures on students, spirituality became a growing interest, particularly evidenced by large enrollments in theology and spirituality courses as well as a greater interest in spiritual direction. In 1987, for the first time in many years, the college sponsored a special retreat for faculty and staff members, in which participants reflected together and separately on the meaning of religion in their lives. In the 1987 summer issue of *SCAN,* President Pampusch noted that all at the college "are fortunate to be in an environment where such activities are not only encouraged, but indeed fostered by contact with a believing community and a variety of support groups, counseling services and Campus Ministry activities, along with liturgies and academic work." Campus Ministry had prompted many of these initiatives. A peer ministry program elicited positive experiences for those in the group, though efforts to generate renewed interest among others on campus received a mixed response. Monday communion services were not well received, and attendance at weekend Mass decreased. Nevertheless, those who worked in Campus Ministry were motivated by active faith commitments generating energy and positive relationships across the campus community. Members of the Campus Ministry team joined with ministers from St. Thomas in coordinating Volunteers in Action, its purpose to transform the concerns and abilities of students into constructive, directed action for the needy. VIA programs included work with KIDS, the Minneapolis Catholic Youth Center, the YMCA of Greater St. Paul, the Archdiocesan Office of the Deaf, the St. Paul Rehabilitation Center, and the St. Paul Society for the Blind. Volunteers offered services at Children's Hospital of St. Paul, Hallie Q. Brown Community Center, Riverside Medical Center, St. Joseph's House for Battered Women, St. Paul-Ramsey Medical Center, and United Hospital. Other programs included work with senior citizens and tutoring and educating the underprivileged.

Supporters on all sides encouraged strengthening the college image as that of one focusing on the needs of women in modern times. Women's colleges historically had great success in training women for leadership positions, and the College of St. Catherine was in a more favorable position than others reconsidering their missions. This provided a strong incentive for retaining its focus on women. Rosemary Fallon Nichols '51, writing in the spring 1987 *SCAN:* "If we examine the Christian religion from the earliest time, we will find women in the forefront in ministry and intellectual achievements. Surely Joan of Arc, Teresa of Avila, Catherine of Alexandria, Elizabeth Seton, and in our time, Mother Teresa and Sister Teresa Kane have stepped out and shown the way to bring Christianity into daily living. Today's Christian women need to be encouraged by our foremothers and support one another in defining and espousing our feminine experiences of the gospel. We have a rich heritage to pass on to those who will come after us. I believe women have a talent for overcoming adversity, and it seems to me that the time to share our deepest needs and hopes for Christianity is now. Our Church needs to inspire and model the gospel truths as we live them in our lives."

As an outgrowth of the SLRP established by Sister Catherine in 1983, a task force on women's research and scholarship (related to the former ad hoc committee) and another on a women's resource center (related to the student project) had both recommended in May 1985 the formal establishment of a women's center. Pampusch suggested the two groups join to form the Women's Research, Resource, and Scholarship Center. It was to have a prominent space, a director and a secretary, and a collection of materials by and about women. A search committee recommended that Catherine Lupori begin work in September 1985. In a small room in St. Joseph Hall, on March 10, 1986, Abigail Quigley McCarthy spoke at the dedication of the Abigail Quigley McCarthy Center for Women's Research, Resources, and Scholarship. She spoke of the strength drawn from community and of the role of colleges in women's lives: "Half of the women in the United States Congress . . . a full half of the congresswomen, were graduates not only of women's colleges but of *Catholic* women's colleges. A small minority of colleges produces half the women officeholders." When she asked why, they said "they had been given the sense in their colleges that the sky was the limit, that there was nothing they couldn't do . . . They had strong role models, but also they learned by example and by precept that the goal of life was service to others . . . the combination of self-confidence and the desire to serve . . . brought them where they were."

Facing increased numbers of requests to cosponsor women's events, the center had marked visibility in 1987-88. It gained full membership in the Minnesota Women's Consortium, cooperated in the metro-state grant proposal for incorporating gender and cultural diversity into the curriculum, helped regularize the Introduction to Women's Studies course, and secured an agreement with Hamline University to alternate its offering between the two campuses.

Administrative changes had brought new women to new roles as models for leadership. Marilou Eldred was now vice president for administration. Maureen Evans was named vice president for academic affairs, and Jeanne McLean became academic dean. Colleen Hegranes, formerly associate dean of students, became dean of students. At St. Mary's Campus a new Student Personnel Office consolidated the services for visually and hearing impaired, resident life and student activities, counseling, health, community awareness, and peer tutors, all under the direction of Sister Karen Hilgers '63.

Writer Meridel Le Sueur and Catherine Lupori, director of the Abigail Quigley McCarthy Center for Women's Research, Resources, and Scholarship on campus, took part in designating the center an official peace site.

On the St. Catherine campus, great strides were taken to raise awareness of cultural diversity. Programs fostering the development of all on campus as sensitive and constructive members of the global community focused on making individuals aware of the history, cultures, and philosophies of other peoples as they developed their own leadership qualities. Such mutual awareness of diverse cultural patterns would better enable all to contribute to world cooperation. International study programs were evaluated and upgraded to guarantee their support of the campus mission as well as to ensure student outcomes stipulated by the academic community. Though there was a greater concern for the needs of culturally diverse students attending the college, international and minority enrollment fluctuated. In 1986-87, sixty-nine students of minority or other national cultures enrolled, including 3 American Indians, 20 Asians, 25 Hispanics, 6 from Guam, Puerto Rico, and Saipan. Seven were minorities of permanent resident status. The sharpest drop in minority enrollment was among American Indian students, followed by African-Americans. Asian student enrollment was increasing, while Hispanic enrollment remained relatively stable.

While freshmen enrollment declined from that of the 1970s, the number of first-time transfer students rose, adding to diversity among students. The increase of graduate students at the college also indicated the multiplicity of women's needs being addressed. In 1986-87 there were 77 total class enrollments in the theology master's program, 266 in MAOL, and 373 in the adult nurse practitioner programs. The tremendous growth of the master's programs, particularly the MAOL, attested to the tenacity of the president, Anita Pampusch, long an advocate for graduate programs at the college.

Bold plans for development went on despite the cloud of economic recession hanging over the nation during the last half of the 1980s. To cushion adverse effects of the economy on long-range planning, the college procured a grant from the Consortium for the Advancement of Private Higher Education (CAPHE Project) to involve faculty and administrators in creating a resource allocation process based on stronger links between planning and budget processes. In 1986 CAPHE involved faculty members and top administrators in projecting best/worst-budget scenarios for 1990-91. These scenarios were based on the college long-range plan, environmental and market trends affecting higher education, and reallocation of resources based on enrollment.

The Abigail Quigley McCarthy Women's Center presented the panel discussion "How Do We Acknowledge the Cultural Diversity of Women in Our Campus Life?" as part of a Ford Grant consortial program on April 18, 1989. Participating were, left to right: Bonnie Wallace of the American Indian Support Program at Augsburg College, Ngo Pham Tran '56, Regina Laroche-Theune '84, Elizabeth Gurrola-Dorado '71, and Sister Sharon Howell, director of Minority Student Affairs at St. Thomas.

CAPHE was intended to increase faculty and administrative staff commitment to the long-range plan by reallocating resources and clarifying the roles of constituent groups. By increasing faculty understanding of and contributions to budget and financial analysis and planning, the administration hoped to increase the acceptance of difficult financial reallocations. Ownership in the process might keep morale from plummeting when allocation shifts adversely affected various departments. But the highly tenured faculty members of small departments, which considered their very existence jeopardized, were wary of the CAPHE recommendations. Most faculty members felt that personnel cuts might hamper the caliber of programs already in place or have an adverse effect on enrollment in the long run. And fear of personnel retrenchment colored every discussion involving planning.

Another financial problem facing the administration in the 1980s was the use of the O'Shaughnessy Auditorium, formerly a money-making enterprise. With construction of the Ordway Music Theatre in downtown St. Paul, the Minnesota Orchestra, Minnesota Chamber Orchestra, and Minnesota Opera Company moved their operations from the auditorium, and the college lost rental revenues. The auditorium served the college and the general public throughout the 1980s, providing educational, performance, and conference space, and while use of the facility was high—124 events in 1986-87—the rentals generated $178,000 in income but $223,000 in expense. The college aggressively sought new clients.

Financial problems in no way dampened the energetic leadership. Efforts made to balance the budget stopped the trend toward deficit budgeting, and in 1988-89 the college achieved a balanced budget, began reduction of the internal deficit, and revised investment procedures and strategies to make the endowment grow. Financial prospects for 1989-90 were good. Enrollment proved more positive than had been projected by CAPHE, and the picture of increased enrollment on St. Mary's Campus offset the decrease in first-year students on the main campus. Enrollment on both campuses exceeded the projections for traditional-age transfer students. Most encouraging of all were signs of good retention for currently enrolled students. While these figures helped boost morale, President Pampusch addressed concern about less positive demographic trends in listing primary goals for 1988-89 as recruitment and the launching of a major capital campaign. She noted the need for strong visibility and promised to devise a plan for developing a more humane and productive environment on both campuses.

Comedian Lily Tomlin's popular Broadway show was also a hit at O'Shaughnessy Auditorium.

After three years, administrators assessed the advantages of the St. Mary's venture: "Together we have many more resources than either of us had individually . . . serving a diverse group of students . . . has allowed administrators to think creatively about programs. In acquiring St. Mary's, the college gained substantial assets—valuable property near major medical facilities, an institution in excellent financial condition, and a sound addition to its endowment." Consolidation at administrative and support service levels resulted in greater efficiency. All records were integrated into the St. Catherine computerized administrative record system. Still, because the two campuses are geographically separate, some services—admissions, financial aid, registrar, academic dean, bookstore, business, and housekeeping—had to be duplicated.

In October 1988, the academic deans of the two campuses presented a joint five-year plan for academic development for 1989-94. The plan examined the mission and identity of the two campuses and suggested program priorities and areas for collegewide revision and development. It addressed future directions for each campus, as well as new shared programs calling for closer collaboration. Ultimately these initiatives became part of *Strategic Directions*, presented to the Board of Trustees in January 1989. Despite some delays in implementation, the plan engaged the two campuses in positive dialog.

The year 1989-90 produced record enrollment at St. Mary's Campus. Predictions for the next school year were similar. St. Mary's Extended Program, designed for students admitted to the campus but to no particular program, was expanded. Aimed at helping undecided students find themselves and the areas of study most suited to them, the Crossroads Learning Center (now simply the Learning Center) enhanced its services—learning assistance in basic skills as well alternative testing and note-taking services for students with special learning needs—in the effort to help and retain these students. And St. Mary's Campus began to require computer literacy of its students, making the two campuses consistent in this area.

Changes in student body composition and program offerings required changes in administrative organization of the college. During 1988-89, the academic dean's office, for instance, consisted of three full-time professional staff and two full-time support staff. Jeanne McLean, academic dean, and John Dwyer, associate dean for academic support programs had held their positions from the summer of 1987. Anne Swanson, associate dean for graduate and nontraditional programs, started in the summer of 1988 in a position created by the departure of Maureen Evans, who had found the position of academic vice president ill-defined and imposing on others. Her departure meant job clarification and administrative growth among the academic administrators.

Taking leadership issues seriously, President Pampusch used her goals for 1988-89 as a model for other college professionals. She became involved in activities with outside persons and groups that influenced and made policy in higher education, especially for institutions like the College of St. Catherine. As chair of the Women's College Coalition based in Washington, D.C., she was actively involved in telling the story of women's colleges, their rationale, and success. The coalition sponsored a study of the role of women's colleges in educating adult learners and worked for creating a stronger database on women's colleges in the United States (numbering 94 in 1991).

Pampusch served on the President's Committee of the Public Leadership Education Network (PLEN), an organization committed to the development of women in general and women in public life in particular. PLEN, which, among its other activities, sponsors student internships in Washington, D.C., lauded the college's efforts in leadership development. And as a member of the Board of the American Council on Education, she served on a committee reviewing congressional initiatives regarding volunteer service for college and university students. She was also involved in major projects regarding the teaching of foreign languages. This endeavor has held hope for establishing an endowment similar to the National Science Foundation and the National Endowment for the Humanities. President Pampusch was determined to keep the College of St. Catherine active in the Council for Independent Colleges. This group, organized to assist small colleges and universities, included the college in its studies and grant projects, and from 1991 to the present, Anita Pampusch has served as chair of its executive committee.

That the college be actively affiliated with national organizations for the promotion of Catholic higher education was important to college administrators and sponsors. President Pampusch was named to the Bishops and Presidents Committee of the Association of Catholic Colleges and Universities (ACCU), meeting twice annually to discuss issues involving Catholic institutions of higher education and their teaching function in relation to Church teachings.

Curriculum revision continued. Full implementation of the curriculum for the Minnesota Intercollegiate Nursing Consortium (MINC) was slated for fall 1989. Members of the St. Catherine nursing department had worked hard in collaboration with the other participating colleges to finalize that curriculum, though some members of the nursing faculty still expressed reservations about the program. Two years later the department did withdraw from this venture because of a difference in underlying philosophies and the cost of the program.

Another academic joint venture needing revision was the St. Catherine–St. Thomas communication/telecommunication/theater department. In the fall of 1990, the department, known by several names over the years, was discontinued as a joint venture. The two colleges maintained a joint theater program with shared costs, but each developed its own communication program. St. Thomas had plans to establish a telecommunication major, whereas the College of St. Catherine planned to focus on communications and rhetoric

After much dialog among faculty members of both St. Catherine campuses, the Montessori certificate program for preschool educators was transferred to St. Mary's Campus, which had developed an associate degree in early childhood development. This decision raised questions about Montessori accessibility to St. Catherine education majors and prompted the education department to explore ways of reintegrating that program into its curriculum. In December 1990, the Montessori Program was reinstated on the St. Catherine campus when the Montessori School and the Child Care Center became a combined Early Childhood Center. Consolidation of the two programs led to improved cost efficiency and a reduction of paperwork. Because of building renovations in Mendel Hall, the center was relocated on the ground floor of St. Mary Hall.

In response to student interest in professional departments and to the leadership thrust of the college administration, new master's programs were proposed. By 1991 proposals for master of arts degrees in nursing, social work (a joint program with St. Thomas), occupational therapy, and physical therapy (with the St. Mary's Campus) had received all necessary approvals for implementation. These would enrich the series of graduate programs—organizational leadership, theology, and the Nurse Practitioner Certificate—already in place.

The development of these programs had prompted their assessment in relation to the mission statement of the college. Study of the issue affirmed the trend with this statement in 1988-89: "The College of St. Catherine offers selected graduate programs in areas in which the college has developed a reputation for quality and has judged that it can fill an unmet educational need. All graduate programs are committed to excellence and to the integration of the liberal arts with the particular discipline. Central themes interwoven in these programs are: ethics and leadership, holistic view of the person, including the spiritual dimension; social justice; critical analysis; and interactive, integrative learning. These themes shape the graduate learning experience and reflect the mission of the College of St. Catherine."

Also examined were interrelated issues including graduate tuition, services to graduate students, compensation for faculty members teaching graduate courses, teaching load/release time for graduate teachers, expectations of graduate faculty for research and scholarly work, and research support.

Into the 1990s

At the threshold of a new decade, the College of St. Catherine reflected a Catholic Church modified by ecumenical orientations. A shift in the religious affiliation of its students was just one aspect of a gradual transition in the Catholic nature of the college. At the same time the decreased number of religious on the faculty and fewer religious on campus mirrored the declining number of Catholic priests, brothers, and sisters throughout the United States. The predominantly lay makeup of the college Board of Trustees, with two-thirds laypersons and one-third Sisters of St. Joseph, also reflected trends in the Church as a whole. The Sisters of St. Joseph, however, retained ultimate control of the college. Without their formal approval, property could not be sold, major debts could not be incurred, and the threefold college mission—that of a Catholic, women's, liberal arts college—could not be altered.

The fresh air of Vatican II had permeated the college community, opening decision-makers to the signs of the time and the needs of a changing world. Students were encouraged to acknowledge a creator and to connect with Him/Her through prayer and to serve others as they pursued spiritual realities. Being Catholic meant not only praying but also growing in love of God and neighbor. Theology courses developed from the 1960s emphasized the new orientation with greater thrust toward ecumenical studies, use of guest lecturers from other religious affiliations and theological orientations, and incorporation of contemporary theological and moral issues into class offerings and public lecture series. All of this put the St. Catherine theology department on the cutting edge.

The Catholic character of the college remained a special concern of sponsors and administrators throughout these changes. In the late 1980s, the college organized a Catholic Character Task Force and charged Campus Ministry with implementing its recommendations. These included increased attention to liturgical services, greater emphasis on social justice, recognition of the diverse religious traditions of students and entire college community, and attention to the expression of its Catholic character in curricular and noncurricular activities.

Academic affairs had claimed much attention during the 1980s, with graduate programs and the liberal arts receiving most attention. The policy for transfer students was revised to establish sound criteria for admission. A revised faculty constitution and by-laws was given final approval and made operative. Approval by the Higher Education Coordinating Board of Minnesota of four new master's degree programs—social work, nursing, occupational therapy, and physical therapy—was a major achievement. The North Central Accreditation Board, after a site visit in June 1990 to assure that the college could support these programs academically, financially, and in terms of its mission, gave final approval by the end of the year. The physical therapy graduate program was to be housed primarily on St. Mary's Campus in Minneapolis, the social work program on the St. Catherine and St. Thomas campuses, and the others on the St. Catherine campus.

The faculty had worked hard during the late 1980s to revise the liberal arts core after the college was selected by the Association of American Colleges as one of twenty-seven to participate in a nationwide project on the development of core curricula. Dean Marilou Eldred and faculty members from the Educational Policies Committee attended a national workshop in the summer of 1990, bringing back ideas and advice. Throughout 1990-91, faculty members and administrators continued to discuss and work on a new core curriculum.

The seriousness of the task plus the determination of faculty and staff to retain the liberal arts tradition in viable form lengthened the process. What configuration would the new list of required courses take? More interdisciplinary approaches to higher education seemed in order.

The St. Mary's Campus faculty was by 1990 moving toward a proposal for an associate of arts in liberal arts transfer degree. This degree, envisioned for students admitted at St. Mary's Campus with plans to transfer to a four-year college, favors transfer into the St. Catherine four-year liberal arts program and is consonant with its new transfer policy.

Initiatives addressing commitment to cultural diversity on both campuses became enrollment goals for the college. In 1989-90 minority enrollment was at about 10 percent for St. Mary's and 4 percent for the St. Catherine campus. The college aimed to increase both, hiring more staff members for minority support programs. For culturally diverse recruitment, the college implemented its 12 Point Plan, enthusiastically endorsed by the Board of Trustees. Funding was developed for continued operation of the plan as well as for Un Primer Paso. The 1990 opening faculty/staff workshop focused on cultural diversity.

At the same time, the president and dean of students initiated Leadership St. Catherine, a comprehensive cocurricular leadership program offering opportunities for leadership experience, involvement, and training. A leadership team including several successful alumnae in a variety of fields was organized to launch the program. The college received grants to implement this and other programs in community service, minority programs, volunteer programs, and alcohol education. In another leadership initiative, the development of a health care ethics program involved both campuses with the Riverside Medical Center, cosponsored by the Sisters of St. Joseph and the Fairview Health Corporation. Given the health care problems facing larger society, the college worked to assure a Catholic professional presence in the arena of ethics in health. The program was modeled on the ethics program for business and nonprofit agencies already in place at the college, with hopes that it might be included within a new Institute for Leadership.

To achieve a fuller leadership role in the community the college needed improved public relations, and that department underwent considerable change. An institutional marketing plan was prepared and targeted efforts were undertaken to enhance college advertising, visibility, and admissions efforts. Visits to editorial boards were used to bring attention to the college. College publications were reviewed and revised as appropriate. The alumnae magazine, *SCAN,* was oriented to the full constituency of the college, and *Currents,* a quarterly publication for donors and friends, was replaced by the *Leader,* a full-color newsletter with an increased audience and changed editorial focus.

The college achieved nationwide visibility toward the end of 1989-90, ironically because of the difficulties of Mills College in Oakland, California. That college decided to become coeducational, then reversed its decision after student protests, resulting in considerable media attention to the advantages and disadvantages of women's colleges. St. Catherine students played a leading role in drawing attention to the strengths of women's colleges. President Pampusch, chair of the Women's College Coalition, was widely interviewed and quoted on the national broadcasting networks. Coverage by local newspapers and the archdiocesan *Catholic Bulletin* put the college in a favorable light.

In spring 1991 the college opened a downtown center in Galtier Plaza, St. Paul. Eager to reach a diverse student population, the college began offering

---

The College of St. Catherine Leadership Statement

The College of St. Catherine is committed to the development of effective, ethical leaders. Through study, practice, and life experience, individuals have opportunities to enrich the knowledge, refine the skills, and clarify the attitudes essential for responsible action. In varied roles and settings, the College of St. Catherine leader:

- lives a commitment to the values of justice and caring
- acts from a strong self-concept
- thinks critically and creatively
- communicates and interacts effectively within groups
- takes risks willingly
- exercises power appropriately
- articulates a positive sense of direction
- and evokes hope.

credit and noncredit programs to students and professionals working in downtown St. Paul. A noon series entitled "Finding Balance in Work and Life: You Can Do It!" was well-received by working women, and the center offered credit courses on weekday evenings as well. Subjects included business, fiction, and communication. Students could take classes on a course-by-course basis or enroll in a degree or certificate program.

In 1989-90 the college moved toward a healthier financial situation, reaping the results of stronger financial management and controls, increasing income and decreasing expenses, and close surveillance over financial policies. That year saw an operating surplus, an increase in market value of the endowment and similar funds by nearly 25 percent, a decrease in long-term debt of 10 percent, and an increase in fund reserves of $400,000. Fundraising that year topped $2.4 million, good news for the college in the light of continued cutbacks in government tuition grants for higher education. The ability of the college to offer financial aid to prospective students was a key factor in recruitment for the next several years. Both campuses were prepared for the impact of legislation that would adversely affect enrollment in the early 1990s. This was a special challenge for St. Mary's Campus because of its large number of single parents and low-income students.

Challenges for the last decade of the twentieth century included strengthening the ties of two campuses by implementing and revising as appropriate their academic organization, particularly with regard to faculty personnel issues, joint appointments, and student policies, such as financial aid, billing, and transfer of credits.

With the capital "Campaign for St. Catherine's" well on its way, the renovation of Mendel Hall began during the summer of 1991. The groundbreaking for a new sports and fitness facility including a swimming pool was scheduled for the following year. By February 1992, total fundraising for the campaign had reached $11.8 million, 76 percent of the goal. The monies would finance Women in Science, Women in the Arts, and leadership initiatives, scholarships for students from diverse cultures, faculty development, and renovation of Old Main at St. Mary's Campus.

Above all, the College of St. Catherine aimed to develop a more humane and productive college environment. Plans included a pay-for-performance program for administrative staff and a merit system for support staff. Meetings and workshops on ethical leadership continued to focus on the threefold mission of the college as a constant common goal for all college constituents. President Anita Pampusch planned an expanded series of informal gatherings of faculty, staff, and students with a view toward meeting a broad cross-section of college community members so that their issues and concerns would continually be addressed.

With dedication and commitment, the college continued its challenge to women leaders in a changing world—to be women of faith, integrity, and cultural achievement, to better society, to pass on the dream, and continue to make the dream real.

A note about sources

Most of the sources used in preparing this volume are available in the College of St. Catherine (CSC) Archives in the St. Catherine Library. General sources include campus and alumnae publications—*Alumnae News, Ariston, The Catherine Wheel, College Bulletins* and *Catalogs, Currents, Etos, La Concha, The Lantern, The Leader,* and *SCAN*—as well as issues of *A.I.D. Dialogue, The Catholic Bulletin, One Voice* (Birmingham), *The American Library Association Bulletin, Minneapolis Star, The Highland Villager, St. Joseph Magazine, The National Catholic Council on Home Economics Bulletin,* and *News from the Ford Foundation.* Most uses have been cited in the text.

Research for chapters 1-4 included oral histories, transcripts of interviews with, written memoirs of, speeches by, and/or letters to and from Elizabeth Cochran, Mabel Frey, Agnes Keenan, Joseph Ryan, M.D., and Sisters of St. Joseph Bridget Bohan, Eucharista Galvin, Marie Philip Haley, Mary Edward Healy, Alberta Huber, Helen Joseph Sanschagrin, Teresita Judd, Agnes Rita Lingl, Antonius Kennelly, Antonia McHugh, Magdalen Schlmanski, Mona Riley, Alice Smith, and Antonine O'Brien; and from Mary Joseph Calasenz, SNJM. The quotations at the openings of chapters 1-4 are from the speeches or writings of Sisters Antonia McHugh, Eucharista Galvin, Mary William Brady, and Alberta Huber, respectively.

Research for chapters 1-5 included reports of administrative offices of the college including those of the president, academic dean, dean of students, and financial directors for the years discussed; reports of various academic departments, the library, student services, and language institutes; reports of various commissions, task forces, and studies of the college; of accrediting teams, foundations, building contractors, student organizations, and the Abigail Quigley McCarthy Center for Research, Resources, and Scholarship; as well as speeches, position papers, and intercollegiate and interlibrary reports. The opening quotation for chapter 5 is from a speech by Anita Pampusch.

For further reading, see the following:

Chase, Mary Ellen. *A Goodly Fellowship.* New York: Macmillan, 1939.

Goulet, Anna, CSJ. *A Pageant of Our Musical Heritage.* 2 vols. St. Paul: College of St. Catherine, 1936-37.

Graham, Clara, CSJ. *Works to the King.* St. Paul: North Central Publishing Company, 1950.

Harvey, Anne, CSJ. *Rhythms and Dances for Pre-School and Kindergarten.* New York: G. Schirmer, Inc., 1944.

Hurley, Helen Angela, CSJ. *On Good Ground.* Minneapolis: University of Minnesota, 1951.

Kennelly, Karen, CSJ. "The Dynamic Sister Antonia and the College of St. Catherine." *Ramsey County History,* Fall-Winter 1973.

Peck, Helen Margaret, CSJ. "Growth and Expansion." Unpublished manuscript. CSC Archives Box 22.

Schmidt, George. *The Liberal Arts College: A Chapter in American Cultural History.* New Brunswick, New Jersey: Rutgers University Press, 1957.

Toomey, Teresa, CSJ. "Chapters for a History of the College of St. Catherine." Unpublished manuscript. CSC Archives Box 8.

Woody, Thomas. *A History of Women's Education in the United States.* New York: The Science Press, 1929.

Index

All sisters listed here and throughout this volume are members of the Sisters of St. Joseph of Carondelet (CSJ) unless indicated otherwise. Other names by which individual sisters have been known are shown in parentheses. Alumnae are listed in the index by their current names.

Aberwald, Ruth Weber, 42
Abigail Quigley McCarthy Center for Women's Research, Resources and Scholarship, 124-25; programs, 132; resources and scholarship, 131
Abzug, Bella, 88, 124
Accreditation, 31; education, 67, 117; evaluation process and, 66-68; funding and, 7-8; music department, 117; nursing department, 117; Organizational Leadership master's program, 129
ACTC. *See* Associated Colleges of the Twin Cities (ACTC)
Adath Jeshurun Synagogue (Minneapolis, MN), 87
Adler, Mortimer, 50
Administration and administrators, 114, 120-21; change in, 63-64, 126; future planning and, 127; organization, 134; and St. Mary's merger, 128
Administration Center, 126
Administrative Council, REAP and, 122
Admissions (*See also* Enrollment): transfer students and, 136
Adult education (*See also* Continuing education; Reentry Adult Program (REAP)): development of, 37-38; faculty, 109
Advertising. *See* Public relations
Afro-Americans. *See* Minority students
Ahern, Reverend Barnabas, CP, 75
Ahern, Pamela, 81
Akes, Sheryl, 94
Alberta, The (student housing), 100
Allers, Rudolph, 50
Alonso, Madre Elena de Cruz Vincente (Sister Helen of the Cross), RMM, 104
Alumnae Lending Library, 38
Alumnae News Letter, 20, 37
American Association of University Women, 7
American Council on Education, 34, 134
American Library Association, Board, 66-67

Anderson, Hurst, 55
Angers, Reverend Joseph, OP, 50, 81
Appleby, Barbara, 124
Archbishop Ireland Educational Fund, 19
Area Studies program: development, 56-57, 76-77; enrollment, 57; faculty, 56-57, 63, 75; Fine Arts Festival and, 57; funding, 96; grants, 77; televised classes, 65
Ariston, 120; format, 3; on accreditation, 8; on Homecoming, 20; on library, 22; on Sister Antonia, 28-29; on WWI, 18
Armajani, Yahya, 56
Armsey, James W., 82
Armstrong, Earl, 34-35, 68; teacher education curriculum and, 35-36
Armstrong, Jack, 97
Arntson, Mie Nkatsu, 80
Art department: building, 99-100; development of, 14-15; faculty, 14-15, 48, 71; in Mendel Hall, 22
Ashton, Sister Alberta (Mary Madonna), 44
Associated Colleges of the Twin Cities (ACTC), 97
Association of American Colleges, 7, 121
Association of Catholic Colleges and Universities (ACCU), Bishops and Presidents Committee, 135
Association of Collegiate Alumnae, 20
Association of Minnesota Colleges, 28
Auditoriums. *See* Jeanne d'Arc Auditorium; O'Shaughnessy Auditorium
Augsburg College (Minneapolis, MN), 105; Associated Colleges of the Twin Cities, member, 97; East Asian studies, 96; library consortium member, 95
Auxiliary Services, 121, 126

Baccalaureate Mass, 46
Bacigalupo, Dave, 24
Bambenek, Helen Boening, 39
Bandas, Reverend Rudolph, 49
Barbeau, M. Marius, 48
Bardon, Sister Frances Clare, 3

Barrett, Lawrence, 93-94
Baumgartner, Sister Aline, 55
Baumgartner, Very Reverend Monsignor, 114
Beaubien, Celine Abbott, 47
Bendel, Kay Sullivan, 99
Bennett, John, 77
Bergh, Kjell, 80
Bergh, Mary Rose Ryan [Mrs. Kjell], 79-80, 82
Berghs, Sister Monica, 2
Bergstrom, Jennifer, 120
Berrigan, Reverend Daniel, SJ, 98
Berthiaume, Marie Brule [Mrs. Fred], 60
Berthiaume, Sister Stella Marie, 47, 61, 74; scholarships, 65
Bethany, 126
Bethel College: library consortium member, 95
Bethune, Ade, 50
Bettendorf, Nadia Saad, 80
Biales, Albert, 95
Big-Little Sister Luncheon, 46
Big Sister program, 97
Binz, Archbishop Leo, 76
Biology department, 116; faculty, 49
Birder, Cecil, 27
Blackhurst, Ruby, 16
Bledsoe, Jacqueline Bowman, 105
Board of Trustees, 116, 126; duties, 19; first meeting, 19; future planning and, 127; members, 19, 76, 136; number, 113
Bohan, Sister Bridget, 2, 8
Bohnet, Agnes Belair, 47
Bolton, Mother Margaret, 33
Bonemeyer, Sister Cecilia, 40, 68
Bonnett, Sister Jeanne Marie, 9, 31; death, 69; education, 9; general education curriculum and, 35; and occupational therapy department, 47-48; religious instructor, 32-33; student teaching curriculum and, 36
Boog, Sister Berissima, 14
Boughman, Ruby, 16

143

Bourgois, Irene, 6
Bowers, Susan, 124
Boyce, Barbara, 95
Boyd, Reverend Angelus, OP, 81
Bracamonte, Laura Ines, 79
Brady, Sister Mary William, 47, 60, 115; background and education, 63; libraries and, 72-73; on Catholic education, 70; on library school evaluation, 67; on liturgy, 86; on the College of St. Catherine, 114; as president, 24, 63-64; television classes and, 65
Brady, Archbishop William O., 37, 49, 63-64, 73, 75; death, 76
Brandt, Reverend Gavin, OFM CAP, 107
Brandt, Marion Connole, 6
Brandt, Mary O'Connor, 108
Breidenback, Gertrude Nelson, 51
Britts, Therese Bailey, 105
Broderick, Mary, 128-29
Brombach, Ruth Haag, 127
Brown, Wes, 93
Bryan, Wilhelmus, 55
Buckanaga, Gertrude, 105-6
Bullock, Reverend William, 76
Burgess, Linda, 104
Burns, Mary Jo Lamb, 69
Burton, Evangeline, 97
Burton, Marion Leroy, 19
Burton, Richard, 10
Busch, Reverend William, 32
Bush Foundation, 121
Busian, Lillian Lord, 20
Business administration department, 91; College of St. Thomas and, 93, 103; continuing education, 110; degrees, 94; development, 116; enrollment, 122 evening classes, 125; faculty, 91
Butler, Nicholas Murray, 40
Butler, Robert, 42, 65
Butler, Sandra Kamman, 99
Buttrick, Wallace, 19
Byrne, Donald, 89
Byrne, Archbishop James J., 62, 80

Caecilian Hall, 19, 21; music library in, 72; renovation, 120
Calasenz, Sister Mary Joseph, SNJM, 4
Cameron, Sister Mary Ellen, 54-55
Campus (*See also* Galtier Plaza center; St. Mary's Campus of the College of St. Catherine), 17; Dew Drop, 21, 24; fencing, 20; gates, frontispiece, 20; gardens, 23-24; landscaping, 19; location, 1-3
Campus Ministry, 107-9; development of, 123-24; programs, 130, 136; and Social Justice ministry, 108-9
Caniaux-Reed, Marie-Thérèse, 64, 79
Cardinal, Barbara, 51
Carlin, Thomas, 113
Carmody, Marcia Black, 51
Carnel, Sister Margaret (Mary Cecilia), 20
Carroll, Dr. William C., 19, 42
Cashman, Mary McNally, 7
Castaneda, Julio, 77, 81
Catherine Wheel, The, 120; on Our Lady of Peace shrine, 45; on pageants, 27; on post WWII era, 45; on St. Joseph Hall, fundraising, 60-61; on theology curriculum, 89; on WWII, 40-41

Catholic Character Task Force, 136
Catholic Association for International Peace, 40
Catholic Bulletin: on enrollment, 19; on Mendel Hall, 22; on Our Lady of Victory Chapel, 20; on St. Catherine's buildings, 17; St. Catherine's advertising in, 2, 6
Catholic Church (*See also* Liturgical movement): lay participation, 89, 91-92; liturgy, 86, 89, 107-8; peace movement and, 40; Vatican II, influence of, 86-87, 91-92, 107, 118, 136; women and, 126; women's movement and, 91-92
Catholic Extension Society, 26
Catholic Evidence Guild, 50
Catholic Worker, 50
Center for Ethics, Responsibilities, and Values, 127
Center for Senior Citizens' Education, 129
Cerri, Evelyn [Mrs. Salvatore], 24
Cerri, Salvatore, 17, 24
Chaix, Mary Frances O'Grady, 47
Chapel. *See* Our Lady of Victory Chapel
Chase, Mary Ellen, 10-11, 50; on maintenance, 24; on Sister Antonia, 28
Chaves, Jose Maria, 77
Chavis, Geri, 124-25
Chemistry department: expansion, 85; facilities, 23 faculty, 10, 17, 43, 50, 58, 69-70, 89, 121; grants, 70; research program, 69-70; Sister Marie James on, 69; students, 116, 138
Chester, Sister Vera, 89-90
Child care facilities, 22, 135
Choral works, 86-87
Choruses, 86-87
Christian-Jewish relations, 86-87
Christmas Party, 46
Civil rights movement, 85, 88
Clark, Alice, 60
Classics department, 9-11
Classrooms, 5
Cleaver, Eldridge, 105
CLIC. *See* Cooperating Libraries in Consortium (CLIC)
Cochran, Elizabeth, 32
Coeducation, controversy, 87, 102-3
Cole, Reverend Russan, OMF, 86
College Association Governing Board (CAGB), 97
College Bulletin, 6, 15
College Center Planning Committee, 126
College Hall. *See* Whitby Hall
College of St. Thomas. *See* University of St. Thomas
Colwell, James, 77
Committee on Women's Studies, 125
Computer facilities and services: academic computing, 121; computer center, 125; staff, 125
Computer science, 121
Concordia College, 95
Confraternity of Christian Doctrine (CCD), 32-33, 81
Connole, Reverend Roger, 54-55
Consortium for the Advancement of Private Higher Education (CAPHE), 132-33
Continuing Education: curriculum, 117, 122; development of, 122-23
Convocations, 18, 50

Cooperating Libraries in Consortium (CLIC), 95-97
Corrigan, Mairead, 115
Corrigan, Marie, 75-76, 109
Cortot, Alfred-Denis, 9
Coughlan, Sister Helen (Jeremy), 60, 92
Coughlan, Katherine Callaghan [Mrs. T. Merritt], 60, 73
Coughlan, Thomas, Jr., 116
Coughlan, T. Merritt, 60
Council for Independent Colleges, 134
Craigie, Henry, 12
Crandall Hall, 100
Crawford, Jacqueline, 110
CREATE, 128
Credit for Academically Relevant Learning (CARL), 110
Crowdy, Dame Rachel, 26
Cullen, Mary Tester, 70
Culver, Dwight, 85
Cummings, Genevieve (Sister Miriam Joseph), 69
Curie, Irene, 14
Curie, Marie, 14
Curriculum (*See also* Honors programs, *and* under individual departments), 103; Christian humanistic thought, 116; cooperative studies, 33-35; development, 9-10, 33-34, 85; high school enrichment program, 129; humanities classes, 33-34; initial curriculum, 2; interdisciplinary courses, 116; international study, 132; language study, 25; liberal arts curriculum, 116, 121-22, 127, 136-37; MAOL, 132; Native American studies, 105-6; postsecondary program, 129; revision, 135-37; Women in America, 92; Women in Art, 92; women's studies, 125, 131; WWII era, 30
Curriculum Committee, 67, 70
Cushman, Robert, 10

Dahm, Sister Mary Therese, 65
Daly, Reverend John P., SJ, 102
Damianos, His Beatitude Archbishop, 115
Dances, 46
Daniewicz, Catherine, 69
Daves, Allayne, 71
Dawn-to-Dusk Read-a-Thon, 93
Day at St. Catherine's, A, 7
Day, Dorothy, 50
Day, Mary Kee Kersten, 124
D'Costa, Martha, 79
de Hueck, Baroness Catherine, 50
DeHorn, William, 10
De Koninck, Charles, 50, 88
Denis, Sybil Murray, 105
Denny, Eleanor McCahill, 7
Depression (1930s), 31
Derham Hall, viii, 21, 76; addition, 17; elevator, 26-27; facilities in, 120; library in, 72; naming of, 2; statuary, 20
Derham, Hugh, 2, 14
De Smedt, Imogene, 81
Devaux, Sister Marthe (Madelaine Alice), 25, 27
Dew Drop, 21, 24
Dezurik, Florence, 51
Dillery, Louise Gradstein, 52
Dillon, Michael J., 19
Dillon, Sara, 133

Dinessen, Lois, 46
Diocesan Teachers' College, 54-55
Dionne, Elzire, 60
Dionne, Oliva, 60
Dionne Quintuplets, 60
Doherty, Reverend Richard, 49
Dolan, Mary Frances Hay, 51
Donahue, Reverend Thomas C., 66
Dormitories, 2, 17-19, 45, 100-101, 120; post WWII era, 45-46; regulations, 46; security, 46
Dougherty, Charles, 114
Dowling, Archbishop Austin, 19, 21, 31; on Our Lady of Victory Chapel, 20
Drama department (*See also* Speech-theatre department): development of, 39; during WWII years, 44; faculty, 38-39, 60, 71; golden jubilee productions, 62; productions, viii, 44, 71
Dress, Sister Eulalia, 2
Duchâteau, Françoise Seidenstein, 64-65
Dunkel, Harold, 33
Dupré, Marcel, 9
Durand, Ruth Sawyer, 72
Durkin, Patricia Connolly, 114
Dwyer, John, 134

Early Childhood Center, 135
East Asian studies, 96
Eckes, Sister Jean Ann, 55
Eckes, Sister Maxine, 107-8
Economics department, 116
Ecumenical movement, 86-88
Ederer, Grace Mary, 40
Educational organizations, affiliation, 134-35
Educational Policies Committee (EPC), 67, 119, 136
Education department: accreditation, 67, 117; continuing education, 110; curriculum, 91; Diocesan Teachers' College and, 54-55; early childhood education, 117; elementary education, 117; enrollment, 122; faculty, 9, 16, 91, 106; in Mendel Hall, 22; Montessori School, 91, 135; preschool education, 16, 91, 135; secondary education, 117; St. Paul Public Schools and, 36; student teaching, 35-36; teacher education, 34-36, 67-68
Eisenmenger, Sister Angela Therese, 41
Elderhostel, 117, 122
Eldred, Marilou, 124; as dean, 120, 129; liberal arts curriculum and, 136; vice president, administration, 131
Ellard, Gerald, 32
Ellerbe and Company, 60
Ellis, Reverend John Tracy, SJ, 50
Emmans, Reverend Edward, OP, 49-50
Emmer, Sister Joanne, 55
Engaged Encounter, 108
English department: faculty, 9, 11, 37, 57, 75; interdisciplinary courses, 116; televised classes, 65
Enrollment, 6, 63; decline, 118; initial enrollment, 2-3; post WWII era, 45, 51, 53; recruiting and, 6-7; transfer students, 132; WWII veterans, 45; WWII years, 19, 43
Esterka, Reverend Peter, 89
Etos, 120
Eucharistic Day, 46, 80
Evans, Maureen, 131, 134

Evening classes, 91
Evening College, 125-26

Faculty (*See also* under individual departments), 139; budget cuts and, 118-19; certification requirements, 6; characteristics of, 10-11; constitution and by-laws, 136; education, 8; evaluation, 66; graduate faculty, 135; honors, 125; international faculty, 25-26; international fellowships, 64; lay faculty, 9-11, 118, 136; letters, 11-12; M. E. Chase on, 10-11; number of, 53; salaries, 64, 85; scholarships, 65; social issues activism, 106-7; and St. Mary's merger, 128-29; teaching duties, 8-10
Fane, Reverend Kevin, OP, 108, 113
Far East Area Institute, 77
Farr, Sister Charitas, 8
Farrell, Reverend Allan, SJ, 67-68
Feeney, Tim, 24
FIG, 124
Financial aid, 6, 85, 126, 138; administration, 126; scholarships, 7, 25, 79, 122
Fine Arts Festival, 57, 72
Flynn, Very Reverend Monsignor Vincent, 55-56
Fogarty, Sister James Agnes, 41, 62, 107; scholarships, 65
Foley, Reverend Edward, OFM CAP, 107-8, 113
Foley, Sister Gertrude, 117
Fonseca, Jaime, 77
Fontbonne Fair, 60-61
Fontbonne Hall, 44; custodians, 24; departments in, 23; funding, 23; Katycombs, 107
Fontbonne, Mother St. John, 23
Food service, 23-24, 25; buildings, 59-60
Ford Foundation, grants, 64, 82-83, 85, 99
Ford, Guy Stanton, 31
Foreign languages: expansion, 85; language laboratory, 63, 97
Foreign students, 52, 58, 79-80, 103-4; scholarships, 25; Sister Antonia and, 25; Sister Mona Riley on, 25
Founding, 1-3, 54; diamond jubilee, 114-15; golden jubilee, 61-62; initial funding, 2
France: summer language institutes in, 78-79
Freeman, Elizabeth, 51
Freeman, Reverend Hilary, OP, 88
French department, 10, 31; faculty, 77-78; language laboratory, 63; summer institute, 77-79
Freshman Assembly, 46
Frey, Mabel Meta, 38-39, 44
Friedan, Betty, 85, 88, 92
Funds and fundraising, 125, 132-33; accreditation and, 7-8; alumnae association and, 20; Area Studies, 96; Associated Colleges of the Twin Cities, 97; budget cuts, 118-19; buildings, construction and expansion, 17-18, 59-60; Campaign for St. Catherine's, 138; Center for Ethics, Responsibilities, and Values, 127; chemistry department grants, 70; cooperative classes, 93; debt consolidation, 42; endowment, 7, 19-20; financial management, 138; Fine Arts Center, 99; Fontbonne Hall, 23; Ford Foundation grant, 64, 82-83, 85, 99; and founding, 2; grants, 64, 121; humanities grants, 68; Jeanne d'Arc

Funds and fundraising (*continued*)
Auditorium, 100; language institutes, 77-79; language laboratory, 63; Lending library, 38; lay mission group, 81; liberal arts, interdisciplinary courses, 116; resource allocation and, 132-33; St. Joseph Hall, 60-61; St. Mary Hall, 75; student activities and, 26-27
Furay, Sally, RSCJ, 102
Furfey, Reverend Paul Hanly, 43
Furnishings, 2-3

Gallahue, Sister Candida, 23-24, 25
Galloway, Judith, 114
Galtier Plaza center, 137-38
Galvin, Mother Eucharista, 36; and Area Study, 56; and drama department, 38; education and background, 32; as missionary, 43; on Catholic education, 32; on WWII, 40-41; as president, 31-32, 50; as trustee, 42; WWII, war effort and, 41-42
Galvin, Loretto, 6
Gamble, Modesta Reichert, 6
Garris, Michael, 121
Gavin, Eileen, 125
General education, cooperative study, 33-34
Georgia, The (student housing), 100
Gerendasy, Carrie, 124
German department, 18
Germany: Nazis in, 12-13, 31
Gibbons, Sister Christina, 65
Gibbons, Sister Marie James, 17; and Area Study, 56; as dean, 85; on chemistry department, 69; and St. Joseph Hall, fundraising, 60; travel, 56; undergraduate chemistry research and, 69-70
Gibbons, Sister Seraphim, 65, 93; computer curriculum and, 96; and housing, 100
Gideon, Ann, 60
Gilligan, Reverend Francis J., 36-37
Glarner, Valerie Nash, 82
Glasow, Glen, 68
Gleason, Sister Angele, 9, 12-13, humanities program and, 68; Latin American Institute and, 77; and Liturgy Club, 32; travel, 56
Glenn, Clara, 31
Goerdt, Jean, 86
Goldstein, Jacob, 87
Gonzaga, Reverend Mother Agnes, 21
Goodman, Rabbi Arnold, 87
Goodwin, Larry, 89, 110, 121-22
Gorrilla, Kristine Smyth, 97
Gottlieb, Jack, 87
Gott, Reverend Camillus, OFM, 107
Goulet, Sister Anna, 9, 21; education, 13; music department and, 39
Graduate programs, 58-59, 136; enrollment, 132; evaluation, 66; expansion, 135; library school, 58-59; Master of Arts in Organizational Leadership (MAOL), 129; nursing, 136; occupational therapy, 136; physical therapy, 136; social work, 136; theology, 121-22, 125
Graebner, Alan, 125; and Honors Program, 130; on coeducation, 102-3
Graham, Sister Clara, 8-9
Grainger, Percy, 27
Gray, Hanna, 116
Great Northern Railway, 6
Green, Curtis, 99

Griffiths, G. H., 82
Griswold, Sister Teresa Joseph, 9
Growe, Joan Anderson, 106
Gudgel, Jennette, 117
Guest, Judith, 125
Gurrola-Dorado, Elizabeth, 132
Gustavus Adolphus College: Minnesota Intercollegiate Nursing Consortium, member, 129
Guthrie, Sister Ste. Helene, 8, 11, 21; as dean, 9; drama department and, 38; education, 9

Haaker, Mary Helen Thornton, 24
Haggerty, Melvin, 10
Hale, Phyllis, 24
Haley, Sister Geraldine (Marie Philip), 5; and language laboratory, 63; and NDEA French institutes, 78; as Fulbright adviser, 64; curriculum and, 34; education, 9-10; French summer institutes and, 78; in Georgia, 90; on international outreach, 25; on social work, 16; on theatrical activities, 27
Hamaya, Yukiko, 80
Hamline University: cooperative library program and, 55-56; library consortium member, 95; student housing at, 100
Hand, Patricia, 105
Hanley, Sister Mary Ann (Nathaniel), 77
Harman, Althea Ashton, 47
Harper, William Rainey, 4
Hart, Rosemary, 114, 120
Harvey, Sister Ann, 16, 28
Hasbrouck, Sister Mary, 128
Hashisaki, Mary Jane Kinoshita, 41
Health Center. *See* Fontbonne Hall
Healy, Sister Mary Edward: and Area Study, 56; as dean, 63-64; as president, 75-76, 83, 90-91; background and education, 75; death, 83; Ford Foundation grant and, 82; general education curriculum and, 35; library and, 73; provincial superior, 83; refugee work, 99; scholarships and, 65; social sciences teacher, 35, 37
Heckman, A. J., 56
Hedges Marguerite Gignac, 99-100
Hegranes, Colleen, 131
Heimel, Judy, 92
Helmich, Andrew, 96
Helton, Sonia Daleki, 58
Hennessy, Sister Elerius, 23-25
Henry, Edward, 102
Henry, Kathleen Pull, 47
Hensien, Dorothy Bartelme, 35
Hessian, Marguerite, 117
Higher Education Coordinating Board of Minnesota, 136
High school, 76
Hilger, Sister M. Inez, 65
Hilgers, Sister Karen, 131
Hill, Emma Mae Blackwell, 105
Hill Family Foundation (*See also* Northwest Area Foundation): Area Studies funding, 77, 96; Associated Colleges of the Twin Cities (ACTC), funding, 97; cooperative classes, funding, 93; humanities grants, 68; libraries, funding, 55
Hill, James J., 54-55
Hill Reference Library: Area Study program and, 56-57; libraries, cooperative programs and, 55-56, 95

Hill, Reverend Thomas, OFM CAP, 107
Hinkle, Margaret Rose Polga, 79
History department, 71
Hitler, Adolf, 13
Hogan, Sister Edith, 2
Holmberg, Sister Ansgar, 55
Homecoming, 19-20, 120
Home economics department, 60, 62
Honorary societies, 70; Delta Mu Delta, 128; Delta Phi Lambda, 32; Iota Sigma Pi, 17; Kappa Gamma Pi, 32, 38; Phi Beta Kappa, 16, 31, 70, 81-82; Pi Gamma Mu, 31
Honors Committee, 129
Honors Day Assembly, 46
Honors programs, 129-30; faculty, 70-71, 129-30; Honors at Entrance program, 71; Honors Reading program, 70-71, 129; retreats, 130
Hoover, President Herbert, 28
Houglet, Christiane, 79
Houle, Sister Victoria, 68
Howard, Sister Celestine, 2
Howell, Sister Sharon, 132
Huber, Sister Alberta (Fides), 67, 111; background and education, 85; coeducation and, 102-3; honors, 111; Honors Reading program and, 70; housing named for, 100; humanities curriculum and, 68; on Allayne Daves, 71; on weekend college, 110; as president, 85, 93, 99, 103-4, 109; retirement, 113; and Weekend College, 122
Humanities program: curriculum, 33-34, 68; expansion, 85; faculty, 68; grants for, 68
Humbert, Vernon, 34
Humphrey, Vice President Hubert H., 98
Hurley, Doran, 74
Hurley, Sister Helen Angela, 32
Hurley, Sister Regina (Jeanne d'Arc), 6, 9, 13
Hutchins, Robert, 50
Hynnek, Joann Kvasnicka, 70

Information management, 121
Institute of International Education, 64
Interim, 117; development of, 94-95; discontinued, 119; faculty, 95
Ireland, Archbishop John, 21; founding of St. Catherine's and, 1-3; *The Church and Modern Society*, 2
Ireland, Mother Ellen (Seraphine), 19, 21, 116; founding of the College of St. Catherine and, 1-3
Irish, Jane, 46

Japanese Americans, 41
Jeanne d'Arc Auditorium, 18, 62, 100
Jewish-Christian relations, 86-87
Joe, Mamie Lee, 41
Johnson, Gunnar, 99
Johnson, Hildegard, 66
Johnson, Monica Carle, 92
Johnson, President Lyndon Baines, 85, 98
Johnson, Sister Marie Inez, 39, 65, 74
Johnston, Scott, 66, 76-77
John XXIII, Pope, 86
Jones, Jim, 125
Jose, Sister Marie, 39
Judd, Charles, 7-8
Judd, Sister Teresita, 16-17, 49, 90
Jude, James, 34
Junior Tea, 46

Kacmarcik, Frank, 124
Kalatsu, Sister Madeline Marie, 80
Kane, Sister Teresa, 131
Kapsner, Jacqueline Kavaney, 69
Keating, Sister Anysia, 14
Keefe, Herbert H., 42
Keenan, Agnes, 9, 33, 51, 67; background and education, 37; general education curriculum and, 35; library school and, 59; on Catholic education, 36
Keenan, Reverend Edward, 37
Keenan, Sister Immaculata: and Alumnae Lending Library, 38; education, 37; English, teaching, 37
Kelly, Anne Dolan, 38
Kelly, Mother Agnes Gonzaga, 42
Kennedy, President John F., 85
Kennedy, Senator Robert F., 98
Kennelly, Sister Antonius, 9-10; adult education and, 37; background and education, 43; building expansion and, 59-60; education, 12-14; general education curriculum and, 35; letters, 12-13; and occupational therapy department, 47; as president, 17, 43, 50; retirement, 50; student teaching curriculum and, 36
Kennelly, Sister Karen, 93, 128
Kenney, Katherine Moroney, 7
Kerby, Sister Margaret, 3
Kessler, Sister Catherine (Lucina), 57, 87; Latin American Institute and, 77; scholarships and, 65
Kingman, Richmond, 81
King, Martin Luther, 98
Klasse, George, 10
Knapp, Leona, 6
Koch, Dr. Michael, 79
Kranz, Mary Ruhr, 33, 44
Kresge Foundation, 100
Kreuter, Gretchen, 93
KTCA-TV (public television), 65-66
Kuhlman, A. F., 56

Labin, Rosemary, 121
La Concha (See also *Etos*), 26, 51
Lacourciere, Luc, 48
LaFarge, Reverend John, SJ, 32
Lammers, Dolores Bowman, 34
Lang and Raugland, 73
Lange, Austin, 73
Langevin, Elizabeth Dusek, 51
Language laboratory. *See* Foreign languages
Lantern, 27
La Pointe, Maridee Johnson, 31
La Qua, Sister Edouarda, 36
Larney, Barbara Elden, 125
Laroche-Theune, Regina, 132
Lasich, Celeste, 124
Latin American Institute, 77
Laughlin, Lucille Bettenburg, 91, 103
Lawrence, Jane Schroeder, 74
Lay Apostolate, 81
Lay missionaries, 23-24, 81
Lay Mission Group, 81
Leadership St. Catherine, 137
League of Women Voters, 26; St. Catherine League, 40
LeBon, Karen, 121
LeBuffe, F. P., 32
Leeman, Richard, 65
Lefebvre, Sister Leon, 48

Legal structure (*See also* Trustees): amendment, 42; bylaws, 42; incorporation, 3
Legarda, Carmen, 52
Le Roux, Michel, 78-79
Lesterson, Sheila Krueger, 105
Le Sueur, Meridel, 131
Leverone, Genevieve Ozark, 35
Lewis, Mary Jane, 51
Liberal arts: curriculum, 116, 121-22, 127, 136-37; curriculum study, 54
Liberal Arts Task Force, 121
Librarians, 22, 39
Libraries: *Ariston* on, 22; Charlotte Hill Slade collection, 72; collection, 22; computer center in, 125; consortium, *See* Cooperating Libraries in Consortium (CLIC); construction, 73-74; cooperative library program, 55-56; donations to, 72; evaluation, 66-67; facilities, 73-75; in chapel, 21-22; in Derham Hall, 21; music library, 72; remodeling, 125; reserve library, 39; Ruth Sawyer collection, 72; Sister Antonia McHugh Collection, 72
Library science department (*See also* Information management): accreditation, 22, 58-59, 66-67; in chapel, 21-22; computer curriculum, 96; continuing education, 110; faculty, 22, 57-59; in Fontbonne Hall, 23; master's program, 58-59; undergraduate program, 67
Lincoln, Sister Eleanor (Mary Edmund), 57, 113; Honors Reading program and, 70; televised classes, 65; on Weekend College, 110-11
Lindfors, Vivica, 92
Lindgren, Amelia, 124
Lingl, Sister Agnes Rita, 8, 77; education, 9, 12-14; letters, 12-13
Linn, Sister Mary Jane, 65, 69
Litecky, Sister Catherine (Paul), 58, 71, 90
Liturgical movement, 32, 34, 48
Loftus, Marguerite, 99
Long, Doris (Kathy) Kathryn, 109
Loome, Thomas, 89
Lord, Ellen, 31
Lowry, Douglas, 121
Luedtke, David, 125
Lukoskie, Estella Whittaker, 47
Lupori, Catherine Pribyl [Mrs. Peter], 57, 110, 125, 131; crucifix, library, 75; wedding, 71; and women's center, 131
Lupori, Peter, 60; background and education, 48; crucifix, library, 75; humanities curriculum and, 68; St. Catherine medal, design, 115; St. Joseph statue, 61; sculpture class, 122; wedding, 71; works, 48
Luther, Betty, 33
Luther College (Decorah, IA), 116

Macalester College (St. Paul, MN): Associated Colleges of the Twin Cities, member, 97; cooperative library program and, 55-56, 95
McAulay, Sister DeLourdes, 54-55
McAuley, Sister Philomene, 15
McBean, Dorothy, 105
McCaffrey, Lawrence, 68
McCahill, Lt. Commander Eugene P., 42
McCahill, Mary Rahilly [Mrs. James], 11, 19
McCarthy, Abigail Quigley, 93; adult education and, 38; curriculum and, 33; English, teaching, 37; on Catholic women's education, 88; on women and church, 124
McCarthy, Senator Eugene, 37, 98
McCarthy, Monsignor Louis J., 49, 73
McClosky, Robert, 72
McConnell, Reverend John M., MM, 75
McDermott, Sister Eva, 8-9
McDonald, Grace, 125
McGaa, Ed, 106
McGovern, Ritamary Reynolds, 34
McHugh, Patrick, 3
McHugh, Sister Antonia, 2, 11, 114, 116; *Ariston* on, 28-29; background and education, 3-5, 8; as dean, 3, 6-9, 17; death, 28; education, views on, 28; libraries and, 72; M. E. Chase on, 28; on Fontbonne Hall, 23; on musical events, 27; as president, 9, 21, 42; resignation, 28; retirement, 31; and students' religious life and training, 32; as teacher, 5; travel and, 24-25; as trustee, 42; WWI years, 18-19
McKeown, Anne Condon Collopy, 31-32, 78
Mackey, Sister Marie Teresa, 14
Mackey, Mother St. Rose, 21
McKnight Foundation: grants, 127
McLaughlin, Kathleen, 127
McLean, Jeanne, 131, 134
McMahon, E. (Edward) M., 19
McNamee, Sister Catherine: background and education, 113; budget cuts and, 118-19; pilgrimage, 115; as president, 113-14, 116, 125-126; and SLRP, 131
McVay, Genevieve Ahern, 31
Mahood, Dorothy, 42
Mahowald, Sister Agnes Leon, 43, 69
Maliwa, Emily, 58
Malloy, Gertrude, 3
Malone, Kathleen Daly, 39
Mamer, Catherine Murray, 79-80
Management Development Center for Women (*See also* Weekend College), 110, 117, 122
Manion, Sister Cecilia, 9
Marcel, Gabriel, 88
Marieb, Reverend Raymond, OP, 81
Martin, Mary, 74
Mary Hall, 100
Marzolf, Sister Marie Cecilia, 22, 58-59
Masterman, Helen, 42
Master's program. *See* Graduate programs
Matchinsky, Sister Marie Jose, 22
Mathematics department, 116; computer curriculum, 96; expansion, 85; faculty, 96
Matsuo, Ruth, 41
May Fete, 45-46, 83, 97; cancellation, 98; floats, 52
Meade, Charles, 3
MECC. *See* Minnesota Educational Computing Consortium (MECC)
Mee, Marvel, 41
Mendel, Gregor, 14
Mendel Hall, 14; computer facilities in, 96; construction, 22; greenhouses, 24; laboratories, 23; Mendel Tower, physics facilities, 129; renovation, 135, 138
Meyers, Betty Ann, 33
Meynell, Alice, 37

Michel, Sister Eleanore, 9, 31, 47; alumnae association and, 20; education, 10; German department and, 18; on WWII Armistice, 45
Michel, Reverend Virgil, 32
Michels, Eileen Manning, 93
Micka, Sister Mary Virginia, 57, 114; humanities program and, 68; writings, 57-58
Migrant workers, 106-7
Mikschl, Hilary, 6
Millay, Edna St. Vincent, 8
Miller, Agatha Hynes, 14-15
Miller, Florence Sletner, 51
Millis, Charlotte, 77
Mills College (Oakland, CA), 137
Minahan, Nancy Ploncinsky, 70
Miner, Janet, 127
Minnesota Chamber Orchestra, 133
Minnesota Educational Computing Consortium (MECC)
Minnesota Intercollegiate Nursing Consortium (MINC), 135
Minnesota Library Information Network (MINITEX), 96
Minnesota Opera Company, 133
Minnesota Orchestra, 100, 133
Minnesota Private College Council, 65
Minnesota Public Interest Research Group (MPIRG), 125
Minnesota Women's Consortium, 131
Minority students, 132, 137; African-American students, 37, 105, 132; discrimination, 37; Hispanic students, 118, 123, 132; Japanese American students, 41; Native Americans, 105-6, 132; Un Primer Paso, 118, 123
Missia, Father Francis, 21
Mission and objectives, 3, 54, 139; education of women, 87-88; graduate programs and, 135; liberal arts tradition, 126-27; religious observations, 80-81; Vatican II and, 86-87; women and, 131
Missionary Sisters of the Most Holy Trinity, 6
Missions: summer Bible schools, 81
Mitsch, Sister Barbara Ann, 64, 91
Mlecoch, Colleen, 93
Model Disarmament Conference, 26
Model League of Nations, 26
Moeller, Elizabeth Maguire, 39
Molter, Nadine Winterer, 37
Monastery of St. Catherine of Alexandria, 115
Montessori School, 91, 135
Moore, Sister Catherine (Anne Joachim), 51, 128
Moosbrugger, Bonnie Brink, 69
Morgan, George A., 56
Morrison, Toni, 119
Morrisson, Sister Georgia, 23-24, 100
Mother Antonia McHugh Fine Arts Complex, 99-100
Moynihan, Right Reverend Monsignor Humphrey, 19, 42
Mueller, Franz, 43-44, 48
Muellerleile, Mary Alice (Sister St. Alfred), 111
Mueller, Therese [Mrs. Franz], 48
Mulder, Joan, 25-26
Murphy, Sister Ellen (Agnes), 91
Murphy, Michael, 121

Murphy, Sister Odelia, 23-24
Murphy, Reverend Roland, O. CARM, 75
Murphy, Very Reverend Monsignor Terence, 93, 103
Murphy, Reverend William, OP, 49-50
Murray, Archbishop John Gregory, 31, 42, 44, 61-62, 64
Music department: accreditation, 117; building, 19, 99; development of, 39; event sponsorship, 100; faculty, 39, 65
Muskie, Jane, 37
Myser, Patricia O'Connor, 99
Myslajek, Florence Baskfield, 38

Nachtsheim, Sister Mary Henry, 78, 104
Nadeau, Janice, 125
Nati, Anna Maria, 65
National Association of Schools of Music, 117
National Campus Ministry Guidelines, 107
National Catholic Educational Association, 7
National Catholic Welfare Conference, 26
National Collegiate Players, 38
National Council of Accrediting for Teacher Education (NCATE), 67-68, 117
National Council of Teachers of English, 92
National Defense Education Act (NDEA) Language Development Program, 77-79
National Educational Association, 7
National Endowment for the Humanities, 116, 121
National Eucharistic Day, 44; Federation of Catholic College Students (NFCCS), 46
National League for Nursing, 117
National Science Foundation, 70
Natwick, Mary (Molly) Hauser, 109
Nelson, Carol Hankee, 51
New Mobilization Committee, 98
Nichols, Rosemary Fallon, 131
Nijim, Germana Portesan, 79
Nixon, President Richard M., 98
Noonan, Sister Jarlath, 2, 23-25
Nora, Florence, 41
Normile, Sister Anna Margaret, 9
Noronha, June, 104, 118
North Central Accreditation Board, 136
North Central Accrediting Association, 129
North Central Association of Colleges and Universities, 121; accreditation and, 7-8, 31, 59, 66
Northern Pacific Railway, 6
Northwest Area Foundation, 121
Noyes, Alfred, 50
Nuesse, C. J., 37
Nursing department, 43; accreditation, 117; Adult Nurse Practitioner Program, 129; cadet nursing program, 43; curriculum, 135; enrollment, 122, 132; faculty, 43, 69, 117; master's program, 135; Minnesota Intercollegiate Nursing Consortium (MINC), 129; St. Joseph's Hospital school of nursing and, 43, 69; St. Mary's Hospital school and, 43, 69; students, 47

Oberly, Genevieve Lamb, 6
O'Brien, Alice, 63
O'Brien, Sister Antonine, 9, 66, 76; background and education, 11-12, 53; cooperative library program and, 55; as dean, 38; following presidency, 63; letters, 11-12;

O'Brien, Sister Antonine (continued)
library and, 73; on Phi Beta Kappa, 81-82; as president, 53-54; and Whitby Hall, naming of, 18
O'Brien, Sister Lioba, 11, 20-21
O'Brien, Mary, 26
O'Brien, Reverend P.F., 10-11
O'Brien, Thomas D., 19
O'Brien, Dr. William A., 42
Occupational therapy department: accreditation, 48; continuing education, 110; development, 47-48; enrollment, 122; faculty, 47-48, 69; master's program, 135
Ochs, Mary Domler, 47
O'Connor, Flannery, 57, 68
Octoberfest, 120
Oehlers, Denise, 124
Office of Academic Advising, 128
Office of Continuing Education, 109-10, 122
Office of Institutional Advancement, 127
Office of Intercultural Student Affairs: established, 104; Un Primer Paso, 118, 123
Office of Student Affairs, 123; Academic Advising, 126; Career Services, 126; Child Care, 126; Learning Centers, 126; Security, 126
Ogle, Marbury B., 31
O'Hara, Sister Mary (Kevin), 88, 92, 125
Old Main, 138
Olson, Doris, 42
Onions, Charles Talbot, 12
Opening Celebration, 120
Opening Mass, 46
Ordway Music Theatre (St. Paul, MN), 133
O'Shaughnessy Auditorium, 99-100, 133
O'Shaughnessy, I. A., 60, 100
Otarola, Sister Mary of the Angels Stuart, RMM, 104
Otis, Reverend Stephen, 76
O'Toole, Alphonsus, 31
Ouellette, Sister Adrianna, 61
Our Lady of Peace shrine, 45
Our Lady of Victory Chapel, 20-22, 124

Pacheco, Armando, 77
Palen, Sister Catherine (Elise Marie), 65
Pampusch, Anita (Sister Mary Gabriel), vi; and St. Mary's merger, 128; as dean, 114, 121, 125; as president, 126-28; background, 126; educational organizations and, 134-35; enrollment and, 133, graduate programs and, 132; on spiritual activities, 130; planning and, 139; policy and, 133-34; women's colleges and, 137
Pana, Daria, 83
Parents' Council, 127
Patrone, Margaret Power, 51
Patterson, Frederick C., 77
Pavlik, Margaret, 51
Peace People, 115
Peck, Sister Helen Margaret, 9, 11; as dean, 85; cooperative studies and, 34-35; education and duties, 35; as registrar, 64; student teaching curriculum and, 36
Penny, Polly, 117
Petit, Angele, 25
Petit, Lucienne, 25
Phelan, Anna Von Helmholz, 10
Phillips, Bernard, 77

Philosophy department: curriculum, 49; faculty, 49, 88; interdisciplinary courses, 116; philosophy-theology program, development of, 49-50
Physical education department, 23
Physical therapy department: master's program, 135
Physics department: facilities, 129
Picard-Destelan, Christiane, 64
Piccard, Jeanette Ridlon, 92
Piene, Otto, 111
Pierce, Mr., 5
Planning: academic development, 133-34; finances and, 132-33
Plaster, Susan Woulfe, 92
Poletes, George, 81; children's plays, 71, 97; film series, 100; humanities curriculum and, 68
Polga, Ben, 79
Policy and policy making, 133-34; Academic Integrity Policy, 128
Porwell, Mary Ellen, 114
Pothof, Edward F., 66
Power plant, 39
President (*See also* names of individual presidents): religious duties, 42; term, 42
President's Committee of the Public Leadership Education Network (PLEN), 134
President's Council, 127
Promer, Alice, 51
Psychology department: curriculum, 35; faculty, 9; Sister Annette on, 88
Publications: gender-neutral language in, 92-93
Public relations, 137; advertising, early days, 2-3, 6

Quanbeck, Warren, 86
Quigley, Catherine Heinz, 60
Quigley, Mary Patricia Wollan, 109
Quinn, Muriel, 112

Race relations, 85, 90
Raiche, Sister Annabelle (Aloise), 106
Ramey, Estelle, 115
Rarig, Frank, 10
Rauenhorst Construction Company, 73
REAP. *See* Reentry Adult Program (REAP)
Reardon, Reverend John, 50
Reed, Mae, 51
Reentry Adult Program (REAP), 109, 122; administration, 126; students, 122-23, 125
Rehnke, Mary Ann, 120
Rentz, Anita, 125
Reny, Georgiana Slade, 55-56, 72
Research: chemistry, 89; women and, 116
Retreats, 130
Reynolds, Sandy Schuck, 105
Richard, Helen Miller, 114
Riley, Sister Mona, 9; alumnae association and, 20; curriculum development and, 33-35; education, 9-10; on foreign students, 25
Roach, Archbishop John, 99, 116
Robertson, Maura Coughlan, 60
Rockefeller Foundation, 19
Roosevelt, President Franklin Delano, 31, 40
Ross, G.W.C., 66
Rowe, Norma, 110
Ruud, Martin, 10

Ryan, Joseph, 48
Ryan, Sister Frances Rita, 8-9
Ryan, Sister Mary John, 8-9
Ryan, Sister Rosalie, vii, 76; as director of admissions, 64; library and, 73; theology curriculum and, 89

Sacred Heart (statue), 20
Sadat, Anwar, 115
St. Catherine Alumnae Association, 19, 38, 99; adult education and, 37-38; Alumnae Center, 75; awards and prizes, 26; building expansion and, 59-60; fundraising, 20, 127; publications, 20, 37, 137; trustees, 42
St. Catherine Alumnae Award, 26, 37
St. Catherine of Alexandria (medal), 115
St. John's University (Collegeville, MN), 86, 116
St. Joseph's Academy (St. Paul, MN), 1, 3-4
St. Joseph's Hall, 72; construction, 60-61; dedication, 61-62; departments in, 62-63; dining room, 62; fundraising, 59-61; West Marian Lounge, 126
St. Joseph's Hospital (St Paul, MN), 69
St. Mary Hall, 75-76, 135
St. Mary's Academy (Winnipeg, Manitoba, Canada), 4
St. Mary's Campus of the College of St. Catherine, 128-29; Crossroads Learning Center, 134; enrollment, 133-34, 138; Extended Program, 134; Montessori program, 135; physical therapy graduate program, 135-36; planning and, 133-34; Student Personnel Office, 131; transfer degrees, 137
St. Mary's Hospital (Minneapolis, MN), 69
St. Mary's Junior College (Minneapolis, MN) (*See also* St. Mary's Campus of the College of St. Catherine), 128-29
St. Olaf College (Northfield, MN): joint curriculum, 116; Minnesota Intercollegiate Nursing Consortium, member, 129
St. Paul Chamber Orchestra, 100
St. Paul Dispatch, 6
St. Paul Foundation, 100
St. Paul-Minneapolis Archdiocese: Commission on the Role of Women in the Church, 126
St. Paul Municipal Chorus, 27
St. Paul Opera Company, 100
St. Paul Pioneer Press, 6
St. Paul Seminary, 49-50, 64
St. Thomas College. *See* University of St. Thomas
Sanschagrin, Loretta (Sister Helen Joseph), 49, 65
Sanschagrin, Lucy (Sister Marie Ursule), 26, 60; background and education, 48-49; French language institutes and, 78; student teaching curriculum and, 36
Sarton, May, 57, 124
Savard, M. l'Abbe, 48
Savoy, Ikalina Moore, 105
Sawada, Dorothy Kanegaye, 41
Schaefer, Dolores, 78
Schimanski, Magdalen (Sister Marie David), 24, 40; background and education, 58; humanities program and, 68
Schmidt, George, 1
Schmitz-Dumont, Isabella, 25-26

Scholarships. *See* Financial aid
Schreiber, Sister Angela, 55
Science departments, 22, 35
Scott, Ulric, 88
Secretarial studies department, 91
Sehl, Katherine, 43
Seidenburg, Reverend Frederick, SJ, 15-16
Seiler, Gary, 103
Seliskar, Reverend John, 10
Sellew, Gladys, 43
Sellner, Chuck, 98
Sellner, Vicki, 98
Semans, Margaret Lange, 71
Semester system, 94-95, 128
Senior Send-Off, 120
Seniors Go to College, 122
Sevenich, Roman, 93
Shannon, Right Reverend Monsignor James, 81
Shanahan, Reverend Thomas, 68
Shea, Sister Cosmas, 14-15
Sheed, Frank, 50
Sheed, Maisie Ward [Mrs. Frank], 50
Sheen, Very Reverend Monsignor Fulton J., 50, 60
Shepard, Roger B., 56
Sherlock, Sister Therese, 110
Sinclair, Mary Palcich, 51
Sisters of St. Joseph of Bourg, 25
Sisters of St. Joseph of Carondelet: centennial celebration, 27-28; history, 53-54; St. Mary's Junior College merger and, 128; schools, 1; students, 6; tercentenary, 53
Sisters of the Holy Names, 6
Skaife, Mary Louise Nolan, 33
Slade, Charlotte Hill [Mrs. George T.], 19, 72
Smith, Sister Alice (Maris Stella), 11, 37; curriculum and, 33; letters, 12; on faculty, 9; on *The Fire Bringers,* 28; travel in England, 53; and Whitby Hall, naming of, 18
Smith, Constance Keefe, 60
Smith, Hannis, 74
Smith, Jean Gardiner, 37
Smith, Lucille Bristol, 10
Smith, Margaret, 6
Smith, Sister Margery (Thomas More), 129-30
Social Action Fair, 108
Social Justice ministry, 108-9
Social sciences department. *See* Sociology department
Social work: women and, 15-16
Social work department: continuing education, 110; cooperation, College of St. Thomas, 93; curriculum, 91; development, 90-91; enrollment, 122; faculty, 36-37; master's program, 135
Sociology department: curriculum, 36; development of, 15-16, 36-37
Sodality. *See* Student clubs and societies
Spanish department, 77
Special Program in Education, 82-83
Speech-theatre department (*See also* Drama department), 38; building, 99; cooperation, College of St. Thomas, 93; events, 100; productions, 97, 105
Spellman, Rita Rhodes, 105
Sports: field hockey, 6; horseback riding, 24; swimming, 23; tennis, 7

Sports Day. *See* Winter Carnival
Spring Fling, 120
Stanton, Elizabeth Cady, 87
Stanton Hall, 100
Steenberg Construction Company, 60
Steenberg, Paul, 2
Steinem, Gloria, 88
Stodola, Sister Judith, 55
Stoltz, Spencer, 10, 13, 17
Stoughton, Sister Mary Judith, 81
Strategic Long-Range Planning Committee (SLRP), 124, 131
Stubbs, Donald, 60
Student Activities, 124
Student Affairs. *See* Office of Student Affairs
Student clubs and societies: Choral Club, 27; French club, 27; International Relations Club, 40; Liturgy Club, 32; National Federation of Catholic College Students, 46; Players' Club, 38, 39; Sodality of the Blessed Virgin Mary, 44-46, 81; veterans' club, 45; Western Saddles Club, 24
Student Development Center, 128
Student Project for Amity among Nations (SPAN), 104
Students (*See also* Dormitories; Foreign students; Minority students; Student clubs and societies), 54, 83, 139; academic ethics and, 128; advising services, 128; change in, 127-28; in chapel, 29; cultural diversity and, 137-38; day students, 6; disabled students, 129; dress code, 84, 97; exchange students, 105; extracurricular activities (*See also* specific activities), 97, 120, 128, 138; fashion shows, 92; fundraising activities, 26-27; graduate students, 132, 134-35; initiation, 84; nontraditional students, 117-18, 122, 125; pageants, 27-28, 53; political activity, 26, 40-41, 97-98; post-WWII era, 47; rallies, 112; recruiting, 6-7, 119-20, 123, 127; religious life, 32-33, 44-46, 130; rules and regulations, 97-98; student government, 97, 120; transfer students, 132, 136; transportation, 6, 93; veterans, 45, 51; Vietnam Era and, 98; war effort, WWI, 18-19; war effort, WWII, 30, 40-41, 45; women's issues and, 124; WWII era, 40-41
Student services, 7
Stuhler, Barbara, 93
Subcommittee for Long-Range Planning, 123
Sullivan, J. C., 89
Sullwold, H. A., 20
Support services (*See also* Food services): laundry, 23; maintenance, 23-24
Swanson, Anne, 134
Symbols and emblems, 11; coat of arms, 10; motto, 11

Tabatt, Marlene (Bunny), 129
Talley, Eldon, 71
Tate, Allan, 68
Tauer, Sister Loraine (Catherine Ann), 40, 64-65
Teacher education. *See* Education department
Teacher Education Committee, 67
Tegatz, Mary Wall, 114
Television classes, 65-66
Temple of Aaron (St. Paul, MN), 86-87
Tesha, Daria Pana, 79

Testor, Marguerite McCusker, 3
Theater, 38
Theater department. *See* Drama department; Speech-Theatre department
Theology department: curriculum, 49-50, 71, 89, 136; enrollment, 130; faculty, 49, 71, 89-90, 117; lay faculty, 89; master's program, 121-22, 125, 132; pastoral ministry certificate program, 117
Thompson, Ann, 108
Thompson, Colleen Donahue, 73
Thompson, Sister Mary (Gertrude), 89, 121
Thornton, Catherine, 24
Tierney, Charles J., 60
Timmerman, Joan, 89
Tobin, Sister Mary Luke, 86
Todd, Reverend John, 1-3
Tomlin, Lily, 133
Toolan, Archbishop Thomas, 26
Toomey, Sister Joan, 19
Toomey, John J., 19
Toomey, Siser Teresa, 4, 7, 19, 131; education, 10; general education curriculum and, 35; and National Eucharistic Day, 44; pageants, 53
Tran, Dinh Van, 99
Tran, Ngo Pham "Angie" [Mrs. Dinh Van], 99, 132
Tran, Ngoc, 99
Trojan, Frank, 24-25, 61
Tuition, 119, 125, 135
Turck, Charles, 55
Turrish, Minnie L. [Mrs. Henry], 42
Twin Cities Youth Orchestras, 100
Tyler, Ralph, 33
Tyrrell, Mary Hilbert, 42

University of St. Thomas: affiliation with the College of St. Catherine, 65; business administration, cooperation, 91, 93; Center for Senior Citizens' Education, 129; coeducation, 102-3; communication-telecommunication-theater department, joint department, discontinuance, 135; computer facilities, 96; cooperative education, 93-94, 102-3, 119; cooperative library program and, 55-56; Interim, 94-95; library consortium member, 95; Minority Student Affairs, 132; social activities, 94; students, 62; Volunteers in Action, 108, 130

U.S. Cadet Nursing Corps, 43

Vajrathon, Mallica, 115-16
Vann, Reverend Gerald, OP, 50
Varner, Sister Christina, 59, 73
Vatican II. *See* Catholic Church
Vietnam War, 85, 98
Vincent, George Edgar, 4-5, 7, 19; science department and, 22
Vocations Day, 46
Volunteers in Action (VIA), 108-9, 130
Volunteer Week, 108
von Hildebrand, Dietrich, 50
Vonhof, Albert, 114
von Trapp, Baroness Maria, 50
Vu, Minh Han, 98

Waldorf, Michael W., 19
Wallace, Bonnie, 132
Wallace, Douglas, 127
Walsh, Virginia Bohmer, 46
Walski, John, 125
Walstrom, Sister Marian, 108
Walters, Sister Annette, 33, 60; curriculum and, 34; as dean, 63; death, 109; library school and, 59; on psychology, 88; televised classes, 65
Ward, Charles A., 60
Wartman, Marcella Flaten, 39
Watson, Catherine, 115
Weatherspoon, Cosette, 105
WEC. *See* Weekend College
Weekend College, 110-11; curriculum, 116-17, 122; enrollment, 117
Wegner, Kenneth, 35-36, 41
Welp, Sister Alphonsine, 9
Werden, Sister Hyacinth, 2, 8
Wergeland, A.M., 4
West, Thomas, 89
Whelan, Thomas, 43
Whitby Hall, 21, 62, 107, 120; *Catholic Bulletin* on, 17; construction, 17-18; departments in, 63; Whitby Tea Room, 60
White, Helen C., 50
White House Conference on Child Health and Protection, 28
White, Julie Belle, 125
Wicka, Sunny Bach, 114
Wieland, Geheimrat, 12-14

Wilkes-Karraker, Meg, 119, 125
Williams, Betty Smyth, 115
Williams, Florence, 6
Williams, Louverne Noble, 105
Wilson, Eva, 107
Winter Carnival, 44, 45, 46, 97
Wirtz, Sister St. Mark, 16-17, 65
Wolf, Reverend Lawrence O., 49
Wolkerstorfer, Sister John Christine, vii
Women: Abigail McCarthy on, 124; Church and, 124, 126; higher education, public perception of, 1-2; public life and, 88; research and, 115-16; social work and, 15-16
Women Expand, 91, 110
Women in Management. *See* Management Development Center for Women
Women in Science, 138
Women in the Arts, 138
Women's College Coalition, 134, 137
Women's Interest Group (WIG), 92-93
Women's Issues Week, 125
Women's movement, 91-93, 124-25
Women's Research and Resource Center, 124-25
Women's Week, 92
Woodman, Joseph, 73
Wood, Sister Mary Davida, 65; background and education, 95; and Far East Area Institute, 77; humanities curriculum and, 68; Interim and, 95; mass, 86; televised classes, 65-66
Woody, Thomas, 1-2
World War I, war effort, 18-19
World War II: Armistice, 45; peace movement, 40-41; students, war effort, 30, 40-41
Wylie, Margaret Murray, 35

Xavier University (New Orleans, LA), 105
Yamagiwa, Joseph, 77
Yearbook. See *College Bulletin*
Ziskowsky, Reverend Aloysius, 21
Zrust, Alice, 42